"In clear, rich, personal prose and accompanied by detailed sketches, maps, and blueprints, the author opens to readers one of the most intimate periods of her life. . . . In heartwarming portrayals of locals willing to help strangers and a young couple ready to learn the nuances of a variety of cultures, this work debunks the myths and stereotypes surrounding 'nomadic' travel, unfriendly local populations, and 'the ugly American' often associated with trips that are not reliant on traditional tourism methods. By fusing the insight of Katya Cengel's *From Chernobyl with Love* and the philosophical observance of Robert M. Pirsig's *Zen and the Art of Motorcycle Maintenance*, this book is guaranteed enjoyment for readers of travel essays and travel-focused literature." —*A recommended review by US Review of Books, Nicole Yurcaba, Ukrainian-American poet, essayist, and reviewer*

"*Wherever the Road Leads* is a fond and evocative recollection of a world that has changed beyond all recognition. It's not all roses and gilded sunsets but a heartfelt and sinewy account, full of fragrant moments as they roam free, laying down a bed of memories to treasure and share half a century on." —*Michael Gebicki, travel writer, photographer, and columnist at* www.traveller.com.au

"To travel the world in a Volkswagen van is a dream of many travelers. This account of a young couple who did just that will spark wanderlust and make you ponder the possibilities of hitting the open road. A remarkable adventure and a delightful read." —*Janice MacLeod, New York Times, best-selling author of* Paris Letters *and* A Paris Year

"Lang-Slattery offers some evocative passages that capture her fascination with the ever-changing landscape: 'Clusters of dome-roofed, dry mud villages squatted among the rocks. A camel caravan, the beasts joined tail to nose, plodded forward, one after the other, at the side of the highway.' She also includes some illuminating asides, such as when she and her spouse were forced to find a library so that they could look up the word *Zouave* in an encyclopedia—a window into the world prior to the internet." —*Kirkus Reviews*

"*Wherever the Road Leads* is a joyride of a story, capturing life, love, and travel in an age when people could truly connect to each other and the world around them without an app. A timely book that allows the imagination to wander when travel is limited. This memoir reignites a spark of passion for the people in all our lives who make the ride worthwhile." —*Meg Weidner, screenplay writer, actor, and filmmaker of* Best Mom

"In this charming memoir, newlyweds Katie and Tom accomplish what many have only dreamed of. In the early 1970s, they left their jobs, hopped in their beloved, green VW van, and traveled to the ends of the world and back. Join them on this exciting adventure to experience astounding cultural sights, sounds, scents, and customs in exotic lands. Delightful illustrations and photos enhance the fascinating stories." —*Jill G. Hall, author of* The Black Velvet Coat, The Silver Shoes, *and* The Green Lace Corset.

"This rosy glow follows the couple throughout their escapades and encounters. Recreated dialogue and descriptions lend a 'you are there' feel to the story." —*D. Donovan, Senior Reviewer, Midwest Book Review*

"Along the way you'll share special moments with a young, adventurous couple grappling with stress and emergencies, as well as celebrating the thrill of discovering the world and each other." —*Georgeanne Brennan, author of the memoir,* A Pig in Provence-Good Food and Simple Pleasures in the South of France, *and a James Beard international cooking award-winner*

"Slattery is a good writer. Her smooth prose is injected with warmth, humor, and insightful observations of the many cultures she encountered. I enjoyed the sights, tastes, and details she relates experiencing on travels from Mexico to India, and many points between. . . . Reading this book was experiencing a window of history during a pivotal decade pertaining to travel without the convenience of modern technology." —*Janilyn Kocher for Story Circle Book Reviews, https://www.storycircle.org*

"Youth does have its advantages and the skill and grit these two had was something beyond extraordinary. A delightful read, and one which you can thoroughly enjoy with gratitude—that you are simply reading and not having to tear that microbus apart one more time." —*Carole Bumpus, author of* A Cup of Redemption *and* Searching for Family and Traditions at the French Table

"This tour de force memoir gives a fantastic account of each country, complete with each national dish (which I enjoyed vicariously), landscapes, people's virtues, faults, and fashions." —*Guy Stern, author of* Invisible Ink, *Distinguished Professor Emeritus, Director of the International Institute of the Righteous at the Holocaust Memorial Center Zelkelman Family Campus*

WHEREVER THE ROAD LEADS

A Memoir of Love, Travel, and a Van

K. Lang-Slattery

Published by Pacific Bookworks, Laguna Beach, California.

ISBN: 978-1-7342796-4-1(paperback)
ISBN: 978-1-7342796-3-4 (hardcover)
ISBN: 978-1-7342796-5-8 (Kindle/mobi)
ISBN: 978-1-7342796-6-5 (epub)

Subjects: 1. Volkswagen microbus travels / 2. Road Trips – 1972 / 3. Living in a Volkswagen van / 4. Adventure honeymoon / 5. Travel - Europe / 6. Travel with children / 7. Travel - India / 8. Travel - Iran and Afghanistan/ 9. Travel - Mexico and Central America.

Library of Congress Number: 2020919418

Illustrations by K. Lang-Slattery
Photos courtesy of Thomas Slattery
Cover Design and Map Design by Cole Waidley
Book Design by Lorie DeWorken, Mind the Margins, LLC
Edited by Lorraine Fico-White, Magnifico Manuscripts, LLC

"Love does not consist of gazing at each other, but in looking outward together in the same direction."

to Thomas E. Slattery

Without him, this adventure would not have happened.

Table of Contents

Preface

*"I am not the same, having seen the moon
shine on the other side of the world."*
— Mary Anne Radmacher, author of *Lean Into Your Life*

Among family and friends, I call it "the big trip" or "the honeymoon trip" and they know what I mean. For forty-five years, I have been telling stories from those two years of travel at dinner parties and to new friends, but it wasn't until recently that I was ready to turn the experience into a memoir. Luckily, I have a treasure-trove of memory enhancers at my disposal.

Between September 1971 and August 1973, while Tom and I traveled and lived in our Volkswagen microbus, I wrote more than seventy-three journal-style letters and dozens of postcards. They were mailed alternately to Tom's parents, then to mine, and to a few other friends and relatives, with the request to share them and keep them safe till our return. To this day, I have these letters, each with its stamped envelope, many with sketches in the margins. Each letter was handwritten on thin airmail paper and composed in the few quiet moments I could grab when I was not exhausted at the end of a day. Though they average six to eight pages, they were frequently written in short spurts, the news beginning with the events described at the end of the last mailed letter—sometimes several weeks previously.

The missives often begin with a lament such as this from one dated December 9, 1971.

> *"We are waiting at the Honduras/Nicaragua border till the siesta period is over. Otherwise we will be charged each step of the way for special services. So I will begin the next segment of our journal."*

Though intimate details of my developing relationship with Tom, my new husband, were not included in the letters (after all, I was writing to my parents and my new in-laws), I clearly remember the fights and romantic interludes. As I wrote, I began to realize my intended memoir of exotic locations and van travel in a world before the internet and cell phones was also the story of a developing, new marriage. Those years were filled with good times and bad. Looking back, I realize Tom and I were always at our best as a couple when we were traveling.

Besides the saved letters, my resources included memories from my niece, nephew, and sister, photos taken by Tom, and drawings I did along the way. Tom shared his saved pocket-sized notebooks in which he jotted down every penny we spent during our journey. He also was a great help remembering the details of the months before and after the trip. I still have some of the original travel books we used, especially the Michelin English language *Green Guides*, filled with information on history, architecture, flora and fauna, geology, topography, and food. Illustrated with countless pen and ink drawings, diagrams, and small city maps, the Michelin guidebooks were just the right size to fit easily in our daypack and went everywhere with us in Europe. Recently, I was able to replace the travel book that led us through Central America, and today's internet made it easy for me to fact check background details and world events that affected our travels. I still treasure the dog-eared recipe cards I took with me and the Indian and Afghani cookbooks I bought along the way.

I have written from my point of view and created dialogue based on my knowledge of the characters, how they usually spoke to each other, recollection of the conversation taking place, and the context. The names of all characters except close family members have been changed.

Rereading my letters, poring through old travel books, recipes, and maps, and viewing our long-unseen slides offered the delight of rediscovery. I fell in love all over again with the young Tom who captured my heart, and I could feel the person I was then looking back at me and saying, "Yes, these were the best years of your life!"

K. Lang-Slattery

January 2020
Laguna Beach, CA

Chapter 1

The Proposal

I woke up to a sharp tapping on our windshield and glanced at my new Swiss watch—9:00 a.m. We were in Paris! I rolled over in bed and pulled aside the curtain covering the van window. A French gendarme stood near the rearview mirror of our van, his flat-topped hat perched squarely on his head and his gold-trimmed epaulets glittering in the sun. His face was relaxed, not in the least threatening. He raised his nightstick and tapped gently but firmly on the windshield again. I noticed a glimmer of impatience cross his face. I shook Tom's shoulder. "Wake up," I whispered. "It's time to move the car."

Tom slowly opened his eyes. He sat up straight, swung out from under the blankets, and pulled on his jeans. The tapping on the glass sounded again, more insistent the third time. Tom moved up to the driver's seat, pulled at the snaps that held the front curtain in place, and rolled down the driver's side window. "*Bonjour!*" he greeted the policeman. This was one third of his French vocabulary, his other two words *oui* and *non*, so there was little more for him to say.

The officer stuck his nightstick back into its holster. He waved one hand and spoke so rapidly his words ran together in a dance of lyrical sounds too complex for my high-school French. I understood only the words *tout de suite* repeated several times.

Tom nodded at the officer. "Oui, oui." He turned and started to come back to the rear of the car again. "Where's my shirt?" he asked.

"We need to leave right away," I said. "You can dress later. Didn't you hear him say to hurry up?" I sat up on the edge of the bed with the sheet wrapped around me.

Tom seemed puzzled by my urgency. "It was all French to me."

"Tout de suite. It means hurry up," I explained.

"All I heard was 'toots wee.' Meant nothing to me." He shrugged, settled into the front seat, and turned the key in the ignition. "Off we go," he said. "Toots wee for us."

While Tom waited for the engine to warm up, I struggled into the passenger seat, dragging the bedsheet clutched to my chest, the ends trailing behind me. As the van began to move, I rolled down the window and stuck my head outside. Directly overhead, the iron girders of the Eiffel Tower arched like an intricately woven basket. In the rearview mirror, I saw the figure of the gendarme wave goodbye as we drove toward the Pont d'Iéna that would take us across the Seine to the campground in the Bois de Boulogne.

The genesis of this adventure was Tom's dream to drive around Europe. As a marine engineer on an American President Lines cargo vessel, the SS *President Harrison*, Tom traveled around the world several times a year, making port calls from Tokyo to Barcelona, from Bombay to New York. Besides bulk cargo in the hold, the ship had staterooms for twelve passengers, mostly retired couples in their late sixties with time and money to spare. Each evening the passengers ate dinner with the ship's captain and officers. Tom listened to the stories of the elderly travelers and saw their disappointment when they were often too tired to go ashore during port calls.

"I want to see the world while I'm young," he had told me during our first year of dating. "I don't want to wait until I'm so old and out of stamina or good health."

Tom's shipping job provided a perfect schedule for personal travel—four months on the ship took him twice around the world and was followed by a paid, four-month leave. Previously, he had spent vacations skiing with friends or in Laguna Beach at a relative's tiny beach cottage. Though we now lived together during his vacations, he still kept his parents' home in East Los Angeles as his permanent address. With the benefit of a strong union, his career as a marine engineer paid well, and this, plus no rent or utilities, made it easy for him to save money.

In the summer of 1970, during one of his four-month vacations, he and I tackled our first road trip together. Tom had spent May and June attending a professional course in Baltimore. In July, when his class was over and I was on summer break from my job as a middle-school art teacher, I flew out to join him for a cross-country car trip. We had been lovers for over a year, and this journey would be a chance for us to experiment with travel as a couple. We drove first to Key West, then back across the continent in a Volkswagen bug, the back seat filled with a window air conditioner Tom had bought to keep himself cool in the summer humidity of Maryland.

During the drive across the cornfields of the Midwest, we talked about our common goals and dreams. One evening, during dinner at a Stuckey's restaurant along the freeway, we talked of our mutual interest in travel.

"I especially want to visit more of Spain," Tom said. "I've been to Barcelona on the ship and it's fabulous, but I want to explore beyond.

Madrid. Granada. Places I've never heard of. I can't help but feel seeing only the port cities is akin to only visiting Tijuana and thinking you know Mexico."

"You'd love Spain," I said. "I wish I'd been to more than Barcelona and the Balearic Islands when I was with my parents. I'd love to see the Prado in Madrid!"

"What's that?" Tom asked.

"One of the greatest art museums in Europe. Probably second only to the Louvre. They have the paintings of Velázquez and El Greco."

He looked at me, a light of pleasure in his eyes. "I probably should go to France, too. But I wouldn't know where to begin. I'd need an art guide. Like you."

I waited silently, receptive for whatever came next.

By this time, we had finished our dinner. Tom reached across the table and took my hand. "You should come with me," he said.

"Really?" My excitement mounted. "Do you mean it?"

Tom was a practical man, and I was obviously a good traveler since I willingly shared space in a Volkswagen bug with an air conditioner. "I do. I've been thinking about it all summer," he said. "Would you be able to take off from teaching for a term?"

Joining his dream adventure would feed my own longing to travel the world. I didn't have to think about my answer. "I'm sure I could get a personal leave. I'd love to come, if you truly want me with you."

"Definitely! The trip would be much better shared with you."

"When would we be going?" I asked.

"How about next summer? We should do it soon."

I was thrilled. Though I was comfortable teaching art, the hectic classrooms of rambunctious preteen students could be exhausting and depressing. Classroom discipline was my weak point, and often students signed up for art only because they thought it would be an easy grade. I would be grateful for a semester away from twelve- and thirteen-year-old kids.

Later, as we lay in our motel bed, flashes of light from the truck traffic on the nearby highway illuminated the room. Excitement bubbled between us, and our plans rapidly expanded. By midnight, we had added all the countries of Europe to our itinerary and planned to travel for at least a full year.

"I could do up to two years without losing my union A-rating," Tom explained. "We would have to travel frugally," he added. "Last month there was an article in *Mechanix Illustrated* that showed the conversion of a Ford van into a super camper with a built-in bed, a flip-up table, even a place to cook. Everything except a bathroom. Would you be okay with travel in a van?"

"Sure," I said. "I've done it before, remember?"

Upon graduation from UCLA in 1966, I had opted for graduate work at the University of the Americas in Mexico City because of the Fine Arts Department and the opportunity to live in a foreign country. My time in Mexico included idyllic beach days in Acapulco and driving to the Yucatan Peninsula years before the area evolved into a vacation paradise. This led to another van adventure after my first year of teaching. I had removed the passenger seats from my microbus, packed it with a camp stove, an ice chest, a pad, a sleeping bag, and one suitcase, then set off for the summer on a solo road trip across the country and up and down the East Coast.

Tom's next comment brought me back to the present. "I'd like to save most of the money I've got stashed in the bank for living on when we return."

"I'll contribute what I can save next year from my paycheck." Though my teacher's pay was half of Tom's salary, I saved on living costs by renting a shared (with my father's elderly draftsman) two-bedroom cottage from my parents. If I was careful, I could save enough to contribute something.

"Don't worry about it," Tom said. "I can pay for this. After all, it's my idea." I already knew my lover was both frugal and generous. "If I can get a position on an oil tanker transporting jet fuel to Saigon," he continued, "I could earn enough in six months to finance the entire trip. Tankers pay extra for hazardous duty in a war zone."

"Not sure I like the sound of that," I said. "Hazardous duty sounds scary."

"It wouldn't be much different from going to Saigon on the *Harrison,* which I do every trip."

"So why is it hazardous duty?"

"Well, if an oil tanker takes a direct hit from artillery, the whole ship would explode in one massive fireball. Not likely to happen, though. I'm more worried about a minor injury sending me to the military hospital again."

I knew the story well. In a Saigon hospital, army doctors, used to quick MASH-style solutions, had wanted to amputate his gangrene-infected foot, the result of an improperly cared-for steam burn. Tom had refused the surgery, protesting that his civilian status meant he didn't have to follow their orders. The doctors conceded and, with massive amounts of antibiotics, they saved his foot.

Tom and I met during his recuperation. He had traveled to Mexico City to visit his friend, a man with whom I shared an apartment and a romantic relationship in the final stages of disintegration. While Tom visited, I became his tour guide and companion as his buddy was fully entangled with other commitments. During the week Tom stayed with us, I found myself attracted to this charming, smart, fun, and extremely handsome man. A year later, romantically unattached, I remembered Tom and sent him a Christmas card to which he responded. "And the rest," as the saying goes, "is history."

Outside our motel window, the freeway traffic dwindled and the neon signs from the Stuckey's blinked off. One last idea kept me awake. "Can we go beyond Europe?" I asked. "Would it be possible to drive to the Middle East? Maybe even to India? Seeing Asia is my dream!"

"We could drive overland to India," he said. "That's probably the farthest we could get. Burma is totally closed. And China, too."

My interest in China resulted from reading the complete works of Pearl S. Buck, but India would do. The Beatles' visit to the subcontinent a few years earlier had thrust the country into the news, and though I had no interest in visiting an ashram, the pictures of John, Paul, George, and Ringo, dressed in white with marigold garlands around their necks, projected the allure of the exotic. "Please, let's try to go overland to India," I said.

Tom laughed and gathered me into his arms. "Sweet Jesus, what I won't do for love!" he said. I snuggled into his embrace and drifted off to sleep.

I was barely twenty-seven years old, but travel was deep in my blood. Even as a young child, I knew there was much to the world beyond my hometown perched on the Pacific Coast of California. My father and his mother had been born in Germany, and our home was filled with cherished reminders of their life before Hitler's anti-Jewish policies sent them out into the world. I grew up eating foods my friends found strange—Limburger cheese, pickled tongue, tender and creamy calf's brain, crispy-skinned roast goose, and the citron-and-raisin studded Christmas cake called Stollen.

A shy and dreamy child, I found solace from my mother's strict rules by drawing, creating paper dolls, and reading. There was always a book tucked under my bed, and on Saturday mornings, I reached for it almost before my eyes opened. Stealthily, I would read in bed for the few precious minutes before my mother opened the door, flashed the overhead light on and off, and announced, "Up and at 'em! Chores!"

My favorite books transported me to foreign lands . . . books like the illustrated children's classics *Hans Brinker, or the Silver Skates; Heidi; The Thousand and One Arabian Nights; Jungle Book;* and *The Swiss Family Robinson.* I imagined the fun of living with a kindly grandparent in the mountains of Switzerland or in some far-off place in a home created from the flotsam of a shipwreck.

My earliest travel experiences had been rough and basic. The summer road trips I endured as a child were ladies-only affairs with my mother, aunt, older sister, and two girl cousins. We headed across the burning deserts of the Southwest in our woody station wagon, picnicking on sandwiches of unbuttered bread and bologna. My mother was a camper, and we often slept in blanket rolls among the roadside stones and sagebrush. These grim days were punctuated by the delight of new sights and different ways of living—picking cotton bolls and eating pheasant filled with buckshot at my great-aunt's farm near the Arizona border; soaring on a rope swing and dropping into the cool water of the Gila river; a stop at a New Mexico sawmill where gigantic logs were shaped into rough planks; and an afternoon astride a fence while cowboys branded terrified calves at a Colorado ranch. These trips stopped with the birth of my sister Karen when I was nine.

As I grew older, I loved movies, as well as books. They, too, had the power to transport me to a different world, a place where, unlike my parents, lovers kissed and there was more to family life than chores. Over the years, my tastes moved from *Cheaper by the Dozen*, the story of a happy family with twelve cheerful children, to love stories like *Cinderella* and *An Affair to Remember*, in which Cary Grant falls in love with Deborah Kerr during a transatlantic cruise.

However, it was the unexpected journey to Europe when I was sixteen that sealed my fate. Different from previous summer excursions, this trip was planned (at the last minute) by my father. His interests included art, history, and good food, and mine followed suit. He led my mother, my seven-year-old sister, and me around the cathedrals, museums, and Michelin-starred restaurants of Italy and France, as well as to Germany, where we visited places he remembered from his own childhood. After returning from that enchanted summer, I would be a lifelong traveler.

As soon as Tom and I arrived home, we began preparations for "the big trip." I sold my old Volkswagen van, and together we purchased a gently-used, updated model, one with the new, sliding side door. We studied books about travel in Europe and told our parents about our plans. There was not much time before Tom had to return to his ship for another four months. Further planning would have to wait until his next vacation.

When he returned, after only one trip around the world, he searched for a position on an oil tanker. One day, after a stop at the union hall in San Pedro, we went together to an RV show. Tom wanted to get more ideas about ways to modify our microbus for comfortable travel. We looked at hundreds of trailers with their tiny cupboards, beds, and stoves, and at giant motorhomes with overstuffed furniture and TV sets. Tom took notes and sketched ideas in a notebook while I wondered when he would find time to build what we wanted. Buying a Westfalia Camper would certainly have been simpler, but neither of us cared for the pop-up top, the need to stand outside to cook, or the narrow bed less than the width of the van. These features, fine for camping, would not be comfortable for long-term travel. Near the end of the afternoon, we found a company that did Volkswagen camper conversions.

The owner greeted us and explained how he and his wife had designed their conversion in a carport at a motel in England. "We wanted a self-contained space to allow for travel and camping off the beaten track—you know, places with no campgrounds. It was important to us to be able to cook and stand up inside even in bad weather. And we wanted a comfortable bed. We wanted to avoid motels in the future and be totally on our own."

Tom and I looked at each other, our eyes wide with excitement. "Is this conversion the same as the one you built in England?" Tom asked.

"Well, we found ways to improve the design as we traveled," the owner told us. "Our van was the old style with the double-opening side door. After our return, we redesigned it for the sliding door on the newer models. Let me show you."

We inspected the interior and both loved the special features this husband-and-wife team had incorporated. Tom and I told the couple about the trip we were planning, and they offered us a brochure and their price sheet to study.

The owner's wife stood with her arm loosely around her husband's waist. "It'll be the adventure of your life," she said. "We traveled for almost a year and a half." Her eyes glistened with love for her husband. "We went to thirty-one countries and four continents. All the while, we thought of ways to improve our design. Then, when we were in the middle of the Sahara Desert, he looked at me and said, 'What do you think about building campers for other people who want to travel?' After that, we couldn't wait to get back to California and start our business."

"We make conversions for Volkswagen dealerships to sell," the owner added, "but we prefer building individual conversions for folks like you. We love to imagine our Adventure Campers traveling all over the world. Leave your van with us for a couple of weeks and we'll return it ready to travel."

Soon our converted microbus waited in our driveway while I drove Tom's bug to work every day. In January 1971, Tom was hired as second engineer on an oil tanker delivering aviation fuel to Vietnam. He was told to be ready to fly to Bahrain in two days. The next day, he returned to San Pedro to update his US Coast Guard ID, get the necessary shots for the Middle East at the union clinic, and pick up his airplane tickets and instructions for joining the ship in the United Arab Emirates.

On his return from San Pedro, I greeted him with open arms, anticipating a last romantic evening before our separation, my body aglow in anticipation of the deep kisses we had promised each other.

"Don't touch me," Tom said. He moved gingerly past me into the living room, where he collapsed onto the sofa. "They gave me a slew of shots this afternoon. I feel like a pin cushion." He sighed and his hands hovered over his upper arms, unwilling to touch them. "A couple of those shots, I've never had them before, and they were doozeys. I think it was the cholera shot, maybe the one for plague."

I sat down next to him on the sagging couch, its gold tweed uphol-stery scratchy and rough. Careful not to jar the cushions, I caressed his smooth cheek. I missed the feel of his beard, shaved off that morn-ing for the clean-shaven look required for his US Coast Guard ID. "It's okay," I said. "Maybe the pain will ease up in a while."

"I hope so." He turned toward me without the usual gleam in his eyes. "I so looked forward to making love tonight. It's going to be a long dry spell until I get back."

With sex a now-distant hope, I shifted gears to my other passion—food and cooking. I'm sure I had prepared a delectable meal, probably one of Tom's favorites, Quiche Lorraine. He always joked I had made him fall in love with me when, one month into our relationship, I insisted on preparing him a three-course meal featuring Duck á l'Orange.

After dinner, disappointed with the turn our last night together had taken, we lingered at the dining table. Tom nursed an after-dinner beer, and I sipped my usual hot tea. We went over our plan to get Tom released from his twelve-month contract with the oil tanker company in July. I was to telephone the ship, a difficult ship-to-shore process in those days, with a fabricated message about his father's fatal illness. We reasoned because his father was already in his seventies, it was a believable event and he wouldn't mind the lie, though I doubted we'd ever tell him. The news of a death in the family would allow Tom to fly home without recriminations from his employer. After that, we would have slightly over a month to pack the van and begin our cross-country drive to New York to meet the Jugolinija freighter that would take us to Barcelona, Spain, the starting point for our Euro-pean adventure.

I would request a year of personal leave, and if all went well, I could resign in order to travel longer. Our only limitation was the two-year timeframe needed for Tom to maintain his A-list union status, vital if he was to get a position on a good ship when he returned. We had every-thing under control.

As the conversation hit a lull, Tom's next comment was unexpected. "It's too bad we can't get married," he said in a hesitant voice. "It would make crossing borders so much easier."

I sat dumbfounded for several heartbeats. I was more interested in travel than marriage. Happily-ever-after marriage, promoted by 1950s' musicals and Disney fairy tales, had filled my childhood daydreams. However, my own real-life experience had shown that love and marriage didn't always go together and sexual intimacy was a separate thing altogether, though certainly better with a partner you loved. I believed marriage was only necessary when there were children, though I admit to being attracted by the romance of the ceremony. I was doubtful being married would help much with border crossings, but something in the way Tom worded this challenged me. I vaguely remembered he had mentioned marriage about a year before. It had been offhand, definitely not a question, and certainly not a romantic proposal. I had pretended not to hear him and the conversation moved in another direction. This time I would not ignore Tom's comment.

I kept it simple. "Why can't we get married?"

"Well, you're not Catholic. I don't care about that. I'm pretty fallen away. But . . . my parents. They actually believe all that Catholic stuff. And they would be devastated if I got married in another church. My dad believes it's a sin to go into any church but a consecrated Catholic Church."

Now it was my turn to be surprised. I knew Tom no longer went to confession or to Mass, but a church wedding was far from my romantic, hippie-influenced, agnostic-leaning, nonaffiliated image of what I imagined. "No problem," I said. "I want to be married in my father's garden." Though my mother also loved the outdoors, our family garden, almost an acre of trees and shrubs, both native and exotic, was always credited to my father as he was a landscape architect. Not only was it a perfect venue, it was filled with happy childhood memories.

"A garden wedding? Is that what you want?" he said. "With my Catholic background, it would never have occurred to me. Gardens don't count as sanctified."

"Yes, that's my dream. A small ceremony with lots of flowers and ladies in long dresses. My father does those yearly parties for the Chamber Music Society. He always plants lots of new impatiens all around for the occasion." I visualized the event. We could get married under the big sycamore tree where I had kissed my first boyfriend in high school and where I splashed my little sister with the garden hose.

Tom perked up. "My dad would attend a garden ceremony. Not sure if he'd believe we were truly married, but he'd come. My parents love you and I know they would be happy to see us officially married before we take off on our trip." A man of few words, there was no mention of how much he loved me. "Shall we do it?" he asked. "Do you want to get married?"

I didn't respond instantly. Couched in practical terms about the effect on border crossings, this was a question I needed to consider. If I did get married, I wanted it to be with a man I could build a life with. I valued my independence and believed marriage was mainly a practical and legal agreement, but one which, ideally, would last a lifetime. We found pleasure in love and intimacy already and our travel plans would go forward regardless.

Over the years, we had talked about the importance of family, and I knew we both wanted children in the future. I had been greatly influenced by Paul Ehrlich's controversial book, *The Population Bomb*, and wanted to adopt a baby from China or India, where I knew infants were often abandoned. Tom approved this idea. Though we occasionally had minor differences in the realm of politics—Tom was a fiscal conservative and a social liberal, while he considered me a full-fledged, "bleeding heart liberal"—we were generally compatible. His matter-of-fact engineer's mind helped center my artistic and sentimental inclinations. He was always happy to expand his knowledge into my areas of interest—art, architecture, culture, and literature. He even tolerated and occasionally accommodated my need for romantic gestures, though this was not one of those times.

I loved the idea of a wedding, the ultimate romantic gesture. Our trip would be a test of our commitment to each other, so why not make it also a test of the ultimate commitment—marriage? Pragmatically I knew the worst that could happen would be my return to California alone and divorced. What did I have to lose?

I responded to Tom's proposal with my romantic side, nurtured by Hollywood movies and popular songs. "Yes, sweetheart, let's get married. Our trip will be our honeymoon!"

Chapter 2

A Wedding

The next morning at LAX, Tom and I parted reluctantly, lingering for a kiss near the boarding gate, while passengers surged around us. Tom's broad shoulders and straight back disappeared down the passageway. I turned with a sigh. The weight of missing him for the next six months settled on my shoulders. Gradually the days would pass and I would have plenty to keep me busy. First, I needed to ask my parents if they would host a summer wedding.

Any other mother would have been delighted to hear her twenty-seven-year-old daughter planned to marry the man she had been living with for two years. But my mother and I had a long-standing oppositional relationship. Her straitlaced view of life often conflicted with mine, and my sexual relationships, past and present, were secrets surrounded by lies. Though she liked Tom, my mother held thinly veiled prejudices against Catholics and so far, she had been unable to fully accept him.

Naturally, when I arrived at my parents' home, my father was not around, even though it was Saturday afternoon. His work was his main passion, and he seldom spent time with the family—the siren call of his jobs and clients more powerful. I sat alone with my mother at the dining table and told her Tom and I had decided to add a wedding to the days between his return and the start of our journey. "We want to get married in the garden," I told her. "Do you think Daddy would make it as beautiful as he does for the concert group? I'd only want a few people for the ceremony, but lots of friends and family for a reception afterward. We can do the food ourselves. Will you help me make a wedding dress?" My mind was filled with plans and ideas I needed to share with someone, and my dour mother was the person at hand.

When I slowed down enough for her to interject a comment, my mother looked up, her face stern, without a hint of joy. "I wouldn't count on any of this," she said in her usual precise way. "Tom will be on the ship for months. His talk of marriage was probably simply a whim. For all you know, he has girls in every port. Slow down. See what he says in his letters." She took a sip of coffee and dabbed at her thin lips with a paper napkin. "Wait and see what he wants when he comes home," she said.

I was devastated. This was cold even for my mother. My own father had been in the US Merchant Marines during World War II. His stories of time as a ship's purser and his travels to Japan after the war had delighted me as a child. My knowledge of what it meant to be a civilian US Merchant Marine officer had been one of the things that had originally drawn Tom and me together. I was comfortable with Tom's profession, with the long separations it demanded, and I trusted him totally. Perhaps I should have wondered what my mother experienced when my father was sailing the world, what my father might have done to give my mother these ideas, but I didn't. I saw only her lack of enthusiasm and opposition to my happiness.

"You're wrong," I declared. "We will get married when he gets back. It was his idea, not mine. He meant it." Why couldn't my mother believe in my judgment and understand Tom would make a good husband?

"I hope you're right," she said. Somewhat softened, she allowed the wisp of a smile to turn up the corners of her mouth. "When he tells his parents, then I'll believe he's serious."

As usual, my mother, educated in etiquette by Emily Post, knew what was important. "He promised to write them," I said. "When he does, will you help me plan the wedding? Without your help, it wouldn't be the kind of special day I imagine."

"Of course, I'll help. When he's proved he's serious by telling his parents, we'll start preparations."

My mother was always true to her word, and in spite of everything, I knew her love was dependable. Hadn't she made a beautiful December wedding for my sister when she was only eighteen and had insisted on marrying a man six years older—a man who no one felt was suited for her? My mother would come around.

In those pre-Internet days, long-distance phone calls were expensive and airmail letters took more than a week to arrive from the Far East, so communication between Tom and me wasn't easy. Ship-to-shore radio calls were patched through by shortwave radio, and when Tom called from the other side of the world, it was usually in the wee hours of the morning. Though excited to hear his voice, it was agony to wait until he said, "Over," and clicked the button. During my turn, with weeks of news to share, I had to sort through what was important and remember to say "over" when I finished. After Tom's final "over and out," I usually lay awake, my head filled with things I'd forgotten to say.

Tom called from the ship when he arrived and I reminded him to write his parents about our wedding plans. Two weeks later, the first air letter from him arrived. His scrawled, widely spaced penmanship consisted of a paragraph about life on an oil tanker, and at the end, a few words of reassurance. "I'm so pleased we have decided to marry. I know it'll make the trip better and we'll be happy. I promise I'll call my parents when the ship gets back to Bahrain to pick up more fuel."

"Don't forget to call your parents!" I wrote to the address in Bahrain. "It's extremely awkward for me to talk to your mom when she doesn't know. And she calls me almost every week!" Eventually, Tom's parents called, thrilled with the news. They would do whatever they could to facilitate our wedding. And so, the planning began with the help of my mother, my future in-laws, and my teacher friends.

The days passed and similar to other brides-to-be, I embarked on a strict diet to lose weight. To sublimate my hunger while dieting, I transferred my passion for food into a recipe collection project. I created a file of recipes from all the countries we hoped to visit, recipes I could prepare on two burners and without an oven. My love of cooking would make it possible for us to experience the cuisines of the countries we visited and live within our limited budget. We would shop in village markets and buy local cheeses, bread, produce, and spices.

In the evening, while I sipped a dinner of chicken broth, enlivened by a half cup of cubed zucchini, I pored over cookbooks. I chose recipes to represent the typical dishes of the countries on our itinerary and copied the instructions by hand onto 3 x 5 index cards, which I filed in an orange, plastic, recipe box. I collected recipes for Spanish paella, French cassoulet, German stews, Dutch soups, and Italian pasta dishes. I wrote out recipes for vegetarian curry to make in India and Greek lemon soup with lamb meatballs to prepare in Athens.

I viewed the trip as a culinary adventure. I bought a pricey set of Revere Ware, nesting cookware that consisted of a large, Teflon-coated skillet, two saucepans with lids, and one detachable handle that fit all three pieces. A stainless-steel bowl served as a skillet lid or a mixing bowl and fit over the nested pans for storage. The set was strapped together by a stainless-steel band and took up no more space than a good-sized watermelon. I purchased a pressure cooker to cook in less time, thus using less butane. I would transform tough meats and dried beans into soups and stews in short order. I gathered the essential cooking tools—two sharp knives, a wooden chopping board, a few mixing spoons and plastic bowls, a vegetable peeler, a flat grater, and a strainer—always in the most compact, packable versions. Tom loved to eat my food and he also loved to save money. I would be the perfect bride and serve my new husband tasty meals, even in the confines of a Volkswagen van.

After five and a half months of strict dieting and compulsive recipe collecting, I was twenty-three pounds thinner. I felt beautifully sexy and happily anticipated Tom's return. The "family emergency" call to the ship went as planned, Tom headed home, and I flew to San Francisco to meet my husband-to-be.

The sight of Tom as he came through the international gate at the airport made my heart race. He stood tall, narrow-hipped, and broad-shouldered, his one duffel bag slung over his shoulder, his face aglow with a smile. He dropped his bag and swept me into his arms. His kisses covered my face and found my lips. I relished the feel of his beard, soft against my cheek, and the aroma of his Old Spice aftershave. There is a great deal of truth to the old saying, "Absence makes the heart grow fonder." As we hurried down the causeway toward baggage claim, Tom was obviously excited. "I have a surprise to show you," he said. "I found the most fantastic wedding ring for myself in Bahrain."

"*Your* wedding ring?" I asked, stunned. I was supposed to buy his ring and he was supposed to buy mine! "You bought your own ring?"

"Yes, wait until you see it. You'll love it." This beautiful man simply didn't get the romantic significance of exchanging rings. Our marriage was mainly a practical matter to him, but to me it had become the realization of all my girlhood, Cinderella-and-Prince-Charming inspired, dreams of romance. I wouldn't let this spoil it for me. He could have his version of how things should go, I would have mine, and often enough we would meet in the middle. Wasn't compromise what any good relationship was all about?

As soon as we were in the hotel room, Tom dug into his luggage and displayed the ring gently in the palm of his hand. It was composed of eight narrow gold bands entwined to create a woven pattern. "It's a puzzle ring," he said. "The Arabs believe this type of ring represents the two separate lives of a husband and wife and how together they form a single unbroken circle." He slipped the ring on his finger and held it up for me to see. "I like what it stands for. You have to be careful so it won't come apart into a jumble of pieces."

The ring was indeed beautiful, and I understood to him it embodied the unity and promise of marriage. Tom felt deeply, but his emotions seldom came to the surface. When they did emerge, as had his feelings about the Arabic ring, I needed to hear the significance behind his simple words.

"If it comes apart," he added, "I know how to put it back together. Look." He took the ring off and laid it in the palm of his hand again. With a gentle upward movement and a jiggle of his hand, the gold rings loosened. He took one band between his fingers, and with a shake, the ring dissolved into a pile of senseless interlocking links that looked more like a chain than a ring.

He must have noticed my stricken face. "Don't worry," he said. "I can fix it."

He took out a printed instruction card with a diagram and placed it on the bedside table. After a brief review of the diagram, he gave his attention to the ring. In a matter of minutes, he had eased the links back together until they again formed a perfectly woven circlet of gold. He slipped it on his left ring finger again and admired it there. "I can't wait to wear it all the time," he said. "I would have bought you one, too, but I didn't know what size." He slipped the ring off and placed it in the small box where it nestled on a cushion of blue velvet.

I kissed him and looked into his eyes. "It's lovely," I said. "I only wish I had been able to buy it for you."

He pushed me back against the pillows of the bed and caressed me in the way he knew I loved. "It doesn't matter," he murmured. "Tomorrow we'll find a ring for you." More kisses. Soon we were undressed and our bodies were as entwined as the golden bands of his ring.

*B*ack in Laguna Beach, our home turf, the days were crazy. First, the wedding plans took a new turn. Tom's mother, Mary, was the favorite niece of Monsignor Gross, the senior priest of the new Wilshire Boulevard Cathedral of the Archdiocese of Los Angeles, a high position in the Catholic Church. When Mary notified her uncle that Tom would wed a non-Catholic, she assured him I had been baptized and had attended Sunday school.

This was true enough. Though my parents never attended church, on Sundays, my mother would drive my older sister and me to the local children's Presbyterian Bible classes in order to have a peaceful morning on her own. Most important to Monsignor, my baptism as an infant made me an acceptable bride for his great-nephew. To please Tom's mother who wanted her son to be married in the Catholic Church, Monsignor Gross took matters in hand. He arranged with her local priest to give me "the religious education necessary" to marry a Catholic. Monsignor Gross also gave the priest permission to preside at the garden wedding if we would also exchange vows in the consecrated church the night before. We agreed to this special dispensation on the condition the marriage certificate would show the date of the garden ceremony where we would declare our own personal vows.

To ensure I wasn't pressured in any way, Tom accompanied me to the religious indoctrination. We sat in the sunny, flower-filled garden of the parish church of St. Catherine of Siena and sipped iced tea with the priest. I remember he was over six feet tall, extremely handsome, had large expressive hands, a frequent smile, and a charming brogue that revealed how recently he had emigrated from Ireland. After pleasantries, the priest looked at me seriously and asked if I believed in God. This was a question I hadn't expected, but I could concede a belief in a higher power to please this sexy priest and be able to marry Tom. Next, he turned to Tom and asked the same question. Once he had received an affirmative answer from us both, the priest leaned back. "A common belief in God is a strong foundation for a marriage," he said. "Faith will give you solace when times are difficult and a common ground for decisions about family and your life together." Again, Father turned to Tom. "I understand from your mother that your profession takes you away from home for months at a time. When you and Katie return from your trip together, do you feel the frequent separations caused by your career will be a problem?"

"We've been together for almost three years," Tom explained, "and we believe the separations make us appreciate each other more. Katie has her job, lots of projects, and friends. This fills her days when I'm at sea."

I nodded in agreement. The young priest spoke again to Tom. "Tell me more about what it's like on a ship at sea for months at a time. What exactly do you do on the ship?" For thirty minutes, I relaxed in the sunshine and listened to Tom explain about his work and the exotic places he was able to visit. I was asked no more questions and given no instruction in Catholic doctrine. The priest didn't even ask if I would agree to raise our children as Catholic. Tom and I had both agreed it held slim importance for us either way and it would be years before we needed to make this decision.

When we left the rectory garden, hand in hand, I said to Tom, "Well, that was easier than I expected."

He shook his head in disbelief. "Unbelievable," he said. "Undoubtably, Monsignor Gross had a hand in how that meeting went. It pays to have a relative in high places."

With the mid-August date for our wedding rapidly approaching, the list of details made my head buzz from morning to night. There were fittings with my mother as she completed my dress.

"I wish you hadn't chosen this off-white fabric," she said as she worked. "It advertises you're not a virgin."

This was the type of comment I had learned to leave unanswered. In spite of her attitude, my mother created the wedding dress I had designed—a floor-length, flowing gown of semi-sheer cotton, decorated with lace-edged ruffles and lavender-and-blue satin ribbon streamers.

In addition to my dress, my mother, Tom's mother, and I sewed pretty garden party dresses for a gaggle of young nieces, for my sisters, and Tom's sister-in-law. I made the three-layer cake, my mother arranged all the flower decorations, and my friends and I split the duties of preparing the food for the reception.

Meanwhile, Tom oversaw the auto mechanic who worked on modifications, intended to add power to our van's engine. Tom knew that when our microbus was loaded into the cargo hold of the ship for the voyage to Spain, the keys must be left in the ignition so crew members could move the vehicle, if necessary. To prevent shipboard theft of all our possessions, Tom built a plywood barrier designed to fit between the two front seats. When secured in place, it closed off the rear living area. When not in use, the barrier would be bolted to the outside of the van.

One of the reasons I felt so safe with Tom was his exceptional ability to fix almost anything. For this he needed tools and a place to keep them safely out of the way. He raised the floor on the passenger side of the cab to create a storage space for essential wrenches, pliers, ratchets, and sockets. Luckily, I had short legs and this adjustment was a much-appreciated footstool.

With both a wedding and a two-year journey coming together, my nerves were on edge. The night before our garden wedding, the quick Catholic ceremony at the church was a quiet event, attended only by Tom's parents. Afterward, Tom and I returned to our cottage next door to my parents' home and garden. Besides our draftsman housemate who occupied one of the two bedrooms, my niece and nephew, Mike and Michelle, were being tucked into their sleeping bags on our living room floor by their mother. I don't remember what upset me, but it wouldn't have taken much to shatter my fragile emotional state. I do remember that I ran into the dark and threw myself down on a thick bed of ivy. Unable to pull myself together, I wept sobs of frustration and anxiety into the greenery.

After a few minutes, I heard Tom's soft voice call my name. I responded with incoherent sobs. He found me among the dusty ivy leaves and lay down beside me, stroked my hair, and kissed my tear-damp cheeks. Gradually, his beard tickled away my sorrow. "It's going to be okay, sweetheart. Tomorrow is our wedding and soon we'll be off on the best adventure of our lives." I curled my body into his warmth as if it were a security blanket and responded hungrily to his caresses.

We consummated our love under the stars and moon in the garden of my childhood. That night hangs pleasantly in my memory. At that moment, I knew Tom had the power to make me happy. When we returned to the cottage and tiptoed past my sleeping sister and her children, I had no doubts about marrying this man.

The priest arrived the next day, his snowy-white cassock adorned with a yellow "smile" button. This was not a tuxedo wedding. Tom looked stylish in a pair of bell-bottom trousers and a fitted Italian shirt, which accentuated his splendid physique. We exchanged our vows kneeling on a log, covered with a white-and-burgundy Indian carpet, which added a hint of *Arabian Nights'* magic to the ceremony. At the reception, our nieces ran along the garden paths between the shrubbery, their flowery, party dresses a swirl of color. Champagne flowed and the buf-

Tom and I on our wedding day.

fet table under the Torrey pine tree was piled with homemade salads, quiches, and cheeses. Tom and I cut the cake and fed each other the moist, sweet, lemon confection. It was a perfect day.

But to Tom, the most memorable event was the news the following morning. On August 15, President Nixon, only a year and a half into his first term and long before the Watergate fiasco, severed the link between the US dollar and gold, thus effectively devaluing US currency, a policy decision that shriveled our travel nest egg by a significant amount.

Despite our reduced funds, we forged ahead. Tom and I moved our two suitcases and boxes of essentials into the Volkswagen. Though I would have preferred music, Tom favored news radio as he worked. I was oblivious to the drone of the newscaster as I tried to find space for all our stuff in our mini-home on wheels. Suddenly I realized Tom stood quietly outside the van's sliding door, a carton of my art supplies in his arms.

"Listen," he said. "This isn't good."

I looked up and concentrated on what the news announcer said. ". . . union leaders say negotiations are at a standstill." I looked at Tom, my question hanging in the air.

"It's a dock strike," he said. "East Coast longshoremen have declared a strike. We're screwed."

"But it's almost three weeks till our ship is due to sail. Won't it be over by then?"

"Dock strikes can go on for months. No ships will leave New York or Newark . . . not even Boston." He shook his head and dropped the box with a thud. "Everything will be shut down. No telling how long. I remember one dock strike affected the Gulf ports for six months. Most likely Jugolinija will simply cancel all ships to the East Coast until it's over."

Within a few days, we received notification that our reservation for the crossing to Spain was postponed indefinitely. By the time we received the notice, we were already making alternate plans.

Neither Tom nor I could bear to sit and wait in California. We had both quit our jobs and itched to begin our journey. If we couldn't go to Europe, perhaps we should head south. I was familiar with the beauty of Mexico. The mysteries of Central and South America stretched beyond. Maybe we could get a ship from Brazil to Spain or Portugal. This long way around was not exactly our first choice but certainly better than remaining in California.

Tom talked to people he knew who had traveled to Latin America. I called the AAA Auto Club to find out about the Pan-American Highway south of the Mexico-Guatemala border. The legendary highway, mostly built in the 1950s and 1960s, offered good driving all the way to Panama. In South America, reports claimed it was passable along the entire Pacific Coast to southern Chile. There was one serious gap in the road. The paved highway abruptly disappeared beyond Panama City, not to reappear again until Medellín, Columbia. There was no road through the thick, tangled jungles of the narrow Isthmus of Panama between Central and South America. This section, known as the Darién Gap, remains to this day an impenetrable rainforest for over one hundred miles.

There was no way through it. One had to go around it—which, we learned, wouldn't be easy. Rumors of boats, maybe a ferry, maybe a local freighter from Panama City to Columbia, circulated. Tom was familiar with the Canal Zone in Panama, as he had frequently traversed the Canal by ship. He felt his contacts there would enable us to find a way around the Darién Gap. We decided to head south. If there was a way around the Darién Gap, we would find it and drive on to South America.

Once we had made up our minds, we couldn't wait to start. Three weeks after our wedding, we stashed the remaining boxes and bags, willy-nilly, in the back of the microbus and said goodbye to our families. Our last night at home, we were too excited to sleep and, after several restless hours, we began our journey at 2:00 a.m.

Whatever happened, we would be together.

Chapter 3

A Home of Our Own

To understand the next two years, it is important to visualize our tiny home.

Our living space was behind the driver and passenger seats of our dark-green Volkswagen microbus. The main feature making this space comfortable was the rigid roof which allowed a full six-foot center overhead clearance—standing room, even for Tom at 5 foot 11 ½ inches—without any need to pop it up. The roof unit boasted screened, awning-style windows on each side and an over-the-cab storage area where we kept our suitcases, my nesting cookware, the pressure cooker, Tom's typewriter, and various miscellany.

For newlyweds, the bed was of tantamount importance. We had a full-sized foam mattress supported by a plywood platform that opened like a book with a continuous hinge across the middle. The mattress took regular sheets and blankets, much better for a two-year trip than sleeping bags. The front edge of the bed, when open, cantilevered out

Our Van Home

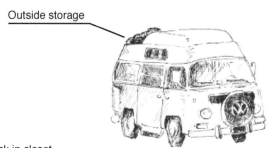

Outside storage

Water tank in closet

Closet

Hot-water dispenser

Sink

Stove

Flip-up counter

Commode in ottoman

Metal grate to separate cab

Overcab storage

Flip-up table

Bench seat

Refrigerator

Sliding door

Fold out bed

Small item storage

Red gasoline cans

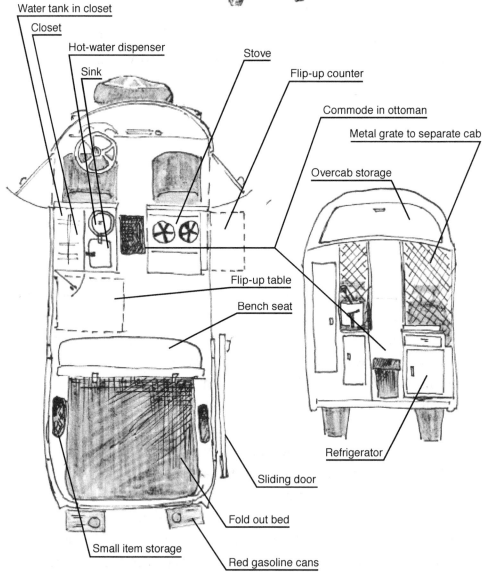

to clear the mini-kitchen by a few inches. I could wake up and put the kettle on the stove without leaving the bed.

My kitchen featured several luxury fittings. There were wood-grained cabinets and marble-patterned Formica counters, including two hinged, pop-up work spaces. Hidden in a cabinet, wedged directly behind the driver's seat was a tiny closet, a sink, and an air-pressurized water tank, which included a charcoal water purification system. All we had to do anywhere in the world was add liquid bleach—yes, regular laundry bleach—to the water tank when we filled it. After passing through the filter, the water flowing from our single faucet tasted sweet and pure. Best of all, we had a hot water dispenser. A tall pot with a spigot at the bottom came with the conversion. It could be filled and set on the stove to heat. Once the water was warm, we hung the pot from a special hook so that the spigot was directly over the sink. Voila! Hot running water!

My two-burner butane stove was behind the passenger seat. A small drawer to hold a few cooking implements was tucked below the stove, and underneath the drawer squatted an electric bar-sized refrigerator! A second, auxiliary car battery ran the refrigerator and two ceiling lights. Tom, always the engineer, compulsively watched the conditions of both car batteries and rationed our use of electricity.

The original Volkswagen bench seat remained in the middle of the car and provided limited storage underneath for canned goods and a few other staples. Above the bed, there were two narrow storage units, one along each side of the ceiling, and a center cupboard with room for a few bowls, plates, and cups. Outside, the custom fiberglass roof was scooped low in the rear to create a place to strap on bulky nonvaluables such as beach chairs, Tom's skimboard, and a canvas bag full of bottles of bleach, paper towels, and toilet paper. Tom mounted two red metal gasoline cans on the back of the van, so we could travel with extra gasoline in countries where stations were scarce.

Blue-and-green curtains and a special snap-on cover for the windshield provided privacy. Although too small to have a bathroom, our cozy van did have sanitation facilities. Our toilet was a fancified bucket, also part of the camper conversion. The green plastic bucket under a plywood seat cut with an oval hole was hidden in a movable ottoman with a cushioned, black Naugahyde, lift-off top. I have to admit I was more nervous about using this bucket in front of Tom than I was about driving to South America. I hoped desperately for lots of easy-to-find campgrounds with flushable latrines.

A second important bucket served for two years as our washing machine. We had gotten this idea from John Steinbeck's *Travels with Charley*, a memoir of the author's 1960s road trip around the United States in the company of his standard poodle, Charley. Steinbeck described his laundry bucket as a smallish plastic garbage can with a tight lid held closed by two metal loop handles that could be attached by bungee cord to a ceiling hook. As he traveled down country roads, the jiggling of the bucket from its bungee tether provided agitation to clean his clothes.

We had no ceiling hook, but the bumpy roads or my hands would work well enough. When not in use, the washing bucket, filled with a box of laundry detergent, rope and clothespins, was lashed to the roof.

After our predawn departure, we arrived at the Colorado River at 8:00 a.m. and found a campground with an entrance sign, "No long hair or hippies." We were given a campsite near a sandy beach. The temperature hovered above 100 degrees Fahrenheit, and the cool river water was the perfect place to de-stress. We had an inner tube and our white plastic water containers strapped on the roof. I reclined luxuriously across the inflated tube, while Tom floated between the tied-together, air-filled water jugs. Together, we bobbed around in the cool river and floated downstream.

Cliffs by our river campsite.

In the evening cool, while burgers sizzled on our barbeque, we sat on beach chairs and watched purple shadows glide over the red-rock cliff on the opposite bank of the river. Later, the air filled with the aroma of roasting hot dogs and the sounds of tired water skiers. The indigo sky filled with countless stars, and we crawled into our bed for the first time. In spite of party noises from the other campsites, we slept peacefully nestled together.

After two days, it was time to cross the Colorado River and leave California behind. Before we reached the outskirts of Phoenix, Arizona, we realized a serious problem brewed deep in the engine.

Nothing is hotter than the land stretching flat and almost treeless on either side of the California-Arizona border. We drove across this inferno, windows open wide to funnel air into the van (that's right, no air conditioning). Tom was unusually quiet. I assumed, like me, all his energy was sapped by the heat. Suddenly, without warning, he pulled to the side of the road and stopped under a scrubby, almost leafless, tree—the only vegetation taller than three feet from there to the distant blue line of mountains on the horizon.

"I heard a metal rattling noise," he said. "And the engine's too hot. I need to take a look." He eased himself out of the car and walked to the rear engine compartment. In spite of the heat, I rolled up the windows. Every fly in the desert had gathered under the same tree to find sanctuary in the only shade for miles around. When Tom came back, shaking his head, he tried to start the engine but it wouldn't turn over. We sat in the sweltering heat. With no pay phones or structures for miles, we wondered when another vehicle might come down the road. Neither of us wanted to discuss our options if the van was dead. The unspoken words hung heavily in the hot air.

After ten minutes, Tom carefully turned the ignition key again. Together we let out a sigh of relief when the cooled engine turned over. "We'll have to find a VW dealer in Phoenix," Tom said. "Sorry. This won't be pleasant, but something is seriously wrong."

I hoped the problem wasn't as bad as Tom believed.

From that day forward, the drama of car repairs and maintenance affected our travels, and as a result, our relationship and how we solved problems. For the next three days, we moved from a repair garage in Phoenix to a VW dealership in Tucson and finally landed at an independent VW repair specialist. We had a new oil cooler installed, our generator overhauled, and our cylinders inspected. After hours with our home on a garage lift, the root problem was solved by the installation of a fifty-five-cent part! The mechanic in Laguna had neglected to change to the larger gasoline jets needed for the enlarged cylinders he had installed, causing the engine to run lean and overheat.

As a result of these problems, Tom, a trained mechanical engineer, became a hypervigilant "car whisperer." He either did the work himself or hovered like a helicopter parent overseeing hired auto mechanics. In New Orleans, our next stop, he bought a book which became his Bible, *How to Keep Your Volkswagen Alive: A Manual of Step by Step*

Procedures for the Complete Idiot by John Muir. I remember it as a spiral-bound book, probably eight by twelve inches, with a blue cover—a book Tom would study before he started any repair project.

From these early days, Tom became the sole driver, fully attuned to the moods of the van, only when behind the wheel. He took care of the engine's needs, checked the oil, monitored the temperature. Nightly, he used his volt meter to keep track of the charge on the two car batteries and set the limits for use of the house lights and the refrigerator. With him constantly focused on the mechanical demands of our home and transportation, my role also became defined. I was the head cook, laundress, and main correspondent, writing journal-type letters home to both sets of parents. This traditional and almost sexist division of labor worked well for us as it was based on our individual talents and interests.

Once the car was repaired, we headed to New Orleans, before crossing into Mexico. Tom wanted to eat oysters, and I wanted to visit my college buddy and his wife. Our visit was short, but one thing I remember clearly—my friend's wife taught me barbering. She instructed me carefully as she trimmed her husband's hair while he sat in the bathtub clad only in his skivvies. She favored the tub location because it facilitated clean-up. Her husband's hair was straight, fine, and thin, and I was skeptical that her technique would work on Tom's thick and wavy mane. But always the optimist, I purchased a pair of barber's scissors and added this to my list of jobs.

On our last morning in New Orleans, our tummies heavy with sweet, rich Bananas Foster, Tom and I strolled around the French Quarter. We stopped at a shop that specialized in Civil War tourist items, mostly tiny model soldiers, books, and other trinkets. Tom was fascinated by the hundreds of toy soldiers uniformed in blue or gray and detailed with touches of color from minuscule ribbons, medals, gold epaulets, and feathers, while I wandered around the cramped aisles examining everything.

Near the cash register, I noticed two packs of playing cards, their backs adorned with colorful illustrations of Civil War soldiers in various uniforms. One deck was labeled, "Uniforms of the Union Army," and the other said, "Uniforms of the Confederacy." Always interested in historical costume, I thumbed through the decks. Most of the uniforms were the expected variations on blue or gray jackets and trousers. But one card in each deck stood out—each depicted a soldier resplendent in Turkish-style ballooning, wide-legged pants, a short open-fronted jacket with swirls of soutache braid, a brightly hued sash, and a fez style hat. Both the Union and the Confederate cards were labeled "Zouaves."

Later, as we drove toward Brownsville, Texas, I continued to puzzle over this strange phenomenon. "Have you ever heard of Zouaves?" I asked Tom.

"Not sure. Sounds foreign." Trees and small towns whizzed by our window.

"Today in the store, I saw several decks of playing cards with illustrations of Civil War uniforms. There was a style of uniform that looked Turkish. You know—harem pants, short jackets and a fez, rather than a regulation cap. Have you heard of this before?"

Tom perked up. "Are you sure? In the Civil War?"

"I saw the cards. These guys were in both sets, North and South."

"They must have been refugees from North Africa. I read somewhere about immigrants signing to join the Union army."

I knew Tom to be well read in the area of military history, yet his answer didn't ring true to me. "I never heard of immigrants from North Africa before the turn of the century."

"People came from everywhere," he assured me. "North Africa, Italy, the Caribbean. Anyone who wanted a better life sailed to New York."

"New York, maybe . . . But I don't think many went to the South. I doubt in 1860 there were enough Turkish or Moroccan immigrants to fill a whole regiment of Northern soldiers, let alone a Southern unit."

Tom thought a minute, then began again. "They were there before the war and got drafted, probably. Couldn't find work in the South

A Civil War Zouave.

because of the upheaval. Or maybe they were southern gentlemen who liked the fancy uniforms because the loose pants were more comfortable in the heat."

I laughed. "I think you're stretching a bit."

Tom looked over a bit sheepishly. "Maybe," he said.

Tom and I were both encyclopedia lovers. I had grown up with a set of *Britannica*, which my father taught us to use whenever we had a question he couldn't answer. Tom's set of *Encyclopedia Americana*, one of his first purchases as soon as he had money of his own, held a place of honor in our cottage and now awaited our return. I wished we had it with us.

Ahead, through the trees, I saw a church spire and a cluster of roofs. "Let's stop," I said. "I bet this town has a library. We could look up Zouave in the encyclopedia."

Tom slowed the van and pulled off the interstate. On the cool shaded streets of this typical small Texas town, it was easy to find the library, a solid stone building adjacent to the courthouse. Our first look at their thick Webster's was not very helpful: "A body of infantry in the French Army, composed originally of Algerians, distinguished for their dash, hardiness, and picturesque Oriental uniform."

We approached the librarian seated behind a wooden podium. "Where would we find books on Civil War history?" I asked.

"In the basement," she said. "All our history books are down there."

In the dimly lit stacks, row after row of tall metal bookcases overflowed with dusty volumes. We found the section on the American Civil War, and I pulled several out. Both Tom and I sat on the cool concrete floor and turned to the index in one volume after another. My eyes scanned down the listings, looking for Zouave(s). "Nothing in this one. No, not here either." A small stack of books at his side, Tom did the same.

I was almost ready to give up when I found the word at the very end of an index. Eagerly I flipped to the appropriate page. "Look at this, Tom. We were both kind of right. It says volunteer units were allowed to choose their own uniform style and the Zouave costume was popular with the men who had seen newspaper drawings of the French soldiers who first wore the Oriental style."

Tom moved closer so he could read over my shoulder. I pointed to the next paragraph.

"Read this, it's perfect. 'In 1859, a drill company called the Zouave Cadets toured nationally, performing light infantry drills with showy theatrical flourishes. Enchanted by the demonstrations and the fancy costumes, Zouave units were raised on both sides during the Civil War.'"

The part I liked best followed. I read out loud. "One of the best-known Zouave regiments was the 11th New York Volunteer Infantry Regiment, made up of New York City firefighters, many of whom were first-generation Irish immigrants who joined as a group."

One of these men could have been Tom's great-grandfather. "Lots of these guys were Irish!" I said. "The New York Zouaves were Irish!"

Back in the van, heading again for the Gulf of Mexico and the border, I giggled about what we had learned. "Irish Zouaves," I repeated. "Tom, when you started spouting off about North African refugees, did you have any idea?"

"No, of course not." His laughing eyes and wide smile united us into the absurdity of the situation. "I thought logic would save the day, but in truth, I was simply bullshitting."

"No kidding! You're a super bullshitter." I grinned to let him know it was okay, but to make it clear I would not be easy to fool, I added,

"From now on, whenever I think you're handing me a made-up story, I'll call you on it. I'm going to call your blow-hard pronouncements Zouaves. You'll know what I mean."

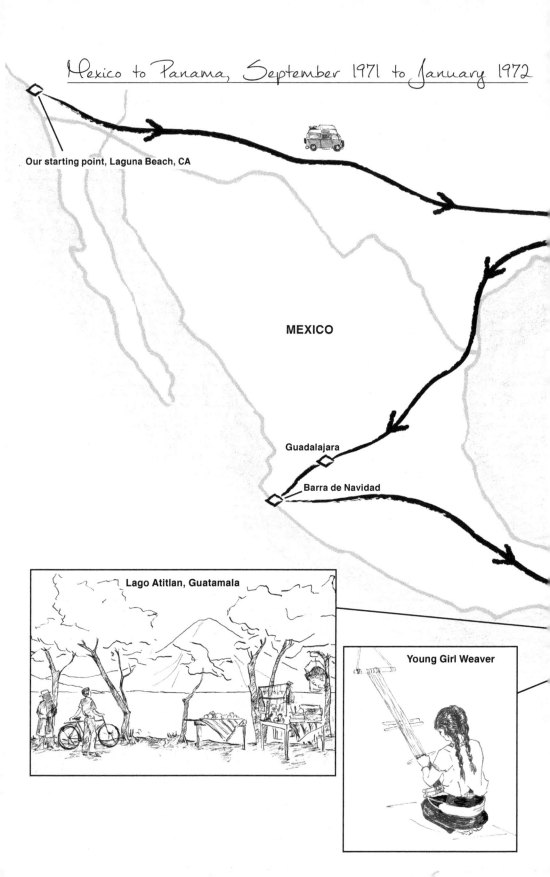

Mexico to Panama, September 1971 to January 1972

Our starting point, Laguna Beach, CA

MEXICO

Guadalajara

Barra de Navidad

Lago Atitlan, Guatamala

Young Girl Weaver

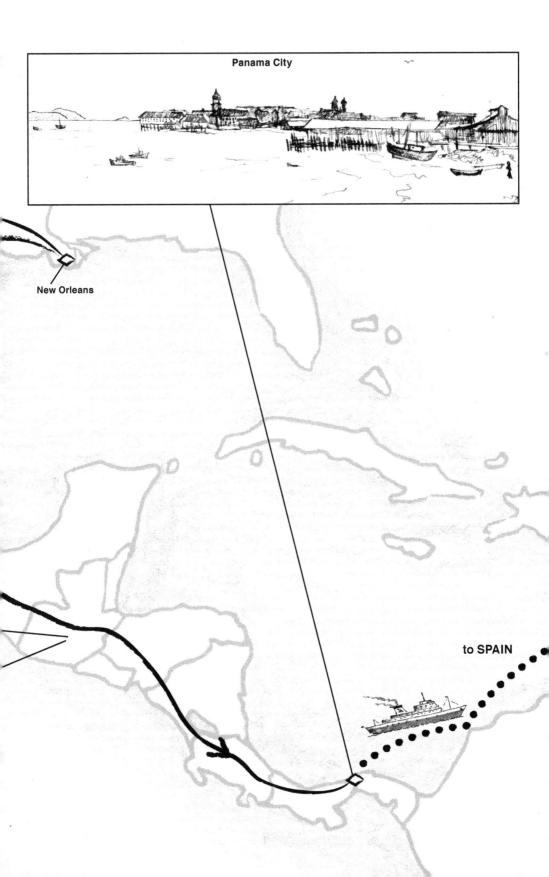

Panama City

New Orleans

to SPAIN

Chapter 4

The Road to Guadalajara

Our goal was to travel an average of 200 miles a day, allowing us to drive slowly and linger at interesting places. We entered Mexico, and for the first two days, we followed our plan. On our second day, we arrived in San Louis Potosi at about 4:30 p.m., not yet tired enough to stop for the night. We bypassed a campground and drove on. This started the saga of one of our first real "in country" experiences.

About twenty miles south of the city, a side road beckoned to us. We would try our first night of free camping. We turned off the main highway and followed the paved country road into the center of a village, nothing more than a row of adobe houses and shops along each side of the street. Soon the pavement became cobblestones, then rutted, hard-packed dirt. The village children gathered to watch and ran alongside the crazy gringo van heading nowhere. A few brave boys even hopped on our rear bumper and rode until the edge of the town. We continued down what had become little more than a trail, hoping to discover a quiet spot to park for the night.

What we found was another village, also long and narrow, and seemingly populated mainly by children. After the last adobe hut disappeared behind us, the dirt road ran parallel to a stream. Barely visible on the other side, I noticed movement, a truck traveling at highway speeds. I pointed toward the speeding, colorful blur. "Look! The highway's over there. This road must meet up with it soon."

Tom glanced over. "Good eye," he said. "All we have to do is get across this stream. Hope there's a bridge."

Though the highway appeared ever closer until the blur of traffic seemed only a quarter mile away, no bridge appeared. I worried we would never be able to cross the river and make our way back to the elusive highway. Tom harbored the same doubts. He stopped the car and walked down the sloped riverbank.

He stood on a sandbar and stomped his feet to test the surface. He pulled a section of twisted tree branch out of the sand and tested the depth of the water and the firmness of the sand. The stream was typical of desert rivers—the bed wide, sandy, and flat, the water slow and shallow, broken into rivulets and pools less than half a foot deep. The opposite bank was an unimposing and gradual incline about three feet high.

"The stream bottom feels solid," Tom said when he got back into the car. "I think we should make a run for it. If we don't slow down, we should be fine. You okay with giving it a try?"

I was willing to do whatever he suggested. He knew cars and was an excellent driver. We were together on an adventure!

Tom put the van in gear and headed across the stream at a rapid rate. Splashes of water sprayed out on either side. We reached the far side without slowing down, until we hit the loose, dry dirt of the far bank. The incline crumbled under our tires. The rear wheels spun and dug into the wet sand at the edge of the stream.

Tom jumped out and climbed to the roof of the van to retrieve our collapsible shovel. "Find me a couple of rocks," he called as he dug around the tires. "Not too big. Flat, if possible."

I located rocks and lugged them one by one back to where Tom knelt in the water behind the van and scooped away wet sand with his shovel. He put my stones under the tires in an effort to establish traction. "I'm going to try again. Stay on the bank out of the way," Tom said.

However, his next try to mount the sandy incline worsened the situation. Now the rear engine rested on the stream bottom and the exhaust pipe was under water. Tom lost no time. Sand and mud flew as he dug a channel in the sand to divert the water away from the engine compartment.

As we worked, local villagers gathered, laughing, talking, and attempting to communicate in rapid-fire Spanish, which we couldn't understand. With gestures and limited Spanish, Tom explained the problem. A couple of the men headed toward a distant hut and soon returned with shovels of their own. They waded into the shallow water and set to work beside Tom.

I stood among the other villagers who encouraged the diggers as they created a channel to move the water away from the rear wheels of the van. Tom looked up at me, relief softening the tense muscles in his neck.

"Katie, can you lighten the weight on the rear? Empty the water tank first and move our food stores to the front?"

I turned on the water faucet in the sink and the purified water from our tank gushed down the drain, out the side of the van, and flowed away downstream. While the men with shovels continued to dig, others gathered dry branches, which they placed under the tires. Children crouched on the riverbank to watch the action as I moved our ample supply of canned goods and fresh produce up to the front seat. They were impressed by the profusion of food, and I joked with them saying, "*Una tienda*" (a store). My rudimentary Spanish consisted mainly of nouns and hand gestures but the children understood my attempt at humor and their laughter made me smile.

By this time, half a dozen men dug to divert the stream and put rocks and branches under the tires. The children and I sat on the riverbank and offered encouragement. When Tom felt all was ready, he climbed into the driver's seat. Six men laid their hands on the back of the van and pushed with all their strength. They pushed and rocked the vehicle, Tom gave it gas, and suddenly the van was up on dry land. A cheer filled the air. We could never have thanked these Mexican villagers sufficiently, but we tried in our broken Spanish. Luckily, we had a bottle of red wine to give the men, and I handed out all our bananas and oranges to the children.

As dusk darkened the cloudless sky, we reached the highway, which was not as close or easy to find as it had appeared. Our wheels firmly on pavement again, we turned back to San Louis Potosi and the campground we had so blithely bypassed earlier in the afternoon. Tom, who was covered in mud, luxuriated in a hot shower while I prepared dinner.

By morning, the experience had taken on the rosy glow of a travel adventure. As we drove down the highway, a few men in the fields recognized our car and looked up from their work to wave. We honked and waved goodbye to the first friends we had made on our trip.

Our first planned stop was in San Miguel de Allende, a classic colonial town I had visited as an art student. On Saturday afternoon, I convinced Tom to forget his car worries and join the crowds coming into town for the La Alborada Fiesta. The main plaza was a sea of celebrants: Indians down from the hills with children in tow; shawl-wrapped babies snuggly carried on their mothers' backs; fancy, big-city Mexicanas, their hair in shiny, jet black curls; American expats; hippie art students; and local residents. The square was lined with vendors. Taco stalls heated bubbling pots of beef and chicken, while cooks flipped fresh tortillas on a convex griddle. Candy and cookie stalls tempted the sweet tooth, and a fresh pancake stall displayed a rainbow array of bottles filled with flavored syrups.

As the sun set, groups decked out in Aztec-inspired costumes danced down the street, followed by floats bearing young women dressed in long, white gowns. Huge flower-decorated structures, each carried by a dozen men, circled the plaza, where dancers stomped and twirled until

San Miguel de Allende from a hill overlooking the town.

the fireworks display started at 10:00 p.m. Tom and I sat on a low stone wall as spinning wheels of sparks flew high into the air and dissolved into a shower of colored pins of light. I breathed out a sigh of awe.

Tom muttered, "It's probably a defective rocket. They'd never pass a safety inspection at home."

"Relax," I said. "It's meant to be beautiful." As more and more twisting, sparkling wheels filled the night sky, even my engineer succumbed to the seduction of the Mexican night.

Car troubles continued to plague us as we continued south.

In Irapuato, a teeming industrial city, Tom realized the oil leak he had found in San Miguel was worse. We spent two days at the VW dealer before mechanics, working under Tom's scrutiny, discovered a serious crack in the engine block. Major engine repair was needed.

Inexplicable battery problems continued to affect the use of our refrigerator, and Tom wanted to replace both car batteries. As we left the dealer, we discovered the garage lift had gouged the tire and now it was flat. Luck was running against us and we needed to decide what to do.

We considered our options while at the hot springs resort of Abasolo, where we found a pleasant, shaded campsite and headed for the pools. Luxuriating in the warm water, steam rising into the cool afternoon, we assessed our situation. We agreed there were three choices.

- Have repair work done in Mexico by local mechanics. (Tom was uneasy about this, plus it would put a serious dent in our finances.)
- Put our van on a truck and go back to California for repairs. (We both vetoed this as it smacked of giving up.)
- Drive slowly to Guadalajara, a larger city where Tom hoped to buy a new engine block and do the repairs himself. (This was our mutual choice. We weren't ready to give up.)

According to our map, a state road offered a more direct route out of Abasolo than the main federal highway to Guadalajara. But maps could deceive and shorter was not necessarily faster.

Though the route wound through stunningly beautiful country, it was a tortuous ride on a narrow dirt road with more ruts and potholes than surface. We bumped along for several hours, jointly scanning the road for unexpected obstacles. Suddenly I felt a sharp jerk and watched our left front wheel wobble away ahead of us and topple over in the dirt. The van slid past the wheel and settled on its axle. Tom's skill kept the car in control and prevented our slide over the nearby embankment and into a canyon below. Within minutes, while Tom gathered up the errant wheel, a Mexican on a bicycle arrived with our hubcap and all five wheel nuts. Local help saved the day for us again.

By the time we arrived in Guadalajara, the city was sunk in twilight, we were exhausted, and all the de-stressing we had gained soaking in the hot pools had succumbed to road-induced tension. Luckily, on the road into town, we discovered a modern trailer park, an oasis of clean water, electricity, showers, a laundry, a snack bar, a swimming pool, and several American travelers who offered friendship and advice. It would be our headquarters for the next month.

On our first full day in Guadalajara, Tom pulled the engine out of the car. This was the first time he performed this feat on the trip, but not the last. I watched in awe as he took the engine apart. By evening, dozens of engine pieces were arranged in rows on a plastic tarp behind the van. How would he be able to get all the parts back together again? Surely, it would be more difficult to reassemble than any Chinese puzzle box or Arabian wedding ring.

When Tom inspected the parts, he found more damage than anticipated. A few engine parts had to be replaced. Others needed to be polished or chemically cleaned. The parts that he needed were not available in Mexico, so Tom called his mother and enlisted her help. Mary would buy them in California and air-freight them to us.

While we waited, Tom continued to solve car problems. Over the next weeks, using the local bus or hitching rides with new friends, he made countless trips to the VW dealer, various auto parts shops, and the local Sears and Roebuck. He cleaned each part meticulously, bought two new tires, and was able to get both our batteries fully charged and operational.

The waiting time was a vacation for me. I shopped at the nearby *tienda*, prepared meals, swam, lay in the sun poolside, read, and painted several watercolors. Together, Tom and I explored the city by bus. We wandered the local parks and munched on steamed corn, rubbed with chili powder, salt, and lemon or bought intensely flavored fruit or nut *paletas* (popsicles) from vendors. At the lively main market, Tom always bought bags of roasted peanuts in their shells to snack on while he worked. We filled our shopping bag with *carnitas* (roast pork) or Chorizo sausage, cilantro, tomatoes, onions, limes, and freshly made tortillas so I could prepare authentic tacos back in the van.

The challenge of preparing meals in my tiny kitchen was satisfying and I learned to combine long-lasting pantry items with fresh produce from the market. I cooked beans or meat in the pressure cooker to produce a luscious stew in an hour and topped it with crumbled fresh Mexican cheese and chopped onions, tomatoes, and cilantro. If we had no time to go to the central market, I could always turn a can of tuna, a can of mushrooms, powdered milk, and a handful of pasta into a skillet casserole.

One night we ate a meal at a popular restaurant, which specialized in *cabrito* (roasted kid). This eatery's front window was filled with a spit where several whole baby goats roasted over glowing coals. A tempting aroma pulled us inside. Cabrito was the only item on the wall menu, but there were choices—hip, ribs, head, leg, and a few other less popular parts. Tom chose the hip, I ordered ribs, and we shared. The meat was accompanied by bean soup and tortillas. We left satiated, wiping the goat fat from our chins.

One weekend, Tom went horseback riding with friends from the trailer park. A good rider, he had become familiar with horses during a summer in his teens spent as a "nanny" for the children of a wealthy, horse-owning family. He was so excited about his afternoon ride, he expended a good deal of effort convincing me to go with him for an equestrian experience. This was not an easy task, as I had a fear of these intelligent animals and had always felt uneasy on horseback. Tom suggested a full day together including a hike in the countryside, so I agreed to the excursion.

I stashed cheese, crackers, and a thermos of lemonade in our daypack, and we set off. The weather was sunny as we trekked cross country, along dirt trails, past hills where homes hid behind white stucco walls topped with bougainvillea. We hiked down a valley with an aqueduct that crossed over our heads and found the makeshift corral where locals brought their horses to be rented out for the pleasure of those rich enough to afford the ten pesos per-hour charge.

Most of the horses looked shaggy and unkempt, but Tom selected two well-cared for steeds, a small mare with a shiny brown coat and calm demeanor for me. With assistance, I mounted into the saddle and the ride began. At first, I was terrified, but Tom was patient and gave me pointers.

"The horse wants to enjoy the ride as much as you do," Tom reassured me. "Sit tall with confidence. If you're afraid, she'll sense it and try to take control."

"That's exactly what I'm worried about." I sat stiffly, afraid to twitch the reins or move my feet for fear the horse would take any movement as an invitation to gallop.

Tom blew me a kiss. "Relax. I'm right here to make sure you're safe."

Gradually my confidence grew as we clip-clopped along at a child's pace, the mare gentle and compliant beneath me. First down the sandy riverbed, then up between low hills to rest in the shade of a stand of eucalyptus. After two hours my poor butt was sore, but I had survived the experience. Still, I much preferred to travel in our fine home on wheels or to walk on my own two feet. To celebrate, we took a bus to town and indulged in triple-scoop ice cream cones at Bling's, a local place similar to the 31 Flavors Ice Cream chain at home.

Chapter 5

Traveling Together

We said goodbye to Guadalajara nearly two months after departing California. Thrilled to be back on the road, the pavement humming under our tires, Tom and I felt renewed energy. Mexico, below the forbidding Sonora Desert, could be lush and exotic, mountainous and green in the center, with each coast a tropical paradise. In 1971, years before the now popular resorts were built on the Pacific coast and the Yucatan peninsula, it was also often primitive.

To celebrate our release from the big city, we headed for the coast. Driving hours encouraged conversation. We discussed where we wanted to go next, shared memories from childhood or school days, and dreamed about our future when we returned home again.

"I like the idea of a name for our van," I said. "Kind of a family nickname or a private vanity license plate."

"Got any ideas?"

"Actually, I do. How about the Turtle?"

"Because we're so slow?" Tom said and stepped on the gas.

I gripped the door handle. "No! Not because we're slow."

Tom eased up on the accelerator. "Why then?"

"Because we have everything with us. The van is our home and it carries us everywhere, like a turtle in its shell."

Tom laughed. "And it's green, too! OK. The Turtle it is."

The road to the beach led us in torturous hairpin turns over several ranges of fantastic mountains, near steep and rocky gorges, and through verdant agricultural valleys. After a final turn, Barra de Navidad lay before us. The blue of its horseshoe bay and the lagoon behind it sparkled in the sun.

The town had no starred hotels in those days, no campgrounds, and no tourists in designer bikinis. It was little more than a village of thatched huts with chickens and pigs roaming in the yards and a small fishing harbor. Beachfront eateries with palm roofs stood in the sand and served platters of bright pink shrimp, crisply fried fish, and a limited choice of beer or coke. We stood in the shade and watched a woman with a grease-splotched apron turn a whole fish in a deep kettle of hot lard. Her fisherman husband snored in a hammock nearby. When she lifted the fish out of the oil, its crispy skin cracked to reveal a hint of the moist white flesh.

"Smells fabulous," Tom said. "Shall we have lunch here?"

I nodded in approval. "Yes, let's. Maybe we can buy shrimp or a couple of smaller fish for dinner tonight, too."

Tom ordered in broken Spanish and the woman nodded. She dropped a handful of potato rounds into the bubbling oil and set out two, mismatched, plastic plates. After a quick swipe with a damp towel across her makeshift tree-stump chopping block, the woman moved the crispy fish to the round wood surface. Tom and I watched in dismay as she raised her big cleaver and brought it down with force, chopping off the fish's head. In rapid succession, she slammed down the knife two more times. Our golden fish was reduced to a mound of crisp skin, glistening flesh, and dangerous bones. The woman's smile was gap-toothed and filled with pride in her work as she lifted the fish in equal parts onto the waiting plates.

Scooped directly from the cooking vat, the fried potato rounds were heaped on the side. She dipped her hand into a nearby red, soft-drink cooler, its long electrical cord dangling across the palm rafters to a lone pole at the corner of the open-air café, and handed me two dripping cans, one of beer and the other, coke. She offered Tom the two plates. With a wave of her hand and a cheerful, "*Buen apetito*," she motioned us to the tables made from upside-down cable spools.

Tom and I sat on wobbly folding chairs, our feet in the sand, and picked carefully through the fish and potatoes, searching for shattered bones. Our chef and hostess brought us a bottle of fiery hot sauce and a bowl of salsa made of minced, fresh tomato, flecks of white onion, and chunks of green chili. One small bite at a time, we worked through the succulent fish. Tom spit countless errant bones into the palm of his hand and built a pile on the side of his plate. My pile of bones was as big as his but more cleanly picked over. I managed to find enough flaky chunks to satisfy my hunger, but it was tough.

Suddenly, Tom slapped his palm on the wooden table and the plates jumped. "I give up!" he said. "There's too many bones and they're all mixed in. What a mess!" He dipped one of the crisp potato slices into the salsa. "I guess I won't starve," he said as he pulled a bit of browned fish skin from the mess on his plate, brushed off invisible bones, then dipped it into the salsa and popped it in his mouth. "Wow, a bit hot for me," he said, "but I'm sure you loved it."

After lunch, we strolled down the sandy beach, breathing in the salt-water smell of the air. Tom and I had each passed countless indolent summer days on the beach as children, and the ocean—whether it was a view of the sea's blue expanse from the hills, the sound of waves, or the embrace of sea water as we swam—was a happy place for us both. With the knowledge of beach people, we had set out from the van, our bathing suits under our clothes. When we reached a quiet cove protected by a jutting sand spit, we stripped down to our suits and ran into the water. The cove was calm enough for me to lie back and float, rocking on top of the gentle swells. Tom swam out to the tip of the sandbar and rode a curling wave back. He glided up to me, wrapped his arms around my waist, and shook his head, spraying me with droplets flung from his curls. "You're so beautiful, your hair all spread out like floating seaweed," he whispered in my ear.

I turned around in his arms and laughed. "Seaweed! What a vision." I threw my arms around his neck and draped strands of my wet hair over his shoulders. "How about a seaweed kiss?" I asked and gave him a big, slobbery smack.

"Any kiss from you will do," he said, splashed me again, then lay back in the water and floated with his hands behind his head.

On our way back to where we had parked the van, we passed a busload of Mexican travelers stopped by the shore for a rest break. They walked near the water line, pant legs rolled up to the knees or skirts knotted and held in one hand, dipped their toes into the curls of white foam, and gathered shells. Unwilling to risk the knife work of our luncheon chef, we stopped at a different seaside café and bought four glistening silver fish. Farther on, three young gringos had staked a claim on the roof of a deserted, storm-damaged house, and they lounged on their sleeping bags.

Reminded of our need for our own spot for the night, we headed to the north end of the bay where we found a flat, dirt area cleared of jungle. Two other VW microbuses were already there. Three young guys in the first van confirmed it was a safe free-camping site.

As soon as we parked, I started our fish dinner. Tom beheaded and gutted the fish for me and handed them back, clean and ready to fillet. With my sharpest knife, I worked carefully and slowly. I wanted to make sure the fish were totally boneless.

After checking the battery and giving me permission to turn on the refrigerator, Tom strolled around the area, sipping his evening can of beer and talking to the other travelers. His ability to start up a conversation with a complete stranger was proving a valuable asset. A consummate networker, he used this talent to gather information about the road ahead, learn the latest news, and find out how other travelers coped with difficulties. During our journey, I depended on Tom's rambling tours of any campsite where other travelers shared the space with us. Whether it was Valencia, Spain; Copenhagen, Denmark; or Istanbul, Turkey, Tom always picked up information and the friendships he started resulted in shared experiences with people from around the world.

Tom returned as I sprinkled chopped cilantro and thinly sliced lemon over a skillet of fish, atop a bed of rice seasoned with tomatoes, onion, and garlic. "The old guy in the dinged-up blue VW is seventy-one years old! He's amazing."

Tom slid onto the bench seat at our table and opened a fresh beer. I ladled fish and rice into our pale-green melamine bowls, set them on the table, and pulled up my folding stool. I was ready to hear all about our neighbor.

"He's a Frenchman," Tom continued. "He's been traveling the world in his van since his retirement in 1960. More than ten years! After dinner you have to come meet him. Speaks good English, too." Tom chewed cautiously on the rice and fish. "Delicious." He smacked his lips and grinned. He put another forkful into his mouth and savored it as he chewed. I watched, proud of my skills. Tom pursed his lips, touched two fingers to his mouth as if to kiss them, then spit into the cup of his hand.

"Did you get a bone? I was so careful," I said, the distress audible. Then I noticed Tom's smile. "Show me your hand," I said. "You're Zouaving me. I don't believe you got a bone."

Tom opened his empty hand. "No bones," he said. "It's ambrosia compared to lunch."

An hour later, after Tom had washed the dishes, he led me over to our neighbor's van and tapped on the window. The Frenchman greeted us, then hopped out with agility that belied his age. He was short and wiry, his gray beard unevenly trimmed, but clean. When Tom introduced me, the Frenchman planted a peck on both my cheeks and shook hands American style.

"*Bonsoir*, Madame Katherine," he said, his elegant accent at odds with our rustic environment. We sat outside his home on folding chairs, and he poured us each a plastic tumbler of red wine. Under the glittering stars, with the sound of waves breaking against the rocks, we chatted about travel adventures and he shared advice about long-term van living. His microbus was neat, with all his possessions in labeled boxes and cubbyholes, easy to find but basic and Spartan. We were happy to return to our cozy camper and our comfortable bed, where we fell asleep surrounded by the familiar sound of the Pacific Ocean through the van window.

"I wonder if we'll be doing this when we're seventy?" Tom mused.

"Maybe. I hope so," I mumbled as daydreams and night dreams blended together.

We lingered only one day at the beach because we needed to get to Mexico City. During much of our journey, a visit to the capital city of each country was necessary. There we could get visas for the next destination, though occasionally a city large enough to have a consulate would do. Because our travel style was unscheduled, we could never estimate when we would actually arrive at various borders farther along our route. Visas, usually valid only for a specific time period, often required a declaration of the date we would enter a country, a date designated as the activation day of the visa. Of necessity, it became our practice to go to the capital city of one country to apply for our visa to the next country we would enter. In Latin America, the US Embassy was also a mail stop where we picked up letters marked, "Visitor Mail,

Hold until Arrival." Our Mexican car insurance coverage expired on November 25, so we had to cross into Guatemala by then. The insurance for Central America, purchased in Oaxaca, Mexico, would only cover us for forty-five days. We needed to be through the Darian Gap and in South America before that insurance expired. Our travels were seldom a carefree adventure—there were always legal parameters, as well as safety and car issues to consider.

The farther south we went, the fewer actual trailer parks or campgrounds appeared, until they were almost nonexistent. If we were willing to stop for the night near a gas station, there was the advantage of running water to fill our water tank, along with the possibility of a usable public toilet. Otherwise, we needed to find a safe spot, a level place which wasn't obviously on private property. We grew to treasure camping freely in the countryside, though a place with water taps was important several times a week.

Free camping also necessitated the use of the "green toilet bucket." I had dreaded its lack of privacy, but this didn't faze Tom. When there was no other choice, I was forced to use the bucket and I amazed myself at how soon my embarrassment evaporated. We established a routine for the placement of the bucket inside its cozy ottoman. At night it was wedged between the driver and passenger seat, easy to get to for predawn use and convenient to our tiny sink—I could wash my hands while sitting on the pot. When we were on the road, the usually empty bucket/ottoman was wedged between the sink and the stove so it couldn't slide around on twists and turns. During the days we stayed put, it was hidden in the corner by the closet. This location offered a modicum of needed privacy for peeing. When the bucket was in use for more serious morning business, the other person would step outside, or if it was raining, sit in the cab of the van and read or look out the front windshield. Still, whenever used, the bucket needed to be dumped. Tom's nonchalance and willingness added the job of sanitation engineer to his list of responsibilities. Each morning, Tom took the bucket somewhere appropriate to dump its contents. He was now mechanic, car whisperer, photographer (he had an SLR Pentax with two lenses), networker, water carrier, and sanitation engineer—truly my hero!

We were both delighted by excursions to local markets. The air, whether open to the sky or covered by canvas awnings or glass walls and a tin ceiling, was always filled with the aromas of spices, the sweetness of flowers and herbs, and the sour smell of rot. We filled our shopping bags from the profusion of produce heaped in piles—bright red tomatoes and chilies, the different greens of limes, lettuce, and zucchini, the yellows and oranges of citrus, pineapple, and papaya, and the browns and whites of potatoes and onions. Stalls displayed row upon row of tubs, each heaped with beans of a different color, from dark red to white, from shiny black to speckled brown. It was fun to explore the stands with packaged and canned goods, too. I found unusual spice blends and bought rice by the kilo, new shapes of pasta, canned salsas, and packaged soups in flavors unavailable in the United States.

The butcher and seafood sections of the markets kindled my adventurous spirit. We were undaunted by the hunks of red meat suspended from hooks in the open air and visited by the occasional fly; whole chickens strung up by their necks, their heads hanging to one side; rows of glistening sausages; or fresh whole fish, their glassy eyes staring sightlessly at the ceiling. Tom wrote down each item we bought and its cost in a tiny notebook he always carried in his shirt pocket. We would return to the camper with our string bags full of purchases. Each country introduced us to new smells and tastes, different foods that never failed to intrigue us and tantalize our taste buds.

As we neared the Guatemala border, the Mexican state of Chiapas offered us a romantic farewell. One dusk, we discovered a natural spa. Our headlights picked up a small sign near a paved side road. *Balneario.* We knew enough Spanish to understand this meant swimming baths. Soon we found a flat, paved area and stopped. In the quiet night, we heard the sound of rushing water. Unable to explore in the dark, we settled in for a meal made from the bounty bought at the Tuxtla city market earlier that day.

We woke to find ourselves at the edge of a gorge. Nearby, the chasm dead-ended at a rock cliff with a cave from which spilled a torrent of water. The stunning waterfall dropped down to a wide, deep pool. The water continued to rush over and around boulders, formed two more pools, flowed on into the cleft of rocks, and continued down the mountain. Uneven stairs led from the parking area, down the canyon wall, to the pools below. The bottom-most pool, fed by a smaller waterfall, was clear and cold but not freezing—perfect for swimming. As we luxuriated in our haven, a few other people arrived, but they chose the uppermost pool for their swim, and we continued, blessed with romantic solitude.

Tom went back to the car for shampoo, and we bravely washed our hair under our personal waterfall. As I worked lather through my hair, I imagined I was a native beauty posing for her lover. But my imagination got the better of me when I looked up at the top of the precipice where a few branches overhung the cascade. There could be logs floating lazily in the current of the upper river. What if a log was even now approaching, pushed by the water and about to tumble over the edge? I rinsed my long tresses quickly and stepped out from under the waterfall.

In the afternoon, we drove farther up the cloud-shrouded mountains through beautiful wooded country dotted with villages. When we got to San Cristóbal de las Casas, the last city before the border, we went to its market where indigenous people (also called Amerindians) dressed in traditional native costumes as colorful as the produce. Of course, we could not resist buying yet more vegetables and fruits from the heaped displays. We had heard agriculture was not as productive in Guatemala and good produce difficult to find. That night, when we camped beside the road about an hour from the border, bags of oranges, onions, potatoes, green beans, squash, carrots, tomatoes, chilies, and fresh coriander filled the van.

The border between Mexico and Guatemala was our first major international crossing. (For Californians, entering Mexico was second nature.) Would being married make the Guatemala border crossing easier as Tom had suggested? We were both keyed up as we approached the guard office next to the highway.

The Mexicans simply waved us through. On the Guatemalan side, the guards stood in the middle of the traffic lane and waved us over. First, they checked our passports and stamped our visas. Then they asked to inspect the car. They were polite and formal and we began to relax. Tom slid open the wide side door and motioned for them to enter. We were proud to show off our neat and well-stocked home.

Two uniformed guards bent their heads and stepped inside. They looked into the upper cupboards, down under the center bench seat, and into the array of sacks filled with our market treasures. As I watched them open first one bag, then the next, I noticed their smiles fade. Finally, they looked up and shook their heads sadly.

One of the guards stood at attention outside our van while the other spoke in stilted English. "Unfortunately, you cannot take these fruits and vegetables into our country. Agriculture protection is strictly enforced," he said. "You can eat what you want before you cross, or you can cook it, if you want. We can allow cooked vegetables into Guatemala."

Eating our hoard of food would have been a staggering and impossible feat, but I was willing to sit at the border and cook. "I can do it in only a few hours," I said.

Tom looked unconvinced and shook his head. "Don't be ridiculous. You know this is a coup for the guards. It'll feed their families and friends."

"I don't want to give all this to the guards," I said, tears stinging my eyes. "With the pressure cooker, I can cook the potatoes and carrots. Lots of other stuff, too. It won't take long. I can make vegetable stew, enough for a few days."

Tom's unsmiling look and his worried words were unwelcome. "We need to get through the legalities and on our way before they come up with anything else. If we stay here, pretty soon they'll find something else we can't take into Guatemala."

"I want to do this," I insisted. "I don't want to waste all this great food. Who knows what we'll find down the road." My voice rose as I argued about vegetables with Tom while the guards looked on patiently.

"It's only food," Tom said, his voice falling an octave lower, a sure sign he was angry. "We're not going to sit here and cook fucking potatoes to save a few pesos!" He pulled out the bags of vegetables one by one and set our treasure trove on the ground at the side of the road. I stood silent and angry and refused to help. When Tom was done, I climbed into the back without a word and sat stubbornly in the center of the rear seat, my arms crossed over my chest, tears staining my cheeks.

Tom slammed the sliding door shut and returned to the driver's seat. He did not look back at me or suggest I come up front. The guards waved us through the barrier and we moved away from the border station and into Guatemala. Our first crossing had not been easy.

The road wound through a breathtakingly narrow chasm, with a white twist of water hundreds of feet below. High rocky crags rose on both sides of the thin strip of highway. I strained my neck to see the top of the cliffs from the rear of the car. Unwilling to miss the glorious landscape, I moved silently to the passenger seat in the cab. The air between us remained tense.

Neither Tom nor I had yet developed the ability to apologize with ease, but by the time we had reached *Huehuetanango*, the first town of any size, we were speaking again . . . barely. I served a simple lunch of canned tuna and crackers, which we ate glumly, surrounded by Mayan ruins.

The next day, at the first village market in Guatemala, the few stands displayed shriveled and spotted produce. "This stuff is terrible," I said, still mourning the previous day's loss. "I don't want to buy any of it. Look. All the tomatoes are half rotten."

Tom shrugged. "Guess the border guards are having a grand feast on us."

"If I'd cooked those veggies, you'd be the one having the feast, not them."

"These oranges aren't too bad," Tom said as he handed a coin to the vendor and stuffed the fruit in his daypack.

It had been our first real fight on the trip. With the clarity of hindsight, I knew Tom was right and my stubbornness certainly absurd, but for some reason, losing the food had been a disaster to me.

Chapter 6

Bypassing the Darién Gap

ach day, as Tom and I drove into the heart of Central America, stunning sights continued to slide by the windows of our Turtle. The excitement of seeing new places and cultures together was a special kind of intimacy.

Our only guidebook, *Central America: Highways, Airplane, Boat, Train, Travel Guide* by Cliff Cross, was a mishmash of useful information, such as the location of camping spots, the days of local markets, and the hours of various embassies. The book suggested a scenic back road south to Guatemala City. We found the route on our AAA map, a thin black line through mountains and valleys. Tom calculated it would take us about twice as long as the main highway, but we were eager to immerse ourselves in the rural countryside and its people.

We began the detour in the late afternoon and bumped along the twists and turns of a narrow, unpaved, mountain road. As dusk fell, we found another *balneario* (spa) or *Ojo de Agua* (Eye of Water). The beautiful spot was next to a sylvan pool at the bottom of a waterfall, perfect for a morning bath.

The sky was golden with the rising sun when we went down for our swim. Refreshed and squeaky clean, we returned to our home in no hurry to leave. Months before, when I was collecting recipes, I had copied down the instructions for Bannock bread, a traditional Canadian camp food with Scottish roots. That morning, we were out of the soft, square loaves of store-bought Mexican bread, and last week's tortillas were stale. It was the perfect, lazy morning to try the quick, skillet bread for the first time.

I mixed together flour, leavening, and powdered milk (a necessary staple with limited refrigeration), added oil and water, and stirred in raisins and chopped walnuts. The dough was stiff, but it felt good to work it into a flat disk the size of the bottom of my large, well-oiled skillet. I covered the pan with the stainless-steel bowl of the set and put it on the stove over a low flame. After fifteen minutes, I peeked under the cover. The bread was puffed up and the bottom had taken on a golden tinge. The smell of fresh bread filled the van. Five minutes later, I turned the hot Bannock out on a plate. The aroma was so enticing, we broke pieces off to taste, blowing on our burned fingertips as the crumbs slid to the table. I set out a plate of sliced oranges and we slathered the hot, slightly sweet bread with butter. Perfect! Bannock bread, freshly made on our stove, would become a regular part of our diet for the next two years.

After a full day driving through pine-covered mountains, we found ourselves in a fertile valley. Lush fields of tall corn, irrigated by streams rushed down from the hills and adobe villages, nestled among banana trees and bamboo. Men plodded along the side of the road, carrying heavy loads on their backs, the weight balanced from a forehead strap, their sandaled feet kicking up dust. The farmers often wore traditional loose, handwoven trousers, which flapped about their shins. The pants were bound at the waist with a sash and topped by a shirt of colorful stripes. Women, traditionally dressed in a long wrap skirt, a sash, and an embroidered, boxy, loose blouse called a *hupil*, strode with water jars on their heads and often a baby in a sling on their backs.

A young girl worked on a waist loom in front of a palm thatched cottage. Her hands flew as she wove an intricately patterned hair band. The long warp threads of the loom stretched from one of the posts that supported the porch roof to a strap, which encircled the girl's waist. With a small heddle, she lifted the red warp threads alternately and slipped a wooden shuttle back and forth, creating a brightly colored, geometric design. After a few strokes, she pushed her work tightly together using a bone comb.

The girl was shy, but her father came out of the shadowed house and offered a finished strip with large tassels at each end for ten dollars. Sadly, we shook our heads. Tom and I had agreed on an average daily budget of the same amount and we could not spend it all on one souvenir. We needed to be frugal.

Later, we stopped beside the beautiful lakes of Atitlán and Amatitlán for a picnic lunch. There we learned from other van travelers of a local woman who offered meals to tourists in her home. That evening we were served a full meal for two—Chile Rellenos, black beans, vegetables, avocado salad, fresh-made tortillas, and a dessert of bananas cooked in honey—all for a dollar, one-tenth the cost of the hand-woven band.

After getting our visas in Guatemala City, Tom insisted we camp on the edge of town at a Texaco service station where he could do car maintenance. On Saturday morning, glad to have his work accomplished, Tom relaxed in the cab while I toasted up two pieces of bread in a skillet and topped each with a crisp slice from our final can of American corned beef hash and a fried egg. This was one of Tom's favorite breakfasts and he deserved a treat. "We're only a few hours' drive from Chichicastenango," he said. "Do you want to drive back and go to the Sunday market tomorrow?"

"Yes! I'd love to." I hesitated, remembering how hard he'd been working. "You're sure you won't mind the extra drive?" I asked.

Market day in Santo Tomás Chichicastenango, Guatemala.

Katie

"It'd be a pleasant break from crawling around under the car. Besides, I know the last three days sitting here at a service station with all the trucks and heat wasn't fun for you."

"I didn't complain. It's the price we pay for this unbelievable trip."

"Thanks, sweetheart. So . . . Shall we go? I'm ready for a day of pleasure."

The next morning, we entered the market's jumble of stalls, umbrellas, and awnings. The narrow spaces teemed with throngs of Mestizos and indigenous people. Vendors squatted in the patchy shade behind displays of trinkets, prepared food, farm produce, woven goods, candles, and household items. At the far end of the square, smoke rose into the air in front of a white, Colonial-style church. Deserted by its Catholic priests years before, the church had become a center of native spirituality. On the front steps, men and women in native dress waved incense bundles while crowds flooded past them to enter the darkened sanctuary. The nave, presided over by a medicine man, was illuminated by hundreds of candles, their wax dripping down on row after row of raised platforms. The flicker of candle flames filled the space in a magical way, their heat rising to a ceiling covered with decades of soot.

Our journey alternated between three types of days—days of sightseeing, endless driving days to cover ground and keep on our schedule, and tedious days of waiting and/or car repairs. It was already December 6. Spurred on by rumors that the boats we hoped would take us around the Darién Gap suspended operations over the Christmas holidays, we headed for El Salvador where our main mission was to go to the Honduran and Nicaraguan embassies for visas. But as we were finding out, inconvenient timing can change plans. We arrived at the capital of Honduras on the Fiesta of the Immaculate Conception. Once again, stumped by the imperatives of the calendar, we searched our guidebook, which indicated visas could be issued at the border.

The crossing into Honduras went smoothly, and we drove straight to the next border and the consulate there, only to find the Nicaraguan officials continued to celebrate the fiesta. They would have issued the visas with a holiday surcharge, but we decided to return the next day rather than pay the extra two dollars each.

I marvel to think four dollars would make us wait a day. It helps to keep in mind basic costs in the United States in 1971—36 to 55 cents for a gallon of gas (it was before the Arab oil embargo), 25 cents for a loaf of bread, 45 cents for a dozen eggs, and $2,800 for a year's tuition at Harvard!

Stalled at the border into Nicaragua, both Tom and I thought of the spot where we had stopped for lunch on the bank of a shallow river.

"Let's go back to our lunch spot," Tom suggested. "It was level and shady. We can stop at the service station we passed to fill our water tanks."

I agreed to this splendid idea. At the river, several village women crouched in the water in the late afternoon sun, rubbing their laundry on the smooth rounded stones and gossiping. They looked up when we parked but quickly returned to their work.

The eternal romantic, I decided I would do laundry, too. There was always soiled clothing to wash—T-shirts, socks, underwear, and jeans. I gathered a few things and a bar of soap and waded into the river. I was

Village children watch as I wash clothes in the river
near the Nicaraguan border.

proud of myself as I knelt in the cold water, scrubbing socks and Jockey briefs against the rocks. Several young girls came over and watched as I tried to copy their mothers. The current ran faster and stronger than I anticipated and before I knew it, the water stole a sock from my hand, followed by Tom's underwear. As I tripped among the stones, chasing the escaping underpants, the local women looked up, smiles stretched across their faces. I caught the briefs myself (they moved more slowly) and retrieved the sock from the outstretched hand of one of the washerwomen. But I was aglow with pride. I had done it! I had washed clothes in a river.

Guatemala, El Salvador, Honduras, Nicaragua, Costa Rica, and soon Panama. Costa Rica, now so well known for ecotourism and vacation resorts was, in the early 1970s, a country of mountain coffee farms, coastal banana plantations, and high grasslands with cattle and cowboys. The biggest tourist attractions were the woodworking shops with hand-turned wooden bowls, mugs and goblets, tables, and carved replicas of the gaily painted native ox carts used to transport coffee from the hillside plantations to the ports. We traveled faster through Costa Rica than we would have liked, pausing only at the 11,000-foot summit known as *Cerro de la Muerté* (Mountain of Death), in the mist-shrouded mountains. We hoped the complete rainbow that arched overhead was a good omen.

December 15 found us on the hot, humid border of Panama, soon to be my least favorite place of the entire trip.

To be fair, all of Central America was different in 1971 from what it is today, and Panama was perhaps one of the most different. At the time, many of the countries of the region were governed by US-backed military dictators and on the cusp of years of revolution, which would drive waves of political refugees northward. Often economically dependent on US corporations such as United Fruit and definitely underdeveloped, the republics of Central America showed only their placid surface as we drove through. The unrest that fermented beneath remained hidden.

Costa Rica, which had been blessed with uninterrupted democracy since 1948, was the most stable country in the region, but the development of ecotourism was a decade away. Panama, which shared its northern border with Costa Rica, was stagnant under a military government led by Omar Torrijo, who strove for much-needed social and economic reforms. But progress was slow and the concessions he eventually won from the United States to gain control of the Panama Canal were several years in the future. When we arrived in 1971, the Canal Zone was an American Territory, fully governed by the United States.

Eager to get to the capital, we zipped through sparsely populated grassland. Panama City was a teeming city of slums mixed with old Spanish colonial remnants, a noticeable lack of infrastructure, and one colorless market where a few vegetables wilted in the heat, and packets of meat and chicken wrapped in plastic sat on dirty ice. Everything sweltered in the tropical heat, familiar to anyone who has ever traveled near the equator.

We went directly to the port of Balboa to investigate possible transportation to South America. Nobody knew anything about the coastal boats we had heard about. One man suggested that if such vessels did exist, they would likely be at the Caribbean port of Colon on the opposite side of the isthmus. A train ran regularly from Panama City to Colon and we grabbed the next one, parking the van at the station. The train track ran near the canal—familiar to Tom but a first-time thrill for me.

In Colon, at the end of the Front Street Pier, we located a tramp steamer (more on this vessel later), which we were told would leave soon for Uruguay, and a couple of coastal boats. We wandered around the docks. Tom asked several workers if they knew of a boat sailing to Colombia. One man told him he had heard a boat large enough for only four cars was expected in a day or two. It might be sailing south. Our first day of research turned up little that would help and we returned to the Pacific side.

The only safe camping spot near Panama City was the Hippodrome, a large open parking lot where travelers slept, including a Canadian couple, Robert and Marie, we had met on the road in Costa Rica. The plus side of the Hippodrome, a sports center and race track, was the availability of an Olympic-size pool and showers. The disadvantage of the site was the hot, black expanse of asphalt that offered no respite from the equatorial sun. Without a tree in sight, it was a hellish place during the day, and at night, the tarmac radiated heat.

Most of the travelers settled down at the Hippodrome were trying to get to South America. A sense of community had developed and information was shared. We learned the boat heading for Colombia had been expected for several weeks. Her lady captain had a bad record for accidents, the boat had only one engine, and the cost of the trip was to be shared out at twenty dollars per person (more for cars). Tom declared this vessel too risky.

Over the weekend, we returned to Colon for a magical respite with a friend Tom had unexpectedly run into, one of his old classmates from the California Maritime Academy and now a Canal pilot. Crossing into the Canal Zone, we entered a time warp, a kind of mini-USA sanctuary, a land of small agricultural fields, green lawns studded with American military-base style houses, clean restaurants, a laundromat, a movie theater, a US post office, picnic grounds, a PX, and a commissary.

Because of Tom's friend, our own US passports, and Tom's US Coast Guard license and US Naval Reserve status, we were able to access most of the facilities. We did laundry, sent packages home, saw a movie, had dinner with our friends, went to the post exchange (PX), and with permission from the Zone police, camped at a lovers' point. Best of all, we learned about a Chinese family with permission to grow vegetables on US government land. Descendants of Chinese laborers from the days of building the canal, this family had a farm stand that sold produce to the American residents. We filled the van with veggies, including Chinese long beans, the first I had ever cooked.

It was obvious we would be in Panama over the holidays. We had quickly formed a friendship with Robert and Marie and talked about the possibility of caravanning with them, if and when we made it around the Darién Gap. Robert, who had previously worked at the Edinburgh Zoo, dressed in his Scottish kilt for special occasions. He insisted it was cool on hot evenings because it allowed air to circulate. I was convinced he wore it more so he could get feisty with Panamanians who found it strange to see a man wearing a "skirt." He and Marie had a four-wheel drive truck with a camper unit on back, topped by an unusual Plexiglas dome. At night when the lights were on inside, the dome reflected the inside of the truck outward, often providing entertainment for neighboring campers as the couple undressed for bed.

A few days before Christmas, Robert, Marie, and Tom drove to the city together to do more shipping research. I remained at the Hippodrome to guard the parts of a disembodied engine (yes, car work in progress on our van, again and constantly). Admittedly, I was also left at "camp" because I was a miserable, whiny mess. The night before Tom and I had stood outside in the cooler night air and chatted with our friends. While we talked, I had noticed pinpricks of pain in my legs and kept rubbing and swatting at my calves. It took me a while to realize I was being attacked by sand fleas, a voracious, bloodsucking bug nicknamed no-see-ums. By morning, my legs, from ankle to mid-thigh, were covered in hundreds of miniscule red bites, which itched with a vengeance. All I wanted to do was lie in the back of the van with wet towels over my legs and suffer.

When the group returned, Tom looked as morose as I felt. "Nobody knows about regular boats going around the Gap," he told me. "Nothing but a rumor with no truth to it at all!"

"How could we all have heard this rumor, even back in the US?" I asked. "I wonder how long this lie has been floating around."

With Christmas only twenty-four hours away, Marie and I switched our concerns to planning a holiday dinner. She had an oven inside their camper and volunteered to cook a turkey. In spite of the sweltering heat and the ventless Plexiglas dome, she managed to produce a tasty bird stuffed with bread and dried fruit. According to one of my letters, I made carrots cooked in wine, cranberry sauce, gravy, and plum pudding with lemon sauce. I'm sure I didn't make the plum pudding from scratch, and I have no memory of how I got it. Perhaps at the PX? Robert honored the celebration by wearing his kilt. We ate the meal under the stars, drank wine, and talked of family back home—ours in California, Marie's in Canada, and Robert's parents in Scotland. Later, two Norwegian guys who slept in a nearby tent passed around bowls of the traditional Scandinavian rice pudding flavored with sugar and cinnamon. Among the creamy grains of rice, I found the hidden almond that foretold a good-luck year ahead! Another couple passed around delightfully alcoholic Costa Rican-style eggnog.

With the New Year so close, it was time to take stock of what we had learned.

- Most small vessels to Colombia allowed only cargo, no passengers.
- The coasters and flatboats were almost nonexistent and dropped passengers illegally on the beach. (Think illegal immigration.)
- There were horror stories about the dangers of driving in Colombia.
- The Mexican vessel heading through the canal in a few days would not stop.
- The only hopeful news was of an Italian passenger/cargo liner scheduled to dock in Colon the first week of January. It could take us to Colombia for $400.
- Another ship of the same company would dock in Balboa on the Pacific side at about the same time and travel down to Chile, with its first port of call in Ecuador.

The most talked about news at the Hippodrome regarded the tramp steamer we had checked out on our first day in Colon. Fast becoming a legend, this was the same ship Tom had noticed because of the odd way it was double-parked at the dock, bobbing high in the water as if it were empty. Six to eight campers and cars and one motorcycle had been on the open deck and several people walked back and forth across the adjoining ship, carrying bananas, boxes of crackers, and five-gallon containers of water. At ease around ships, Tom had followed them onto the old tramp, leaving me standing nervously on the pier. He returned breathless with information.

"Wow, those guys are in trouble," he said. "The ship's loaded with contraband cigarettes!"

"Illegal cigarettes?"

"Yeah, I guess there's a high tax on tobacco in Uruguay. They're headed to Montevideo. But before they go into the port, they'll have to offload the cigarettes into smaller boats on the high seas. They'll be bobbing around like a cork in a bathtub for days, not to mention for the entire twenty or thirty days it'll take to get there. It'll be a long trip and all those guys in their vans will have to supply their own food and water and do all their own cooking in a greasy galley on deck."

"That's a lot of water. And by the look of what they're taking aboard, it'll probably be a steady diet of bananas and saltines," I said. "Sounds awful."

Tom grunted in agreement. "Awfully dangerous. We're not doing it!"

Now, almost two weeks later, rumors about the ship abounded at the Hippodrome. Originally, its captain had accepted twenty-five men, five women, two dogs, and one baby as passengers, but one smart couple traveling without a car had since deserted ship, as had a Japanese youth who was able to get his motorcycle off. Difficult-to-remove vehicles, including eleven campervans, remained lashed on the open deck, their owners held captive by their situation.

Panamanian authorities had delayed the vessel's departure because the number of passengers required them to have a doctor or nurse on board and better sanitation facilities. Other legal problems plagued the ship, too. Half the crew had been arrested after a barroom brawl over the holidays, and their court appearance was a week away. Add to this, money problems. The ship had an outstanding bill with the Port Authority for half the repair cost of a shed roof they damaged when they docked at the pier.

The Darién Gap was obviously a dead end with no easy way around it. Robert, Marie, Tom, and I joined forces to sleuth for other options. We drove all over Panama City and Balboa, Marie and I often sitting in the broiling cars while Tom and Robert tromped from one shipping office to another. Sometime during the long hot day, I glanced at the printed schedule Tom had brought from the Italian line office. Thumbing through it to pass the time, I noticed the destination for their next scheduled ship was the Mediterranean.

When Tom returned to the car, I showed him the schedule. "Look, the ship coming next week is sailing to Spain," I said. "Why don't we go all the way? That's what we wanted to do in the first place."

He shook his head. "I'm excited about South America. It'll be a place neither of us has been."

Visions of Spain had returned to dance in my head, and I was disenchanted with Panama. I couldn't wait to leave. But Tom was the driver and if he wanted to keep going south, I would follow him to the land of the Incas. After all, I was in it for the travel, pure and simple, so what did it matter where we went? As we drove across the isthmus to Colon, Tom was quiet, mulling over my suggestion.

After a while, he spoke again. "I don't want to spend more than four months in South America," he said. "I'd like to be in Europe by spring."

I nodded agreement. "Spain should be lovely in March or April. Can we do South America in three or four months? It took us four months to get here. Three if you don't count Guadalajara. South America is far bigger and tougher driving. There's the Andes Mountains and so much jungle!"

"I hope it won't be this difficult to find a ship from Brazil to Spain," Tom said. "Rio's a big port, but . . . you're right about Europe. It's what we planned in the first place. Maybe we can come back to South America in the future, after they figure out how to put a road through the Darién Gap."

That evening, we continued to talk as we lay in bed in the oppressive heat. The light sheet tossed aside, our naked bodies glistened with perspiration as we discussed making a hard left and crossing the Atlantic. By morning, our travel plans had come full circle. We moved from the depression and frustration of trying to get to South America to the elation of dreaming of Europe. By noon, our reservation was made and our fare paid. We secured the last double cabin on the SS *Donizetti* for their sailing to Barcelona. We would be on our way in less than a week. The fifteen-day passage for two people and the van cost us $900, a bargain next to the $400 fare for Columbia.

We met with Robert and Marie for a picnic overlooking the Panama Canal and shared our new plans. After lunch, while we stood on a lock observation deck, Tom recognized a friend of his on the deck of the SS *President Garfield* as it rose up on the water in the lock. He waved his

Beside the Panama Canal.

arms over his head. When his friend waved back, Tom climbed to the roof of our microbus and made possessive gestures like a proud father.

Robert and Marie booked passage on the Italian Line ship going down the Pacific coast. We would soon be parting. At a bon voyage celebration, Robert, dressed in full kilt regalia, saluted our friendship with whiskey toasts. As the meal progressed, his Scottish burr became broader and broader. At the end of the evening, Robert pressed his parents' address in Scotland, which he had scribbled on a napkin, into Tom's hand.

"Promise, now," he said, his strong accent rolling the words off his tongue. "Ye'll look up me folks when ye're in Edinburgh!"

Windmill

Winch

SPAIN

Madrid

La Mancha

from PANAMA

Agadir

MOROCCO

Moroccan Djelleba
and Peasant Dress

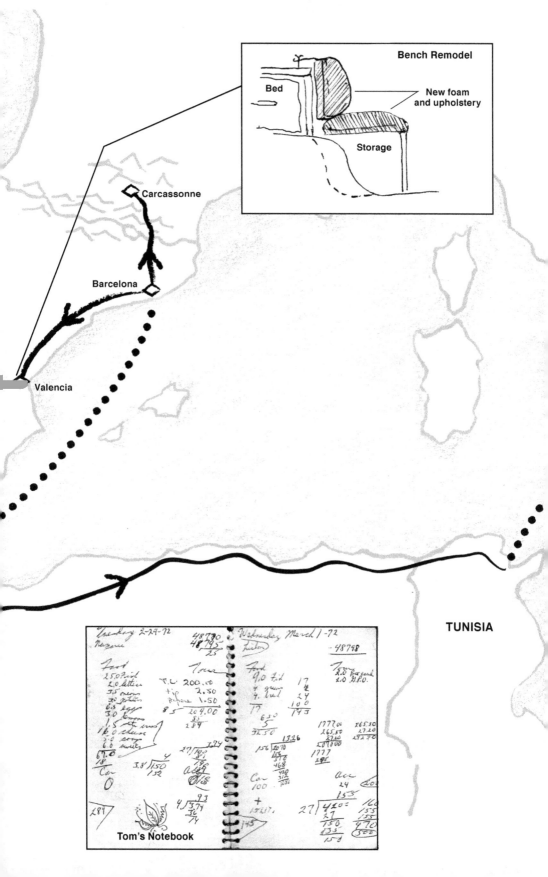

Bench Remodel

Bed

New foam and upholstery

Storage

Carcassonne

Barcelona

Valencia

TUNISIA

Tom's Notebook

Chapter 7

Transition and Family

We boarded on January 6.

The day before sailing, we worked hard getting the van and our possessions organized. It would be the first time we used Tom's plywood divider. We gave away leftover food and maps to friends at the Hippodrome and drove to the Colon area where we would board the SS *Donizetti*. In the morning, while parked at the dock, Tom bolted the security barrier in place between the driver and passenger seats, while I guarded our bags. The longshoremen secured the straps and ropes and Tom carefully inspected each knot and harness. As our green home swung over the ship's bulwark, we hurried up the gangway and over to the edge of the hold to watch our van lowered into place.

When the Turtle's tires touched the floor of the hold, Tom vaulted over the side and scrambled down the ladder. The first mate, standing next to me to oversee the loading of the ship, yelled after Tom, "Stop! Stop! You can't do that!" He reached for his bullhorn and yelled again.

"Get back up! Immediately! Get out of the hold!"

Tom, halfway down the ladder, ignored him. The officer had obviously not anticipated this from a mere passenger.

"Don't worry," I told him. "My husband works on ships. He knows what he's doing." The man looked doubtful. "He's a first engineer for American President Lines," I explained. "He's been up and down ships' ladders thousands of times." I leaned over the rail and watched as Tom inspected the van to make sure all was secure after the stevedore parked it, then strolled back to the ladder and climbed the rungs. "See," I said to the nervous officer, "he's only checking to make sure everything's OK." But the first mate was stiff with his responsibility.

Tom swung his legs over the rail of the hold and landed firmly with both feet on the deck. The officer looked him in the eye. "Don't ever go in the hold again. Not on this ship," he said.

"Yes, sir." Tom lifted our suitcase and turned to me. "Let's find our cabin. I want to check it out before lunch."

Our cabin was almost in the bow of the ship, barely above the water line, its one porthole securely locked and painted over. There was only room for the two bunk beds (Tom graciously took the top), two tiny closets, a chair, and a sink with a mirror. Toilets and showers were not far down the hall. We stashed our bags and went up to the dining lounge, where we hurried through an Italian lunch, then dashed to the observation deck above the bridge. As the ship sailed out of the placid water of the harbor and into the Caribbean Sea, its bow rose and descended on the ocean swells.

Totally exhausted from the heat and stress of the last three weeks in Panama, we returned to our cabin and fell into our bunks to nap until dinner. At 5:30 p.m., when our alarm sounded, we were groggy and feeling peculiar. The sea had gotten progressively rougher and as we walked up the narrow corridor from our cabin to the stairs, the floor of the hall undulated ahead of us. Tom, though a seaman, had a reputation as a kid for being carsick on family trips. His years of working around this weakness sent him ahead up on deck where he could breathe in the sea air. My usually sturdy stomach roiled with each dip of the ship, and I returned to the cabin where I lay supine on my bunk and groaned. Neither of us made it to dinner.

A steward knocked at the cabin door and offered me a pill, which I gulped down gratefully. About half an hour later, when I was already feeling better, he appeared again with a saucer of sliced green apples and crackers. "It's the best food when you're seasick," he said and left me to nibble slowly on the snack. By the time Tom returned and fell into his bunk, I felt well enough to read, the reassuring rumble of Tom's snores above me. Finally, I dozed off, the book across my chest, and slept through the night.

I woke with a start in our pitch-dark cabin and switched on the light. The ship was quiet, the clock showed 8:00 a.m., and Tom sat on the edge of his bunk, blinking away sleep. Now ravenously hungry, we grabbed breakfast and went on deck to watch the activity on the docks of Cartagena. Several of our compatriots from the Hippodrome struggled down the gangway to their cars waiting below. Tom searched the city with new binoculars he had bought in Panama.

That evening, we entered headlong into rough seas and high winds, typical conditions for an Atlantic crossing in January. In spite of the blustery weather, Tom and I felt much better for the rest of the trip. We avoided the long corridor and spent most of each day breathing fresh air on deck and relaxing in the open spaces of the salon and library.

The *Donizetti* was an old-fashioned liner built in the 1950s to carry passengers and cargo. Set meals, not buffets, were served in the dining room at assigned times. Our breakfast seating was at 8:00 a.m., and each morning we were served the same freshly baked hard roll, butter, jam, and a hard-boiled egg. Lunches were ample, as per European custom, and late supper was light, both meals usually featuring tasty Italian cuisine. We loved the variety of cheeses offered after the main course, and once we were served a rabbit stew cooked hunter style, the white meat tender and smothered in a sauce of tomatoes and mushrooms.

Most afternoons, we snuggled in lap robes on deck chairs or braved the wind and spray to march around the decks. Each evening, we strolled hand in hand to the bow of the ship where the tourist-class pool sat empty. More romantic than our cramped cabin, this semi-private retreat became our special getaway. We reveled in the feel of the salty spray on our faces as we stood leaning against the bulwark, our bodies closely entwined for warmth. After a few kisses, we watched the dark waves curling against the prow of the ship.

On days when the sun emerged, we soaked it in, despite the wind. I kept my hands busy with an embroidery project, turning one of Tom's chambray shirts into a hippie shirt with flowers on the yoke, collar, and sleeves. Movies were available in the salon in the afternoon and evening, and if an English language movie was showing, we were sure to be in the front row.

The night before our arrival in Barcelona was especially rough. At the breakfast table, awaiting clearance to go ashore, I fainted, face down into my toast. I revived instantly and looked up puzzled by this unusual turn of events. Tom was more concerned than I, and he settled me into an easy chair in the salon before he went to check on our van and start the customs process. I nodded off, but awoke when I heard a soft voice say my name.

"Katie, are you all right? Tom told me you weren't feeling well."

I opened my eyes. My younger sister, Karen, stood in front of me. "What? Where did you come from? How did you get here?"

"I came from Paris last night on the overnight train," she said as she sat next to me. "I got to Europe night before last. I was so scared I'd miss you."

I looked at her wide-eyed. "We had no idea you were coming."

"I know. I was so afraid you'd get in the car and drive away before I got here. I hardly slept at all for the last two nights. I've been waiting on the dock since dawn."

"What about your classes?" I asked. She was nineteen and supposed to be at university.

"I decided to take off for a semester. I need to see Europe again, now that I'm old enough to travel on my own."

Of course, this made sense. She had only been seven when we went to Europe as a family. Now she was studying languages and European history and culture. Travel would be better than a school field trip.

I suddenly felt refreshed and eager to get going.

Tom, Karen, and I made short work of getting the van back to rights, all possessions stowed where they belonged, and we launched ourselves into Barcelona looking for our first Spanish meal. The gray clouds overhead did not curb our enthusiasm as we walked along *Las Ramblas*, delighted by the stalls selling books and magazines, fresh flowers, and birds in cages. The shop windows revealed fine leather goods and classy shoes. In the main market area, I entered a heaven of food. Fragrant cured hams stood upright in their special wooden holders, the butchers hovering nearby, ready to carve away thin slices of glistening meat. Pale golden wheels of Manchego cheese coated in

I love local markets. Here I select oranges at the central market in Barcelona.

brown wax lay next to creamy white goat and sheep *queso*. Orderly pyramids of bright oranges and lemons from the Canary Islands rose above bins of North African dates, roasted nuts, and black olives.

I turned to Tom. "I adore Barcelona!"

"Lunch first," Tom said. "You can shop later."

We headed into the old town, wandering down twisting streets in search of the perfect Spanish *taverna*. On one of the narrowest alleyways, we found a dark café with no name. The ceiling was black from years of smoke, one wall was lined with old wine barrels, and the other wall offered crude wooden tables and benches, where several groups of men in work clothes ate, drank, and talked.

A partial menu was scrawled on a blackboard, while sandwiches and snacks were displayed on the bar counter. A waiter with a stained white apron took our order. The men at the nearby table drank red wine from a glass vessel used like the traditional goatskin bota bag of the Basque shepherds. Each man took a turn with the carafe, which featured a long spout jutting from one bulbous side. He would tip his head back, open his mouth, hold the carafe so the end of the spout was ten to twelve inches away, and pour a long stream of wine between his waiting lips.

When our order arrived, the food shouted, "Spain!" I devoured my rich rooster soup and slice of Spanish tortilla, a room-temperature wedge dense with egg and potato.

After lunch, we left Karen at her pensión and set off to the outskirts of town to locate the campground. Public transportation back into town was excellent, and that evening and the next day we returned to the city, met Karen, filled our daypacks with snacks at the market and wandered around the central city. On Sunday evening, after a stroll around the exterior of the half-finished Gaudí cathedral, the *Sagrada Famila*, we found ourselves in the large square of Saint Jaime, surrounded by imposing government buildings. In the center of the square, a group of men played traditional music. All around them people formed circles, held hands, and danced, their steps precise and rhythmic.

Karen's Spanish was better than ours, so she asked a gentleman in the crowd what was going on. A feather merchant from Brussels, who visited Barcelona monthly, told us the dancers were all Catalonian nationalists.

Barcelona, in the heart of Catalonia, had been openly anti-Franco since the Spanish Civil War. As a way of suppressing their nationalism, Franco, who was firmly in power at the time, had outlawed their dance and the use of the native Catalan language. But the Catalonians disregarded these laws and came on Sunday afternoons to the square to join hands and perform their traditional dances. The groups were of all ages—young people in their 20s, senior citizens, even children—all dancing in the plaza to assert their opposition to the ruling government.

Barcelona in January, though often sunny, was freezing cold, and when we packed in California, we had not anticipated being there in winter. Luckily, we discovered *El Corte Inglés*, a Spanish department store, where we beefed up our wardrobe with long underwear for Tom, woolen pantyhose for me, and fur-lined leather gloves for us both.

One afternoon, as the three of us ate steaming paella (60 cents per person for a plate of garlicky rice and sausage), Karen described two places she had studied in school and wanted to visit.

"They're across the border in France," she said. "Carcassonne and Albi. Carcassonne is supposed to be the best-preserved medieval town in France and Albi is the birthplace of Toulouse-Lautrec."

Tom spread out our map on the wooden café table. "How far are they from Barcelona?" he asked.

Karen leaned into the map and pointed. "Here. Carcassonne is just over the border," she said.

Tom calculated the driving time in his head. "Hey, look. Andorra isn't far from Carcassonne. We could go there, too. We'd get two new passport stamps in one short trip."

"What about Albi?" I asked. "I'd love to see where Lautrec was born."

"You art students!"

I could tell by the twinkle in Tom's eyes he was teasing and he approved of the excursion. "Let's start today," he said. "We can get out of the city and on the road before dark."

North of Barcelona, we found a place to camp for the night on a cliff overlooking the sea. At this point, the difficult logistics of the three of us traveling together in the microbus became apparent. Where would Karen sleep? The only option was for her to curl up across the driver's seat, the passenger seat, and wedged in the aisle between them, the leatherette ottoman that contained, under cover, our bucket toilet. Karen couldn't stretch out flat across the cab of the van and the narrow seats and the protruding steering wheel made it difficult for her to shift positions. Tom and I, used to our privacy, found a glass jar for midnight urination, and undoubtedly that made Karen uncomfortable, too. In the morning, we all took turns with the bucket, while the other two waited patiently outside in the biting January wind.

Breakfast brought up another issue. I scrambled a large pan of eggs and at the same time, on the other burner, melted butter in a skillet and fried slices of bread, our usual camper's toast.

"I'd rather not have fried bread," Karen said under her breath from the corner of the bench seat where she was curled, wrapped in a blanket. I looked up. "It's too fattening," she added. Karen's timid voice was easy to brush aside.

"It's what I'm serving," I said. "I don't have a toaster. This isn't the Ritz."

Karen didn't complain again, but she didn't touch her bread, either, and I wrapped it up to save for croutons to go with soup for dinner.

The road north to the French border twisted along the deeply indented Costa Brava. From one side of the van, we saw the wave-tossed Mediterranean, the coast studded with villages, hidden coves, and an occasional new development of tall apartments. On the other side of the van, steep slopes planted with ancient olive trees sped past. Occasionally, an inland twist of road took us between fallow winter fields and farm villages, each with its own church. From our prime seats in the front, Tom and I delighted in the sights along the road, while Karen, obviously out of sorts, dozed and nodded in the back seat.

At midday, she jerked awake when we entered Cadaqués, a Spanish fishing town, its narrow streets lined with pastel buildings. Brightly painted boats lined the docks and an old lighthouse stood at the end of the breakwater. We huddled inside the van while gusts of salt spray soaked the car.

France was only a few miles away. In Carcassonne, we located a campground in the river valley at the foot of the castle-topped hill. The wind tossed the nearby shrubs and rattled the windows of the van as we settled in for another uncomfortable night.

The morning revealed a lead-gray sky, soaking rain, and frigid air temperatures. Tom and I donned our new winter clothing and Karen bundled up in her woolen coat and scarf. With only one umbrella to share, we entered the medieval city to explore the narrow streets, the palace, the fortified citadel, and the old ramparts. We bought cheese and sausage and a freshly baked baguette. At a neighborhood bar, we ordered three glasses of local wine and the proprietor allowed us to eat our picnic lunch at a table near a roaring fireplace. In the afternoon, at the city museum bookshop, we bought several English versions of Michelin *Green Guides*, which I loved for their details of art and culture, the pen-and-ink illustrations, and their small city maps.

Eventually we had to return to the campground for another night in the crowded van while the weather continued to get colder. We awoke to a sky filled with dark, rain-heavy clouds. To get to Albi, we had to cross over a steep section of the Massif Central, a highland area of mountains and plateaus. Karen rode slumped groggily in the back, missing most of the breathtaking views.

Gradually the rain turned to sleet. Then, the sleet turned to snow. Tom and I watched the flakes melt as they landed on the windshield, then no longer melt but pile up on the windshield wipers. Soon the entire landscape was covered in white and the air was filled with a veil of falling snow.

"That's it," Tom said. "I don't dare go farther without snow chains."

Struggling out of sleep, Karen asked, "What's happening? Are we there?"

"If you weren't always asleep, you'd know it was snowing," Tom said in a tight voice.

Karen peered out the window, swiping away condensate. "Wow! Snow!" she said, a California girl born and bred. "How much farther to Albi?"

Tom snapped. "Forget Albi. If I don't turn around, we'll be stranded here. And forget Andorra. It's probably snowing in the Pyrenees, too."

Karen leaned silently into the corner of the seat and watched as Tom inched the vehicle around and headed back the way we had come. The return to Barcelona was quiet, the air filled with tension. We traveled through ancient, hilly country, past fields of dormant grape vines and old towns with castle ruins little changed since the twelfth century.

We were all unhappy by the turn our holiday had taken. I was disappointed. Tom was exhausted and had taken on the attitude it was his responsibility to make sure we got the most out of the trip. His irritation with Karen grew as she continued to sleep fitfully.

"Look out the window," he nagged at her when she was briefly awake. "You're missing all this beautiful country!"

Poor Karen would try to pay attention until her head nodded and she was asleep again.

Tom complained to me. "She's a useless weight we're carrying along. She's not getting anything from this trip. And it was her idea!"

It was my first experience of being caught between two people I loved, understanding both but unable to help them understand each other.

Disruptive arguments in families often begin in this way and escalate over the years. We managed to condense the seed of discord into a five-day trip in a Volkswagen van. Karen was nineteen and Tom and I were only six months into our marriage and not yet thirty, so the self-absorption of youth certainly played a part in our problem, not to mention sleep deprivation and lack of privacy. We endured one more uncomfortable night on the road, then we were back in Barcelona.

After a few days apart and a couple of nights of good sleep, we were able to mend our rift and spent one final day together in Barcelona. In the afternoon, Tom went off on his own to pick up our mail, change money, and find a mouse trap (we had heard strange scratching and squeaking coming from the underbelly of the van and found toothmarks in our store of potatoes). Karen and I joyfully strolled the central market, relishing a few hours of girl time. Later, she and I carried my string, market bags laden with groceries to our favorite restaurant where we met Tom for dinner. Our final goodbyes were accompanied with the appropriate hugs, and I was relieved when Tom embraced Karen with warmth as we parted.

Chapter 8

An Iberian Winter

Tarragona was only a couple of hours south of Barcelona. We arrived at dusk and located a campground on the deserted winter beach. Though we spent a few hours in the old walled city and the Roman ruins overlooking the bay, for the next few days, most of our time was devoted to chores. When we were on the road, we preferred free, scenic camping spots, but when we were near a city, we needed to do car repairs or laundry, or if one of us was nursing a cold, we looked for a campground with running water and the possibility of showers.

The camping ground near Tarragona was in a beautiful location, close to the sand on a wide cove. A rocky outcropping at the far end of the beach was topped by a ruined tower. There were showers but no hot water. We soon realized this was common for southern European campgrounds used mainly in summer. With the chilly weather and wind, the idea of a cold shower was off-putting, and we opted to do without and try a sponge bath in the van. We covered the floor with a beach towel, heated up a large bowl of water on the stove, and took turns stripping down and cleaning ourselves with a wash cloth, warm water, and soap. I washed my long, waist-length hair outside in the pale sunlight and wind, Tom pouring pots of warmed water over my head as needed. Uncut for over six weeks, his thick, curly hair was in desperate need of trimming. I preferred to cut his hair dry and dirty when it was easier to handle. With his locks shorn to a conservative length, Tom knelt over the bucket to wash his hair while I became the assistant. This type of primitive personal hygiene became our winter routine.

Laundry was always a perpetual source of angst for us, often the source of a disagreement as to whether we needed to stop as soon as possible (me) or if we should wait longer and hope for a place with a clothesline and hot water (Tom). Public laundromats were almost unknown in Europe at the time, and during that cold European winter, we sometimes washed a few intimate articles in our tiny sink and looped them around the van on zigzagging cords.

In Tarragona, the day was cloudless and sunny, a day that demanded we tackle our overflowing bag of dirty laundry. Tom hauled water from a nearby spigot. I filled our two largest pans and put them to heat on the stove. When the water boiled, I added it to cold water in the laundry bucket. A bit of detergent and a dollop of bleach and the sheets went in to be agitated and wrung out by hand.

Meanwhile, Tom lugged more cold water for rinsing. This procedure was an all-day project, repeated for each bucket-sized load, once for the sheets, once for towels, once for two or three pairs of jeans, and again for shirts, blouses, and underwear. With buckets of wet clothes and linens, the next issue was to get the laundry dry.

In Barcelona, housewives hung laundry from a rope tied to both ends of their balcony rail and held out by a long central stick. The weight of the wet clothes provided tension to keep the contraption in balance. With no trees in sight, we tried the Spanish apartment-dweller method.

Once a similar system was attached to the side of the van, Tom steadied it while I draped the wet sheets over the rope and the sodden towels from a similar setup on the other side. Inside, I strung cord across the rear, from cupboard knob to anything else I could tie a knot around, and hung up our shirts and underwear.

Proud of our work, we strolled down the beach to view the sunset. On our return, the laundry danced in a stiffening breeze. Suddenly, a gust caught one of the sheets like a sail. The whole clothesline flipped off the side of the car, depositing our linens, tangled with the rope and the stick, in the grass. The next gust of wind toppled our towels.

"Damn wind," Tom muttered. He moved the van close enough to the shower house so he could tie one of the lines from the van to an exterior water pipe. With our only bed linens hanging damply outside, we spread beach towels over the foam mattress. The wind whipped around us all night and we hoped it would not bring rain.

The search for cooking butane to fill the tanks underneath the van was another recurring chore. It was difficult to locate a service station or gas wholesaler in each new city. Back in Barcelona, we had met an older couple from Northern California who traveled in a green Volkswagen conversion identical to ours, and we struck up one of those brief friendships that develop between travelers. Tom and the other man discussed mutual mechanical problems and design improvements. The older couple had added an auxiliary gas system to their unit that used International Campingaz, a European product which utilized a standardized, exchangeable gas bottle. Commonplace now, this exchange concept was new in the 1970s, and Tom was eager to set up the system for us. Before we left Tarragona, we bought one of the full, blue, Campingaz bottles and the needed fittings to make the conversion.

As we drove along the coast toward Valencia, we discussed possible places to put the blue gas tank. Finally, Tom said, "What do you think about taking out the VW bench seat in back and building an entirely new seat? It would give us more storage, too."

I envisioned storing potatoes and onions and a hidden place to keep dirty laundry. "What would you build it from?" I asked.

"Plywood should be easy to find. If we keep the design simple, I can cut the wood with my hand saw."

"Can we cover the bench with foam and make it comfortable and look nice, too?"

"Sure, why not? I've watched my mother upholster a few chairs. It's not much different from how you stretch canvas on a frame before you paint on it."

By the time we arrived in Valencia, we were both excited about our project. The first day, we found wood, including cabinet doors the right size for the seat and seat back and the needed hardware. We located sheet foam, and at the El Corte Inglés, we bought strong muslin cloth and a green wool-like upholstery fabric.

The Valencia campground was large, comfortable, had hot water in the showers, and was near a golf course, all of which attracted a few winter campers. A retired British couple came over from their space as soon as we began work to ask why we were dismantling our van. The original bench seat already tipped precariously out on the grass. Tom explained our project while he measured the wood and marked where he would cut. The Brits, John and Sue, fascinated by his ingenuity, came over again to check on our progress after a round of golf.

Tom framed the structure, while I cut the fabric for our new seat. Together we fit the foam to the doors and stretched the muslin over, tacking it firmly in place. We stretched the green fabric over the muslin and tacked it down, pleased at how tight and professional our new sofa looked. The seat back hung from turn screws and was easy to take down at night so we could open up the bed. The padded seat, though heavy, lifted to provide access to the new storage.

With this project done, we were eager to go to town. I had purchased an authentic paella pan earlier at Corte Inglés and was determined to make Paella Valenciana while in its namesake city. It would be a celebratory dinner and we invited John and Sue to share it.

Tom also wanted electrical supplies for new lights he intended to install over my kitchen so I could cook easier on dark, winter evenings. Fluorescents would offer better illumination with less power usage. We tucked our string grocery bags in Tom's daypack and went to town to make our purchases.

By this time, I was familiar with shopping at local markets and knew not to help myself at the produce stands but to tell the vendor what I wanted in my limited Spanish. The seller would select from the back of the pile, leaving his beautiful, carefully displayed goods in front. I was thrilled to find a poultry vendor in the Valencia market who, besides the inevitable whole chickens hanging by their necks, had a few legs and wings laid out on his marble counter. I selected four of each. The vendor wrapped them up in paper, and I left, pleased with my purchase.

I began the paella as soon as we returned to the van. As I cooked, Tom knelt directly behind me to hook up the Campingaz bottle in its new location. I worked with my legs spread, astraddle his feet. First, I made the *sofrito*, a flavor base of onions, paprika, tomatoes, and garlic sautéed in olive oil. When the aromas filled the air, I added the short grain rice, chicken broth, vegetables, and a few slices of chorizo sausage. I laid the prized chicken pieces on top, gently pushed them down into the bubbling rice, turned the heat to low, and stood back proudly. While the paella cooked, I tore lettuce and sliced cucumbers and tomatoes for a salad. Tom, finished with the gas project, was now at work above my head, installing the new kitchen lights and their switches.

We both finished our preparations at about the same time. I tasted the rice to make sure it was done, then covered the pan loosely with a kitchen towel. Our British friends had the bigger van, so we had arranged to eat there. Tom and I carried the dinner over and we four settled around John and Sue's table. John opened a bottle of wine and we lifted our glasses to toast friendships and travel. As we ate, John and

Sue explained they had no permanent address in England, but traveled almost all the time in their camper converted from a Bentley postal van. They had been across Europe, North Africa, Canada and the United States. They were devoted to golf, and in the winter, they usually settled down in southern Spain, where the courses stayed open all year. In summer they headed for Scotland.

I mentioned we intended to drive to India next winter.

"We did the same when we were about your age," Sue said. "And in a Volkswagen, too!" She raised her glass of red wine and took a long swallow. "Two years we stayed in India. What a time! It was our first trip and we got hooked."

I had been so interested in the conversation I had only eaten a few forkfuls of the rice. Now I picked up the chicken leg on my plate and tried to bite into it. My teeth bounced back as if I had chomped into an old rubber tire. I tried again, but the leg was unchewable. I looked up at the others. "My chicken is tough," I said. "Is yours OK?"

"It's tough," John said, "but the rice is tasty."

I glanced down at John's plate. It was empty except for his untouched chicken leg and half a wing. Sue's plate also held untouched chicken. She smiled and nodded. "The salad and rice are super. The bits of sausage are brilliant."

I looked at Tom, a slow eater. He had not yet tried his chicken. While we all watched, he took a bite and tried to chew it, then reached for his glass of wine and took a big gulp. "Sure is one tough chicken," he said. "Maybe it's a rooster."

"I'll bet that's why the stalls leave the heads on the chickens," I said, suddenly enlightened. "So you can tell a hen from a rooster." I was embarrassed. "I'm sorry about dinner. Without the chicken, it's pitiful. I was so excited to find parts, I didn't think."

John and Sue, the epitome of British manners, smoothed the situation over and assured me they had plenty to eat and the flavor of the paella was perfect. Soon we were happily talking of travel again.

The next morning, Tom and I continued down the Spanish coast, rich with fragrant groves of orange trees and almond orchards in bud, then turned inland toward La Mancha, the land of Don Quixote, a high, dry plateau where rows of white windmills, their broad wings turning steadily in the icy air, crowned rocky outcrops. When we arrived in Toledo, I navigated us to a famous viewpoint, which claimed to be the spot where El Greco set up his easel in 1600 to paint *View of Toledo*. As an art student and teacher, I was enraptured by this iconic vista warmed by the rosy glow of the setting sun. The government-run parador, a luxury hotel recently opened to encourage the tourist trade, dominated the slope above, its veranda looking across the sinuous Tagus River to the medieval heart of town. That night, we stayed for no fee at a deserted campground with all facilities shut down, while I dreamed of returning one day to stay in the parador.

Madrid, the capital of Spain, greeted us with falling snow. We had not expected it to be so cold in Spain and it wore us down. However, the original Velázquez paintings of princesses dressed in silver and gold renaissance garments at the 150-year-old Del Prado Museum and Spanish food made up for the cold weather.

For the first time, we tried a full meal of *entremés* (now commonly called tapas). These hot and cold appetizers came in all sizes, and Spanish bars offered at least one free with wine service. Entremés might be as simple as a complimentary bowl of peanuts or as complicated as a terra cotta dish brimming with sizzling pork stew. The tavern bar counter was lined with rows of cold dishes to choose from.

With our first glass of wine, we sampled a dish of tiny fish fillets in oil and garlic marinade, then *pulpo* (octopus) in a tomato sauce, which was so good we ordered a second serving. We ordered two more glasses of wine and shared a hot sandwich of pickled and fried pork loin on a crusty roll. A half-block stroll down the street brought us to another bar and a third glass of wine. Tom tried a fish empanada while I ate a delectable fillet of fried fish with roasted potatoes. The entire lunch,

Street scene in Segovia, Spain.

including our six glasses of wine, cost only $1.50. With this type of food, we lost interest in braving the rain to see historical sights. We would soak up Spain via wine and olive oil!

Madrid, Segovia, Ávila, and Salamanca, then west into Portugal. The high, flat, treeless plateau of central Spain changed to hills, crowned with stands of pine or eucalyptus and groves of olive trees. Sturdy granite houses clung to the clefts of rocky valleys. A kerchiefed woman drove a mule cart laden with fodder. A shepherd with a long, dusty, black blanket draped over his shoulders watched flocks of sheep and goats. Naturally, at the sight of an open market, we pulled over. Women carried enormous bundles of greens on their heads and at the same time hawked fresh fish and eggs in baskets, while the men gathered for a livestock sale, their flocks milling around them.

Guided by our green Michelin book, which gave towns starred ratings, we arrived in Coimbra (two stars) where we found a campground with free hot showers, worth five stars in our opinion. This warranted a day of relaxation. While I drew contentedly in my sketchbook, Tom spent the morning building a small bookcase with a copper-tube railing. Building things was clearly Tom's creative outlet, in the same way cooking and drawing were mine.

Neither Tom nor I knew much about Portugal, so we relied heavily on our guidebook, which led us to Portugal dos Pequenitos, a children's park where miniaturized buildings represented regional styles of architecture. The replicas were built so children could go in, touch, and use everything. I thought of my niece and nephew, aged 9 and 10, as we wandered around the winter quiet of this child-friendly park. "Wouldn't Mike and Michelle love this place?" I said as I peeked inside the windows at playhouse-sized furniture and dishes.

Tom grinned. "It'd be great to have the kiddos see this place! We'd have to stay all day while Michelle played house."

When we visited a beautiful Roman ruin with fragments of marble sculpture, well-preserved mosaics, and a defensive wall, we thought of the kids again. "Mike has a book about the ancient Romans," I said. "He'd want to climb on the wall and pretend to fight off the barbarian hordes."

"They'd both love these public baths," Tom said. "It's cool to imagine real Romans here enveloped by steam and scrubbing their toes. This is the way to learn history!"

An idea grew little by little. We wanted children to share our adventure. No, not a baby, but ready-made school children, curious and eager to learn.

Later, we camped on a high bluff above the fishing village of Nazaré. Huge Atlantic waves pounded against the base of the cliff. A storm brewed out to sea and a high tide was expected. The next morning, the village fishermen, bundled in heavy knitted sweaters and black stocking caps, sat on the sea wall near their beached craft. Their eyes constantly evaluated the surf while their gnarled fingers were busy mending nets.

I had read of Portuguese embroidered linens and popped into one shop after another in search of a tablecloth. Tom had developed the habit of carrying a small notebook in which he recorded each expenditure, no matter how inconsequential. Even minutia, a bottle of beer or a bunch of grapes, was entered under the appropriate heading—food, car, accommodations, or tourism. For each new country, he created a chart of the currency exchange. Portuguese *escudos* were worth 3.7 US cents each. We both scrawled quick sketches in the booklet, too, of things we wanted to remember visually, perhaps a project idea, the costumes of the locals, or an architectural motif. For Tuesday, February 29, 1972, there is a drawing of an embroidery motif, and under tourism, the entry "T.C. 200.00." This is 200 escudos or $7.40 US for a tablecloth, a major souvenir purchase for us.

Portugal was a dramatically beautiful place with castles, palaces, museums, Moorish fortresses, a stunning coastline, and villages barely changed from previous centuries. Yet, what I remember most is the cold, rainy weather, markets with a limited selection of cabbage, cauliflower, and wild, weedy greens, and the rough, rocky cliffs overlooking the Atlantic, so similar to the Big Sur of the California Pacific Coast. One cold evening, I prepared a rough approximation of the traditional *Caldo Verde*. My quick version of this warming potato-and-kale soup used Spanish instant mashed potatoes, the finely pre-shredded kale available in local markets, and slices of garlicky, smoked *Linguiça* sausage.

In the coastal villages, the men, young and old, wore heavy, ankle-length, brown wool capes, the shoulders augmented with extra cape-like layers, the collar often enhanced with fur. These capes, perfect for the blustery weather, reminded me of the greatcoats worn by Napoleon and the Russian heroes in the movie, *War and Peace*. Very romantic! I would have loved for Tom to get one of these cloaks, but I couldn't convince him to even try one on and let me take a picture. I was learning his romantic inclinations were stunted. His engineer's mind was firmly entrenched in the idea that fixing and building was the best way to show his love. As a result, the Turtle was more comfortable than when we started out, but occasionally I longed for a romantic gesture.

Deserted summer resorts lined the road back to Spain where early spring laid a thin green wash of grass over Andalusia. I had recently finished reading *Or I'll Dress You in Mourning* by Larry Collins, a biography of the famous matador, El Córdobes, and I was still under its influence. Andalusia embodied, for me, the essence of Spain—the last stronghold of the Muslim Empire in Europe. Arab atmosphere still permeated the historical cities. The most renowned building of the Andalusian Islamic legacy, the Alhambra of Granada, was a glorious Moorish palace and fortress surrounded by gardens and fountains. In the Generalife, a side palace which had served as a summer retreat for the Caliph, the fountains, view, and gardens filled my head with romantic images of ladies covered in veils reclining in leisure as their sultan, his turban encrusted in jewels, sipped tea and puffed on his hookah. It was a Shahrazad dream.

I leaned against the cool stone balustrade and gazed across to the snow-covered Sierra Nevada Mountains, the ancient center of

Fountain garden in the Generalife, Granada, Spain.

Granada nestled below. Tom stood behind, one arm wrapped around my shoulders. His warmth enveloped me. Silently we breathed in the history-tinged air and the wonder of the moment.

Constantly being slowed by the enchantment of the journey, we were a month behind our proposed schedule. In Europe it was necessary to pick up mail at a central post office, rather than at the US embassy, and Malaga would be our first mail stop since Barcelona.

As we headed to the city center, we were enmeshed in late afternoon traffic. With Tom the primary driver, it was my job to navigate him through unknown towns with the aid of the maps in our Michelin *Green Guides*. The tiny map of Malaga showed the direction of one-way streets with miniscule black arrows, but in the city center I realized a few of the arrows were incorrect. Disoriented, I was soon completely turned around.

"No, not there. Go another block. No, it's one way the wrong way . . . maybe go around the block?"

Tom, never happy with traffic problems, became impatient, swearing angrily. He had no concept of my frustration and I felt unappreciated. When at last we located the post office, parking was almost impossible. Tom found a kind of loading zone, a block away. "Go in and get the mail," he ordered me, his voice harsh.

Already emotionally stressed, I did not want to do it. My Spanish was bad. Tom's was better. I was shy and hesitant in new situations. Tom was not. "No, you go in," I said, my eyes stinging with held-back tears.

"Are you crazy?" he asked. "I can't leave the car. I'm not even sure this is a legal parking spot. What if a gendarme comes along?"

I was beside myself. I didn't want to go inside and deal with speaking Spanish in order to find the stupid general delivery. What was general delivery in Spanish, anyway? "No. Please," I said. "You go. I can drive if I have to. I'm capable of driving around the block!"

A burst of angry air exploded from Tom. "Fuck it! Get inside and get our mail or we're leaving without it."

Missing the letters from home was inconceivable. I got out of the van, slamming the door as I stepped to the sidewalk. I don't remember if I actually had any problem or even if there were letters. I only know, at that moment, I hated Tom for making me do it.

As we left Malaga, I was once again ensconced in the rear seat, turned inward by my anger.

Tom drove silently out of the city, while I stared icily out the side window. He could navigate himself if he didn't appreciate my efforts. We passed a sign indicating the airport was a few kilometers ahead. I'll go home, I thought. He can't talk to me that way. I don't have to stay and take it. I'll demand he take me to the airport.

Why not go home? I would have a teaching job waiting for me in September if I returned now. I needed time by myself without Tom. But what of the good times? Each day, even the hard days, had been a singular lifetime experience. If I left now, I wouldn't see Morocco with all its exotic Moorish delights. And, yes, we were married. I had to remind myself we weren't simply lovers, we were husband and wife. I didn't see myself as the type of person to give up and walk away from marriage. I watched the airport slip away behind us.

Before we reached Gibraltar, I returned to my place up front with Tom. I now realize, on that day as we drove past the Malaga airport, I made a stronger commitment to our marriage than I had at our wedding. When he slipped the ring over my finger, I had been caught up in the excitement of the celebration and the romantic idea it represented. On March 16, almost seven months later to the day, I finally made a firm commitment to our marriage—for better or for worse.

Chapter 9

A North African Spring

The close living conditions of our van made it impossibly awkward to stay angry with each other for long. During dinner, I expressed my pent-up emotions to Tom. "I hate the way I feel when you swear at me," I said. "You know I hate the F word. Why should a word about making love be used as a swear word?"

"Ah, come on, Katie. I didn't say, 'Fuck-you.' I wasn't swearing at you, just swearing."

"Well, it pisses me off. I don't mind some bad words. I just can't stand the F word."

"Sorry. When I'm frustrated it slips out."

I stood and put the water pot on the stove to heat for clean up, then sat back down next to Tom. "We're together 24/7 and the Turtle is way too small for us to stay angry at each other and survive." I hesitated, then added, "Our travels are unbelievable and I'll never be able to thank you enough for making me a part of this grand adventure, but today, when we passed the airport, I thought seriously about going home."

Tom enclosed me in the circle of his arms and kissed my forehead. "I'm so glad you didn't go," he said, his voice low. "We're perfect travel partners on the trip of a lifetime." He leaned in and kissed me gently on the lips. "I'll never stay angry with you. I promise," he murmured as our kiss deepened and I dissolved into the warmth of my husband's body. The dishes would wait until morning.

The next day, we took the ferry from Algeciras across the twenty-one nautical miles (approximately twenty-three land miles) to the Spanish-owned free port of Ceuta where I insisted on stocking our pantry with nonperishable, emergency-type food—Knorr packaged soups, dried sausage, and several large, round cans of Spanish cheese.

Then we crossed into Morocco, an entire country of Granadas! But even more than the architecture, I was enchanted by the people. Both men and women wore long, loose, hooded, outer robes called *djellabas* (the d is silent) and the men often wore a fez—a stiff pot-shaped hat topped with a tassel—or a turban. The women concealed their faces with the edge of their *djellaba* hood or with a veil or scarf. This was long before any controversy about the wearing of a *hijab*, and for me, the use of the veil was an exotic accessory, reminiscent of the Arabian nights, a welcome touch of unchanged, authentic North African culture.

My fascination with traditional costume was an extension of a long-standing interest in clothing. As a girl I had played with paper dolls, dressing them in original costumes I created. As a teen I had dreamed of becoming a fashion designer and constantly drew pictures of ball gowns and dresses inspired by Hollywood movies. My idol was Edith Head, who had earned eight Academy Awards for best costume design and created gowns for Audrey Hepburn and Grace Kelly. Throughout the trip, I kept notes about the different native costumes and illustrated them in my sketchbook.

Whenever I could, I tried to dress like a native, to blend into the surroundings and not stand out as a tourist. In Morocco, I liked to wear a long caftan I had sewed at home—a late 1960s hippie-type garment made of a striped, nubby fabric of various blues. It looked similar to a djellaba, except it lacked the requisite hood to cover my telltale, blond hair. I felt immersed in the culture when I wore my caftan to the *souks* (local markets) and looked for a real Moroccan djellaba to add to my wardrobe.

Our first stop in Morocco was Chefchaouen, a town with nine mosques (six for men and three for women), a *medina* with a red-walled, defensive fort or *kasbah* at its center, and a nearby camping ground. We explored the narrow, twisting lanes the first evening and again the following, sunny morning. The old center of the town was built into the steep hillside. Maze-like alleyways often turned into stairways, fine for donkeys and people but impossible for cars. The babbling of several streams filled the air and a substantial river cascaded along one side of the medina, offering a perfect place for the village women to do laundry. The town's flat-roofed structures were coated in whitewash, which shimmered in the bright sun. But the special charm of Chefchaouen was the glorious, cool cobalt wash painted on the lower portions of the houses. Blue splashed over the stoops and into the streets and reached up the smooth walls to about ten or twelve feet high. In areas of shade, the blue looked icy and the effect was psychologically cooling. We were told the blue wash also helped control insects, especially mosquitoes.

The market was tucked off to one side of the old medina quarter. Stalls hunkered under awnings to protect the produce from the strong North African sun. Shops leaned against the old walls of the medina and offered spices, staples, shoes, clothes, cookware, and fabric.

Not far from the ferry from Spain, the town was accustomed to tourists who arrived by bus. There was an abundance of hustlers and we soon had our own pair of tagalongs. A teenaged boy found us first. He professed to be a student of English and promised to take us to the shop owned by his brother-in-law. Tom, who had experience in the port cities of India and Pakistan, rebuffed him at first, but the youth

The narrow blue streets of Chefchaouen, Morocco. Katie 1972

was persistent and would not leave. Soon, a lad of about six or seven joined us, his smile and manner infectious. The little kid spoke only Spanish and Arabic. He became my sidekick while I shopped for mint and bread. It was impossible to shake our boys and, as they were pleasant company, we gave up trying to shoo them away. When we returned to the car, they asked for nothing—no handout, no request for money. I was so charmed by my small companion that, in spite of Tom's scoffs, I offered him candy from our stash. A smile lit up his face, all the thanks I needed, and he ran off, his pockets stuffed with sweets. As we watched, a straggle of kids greeted him at the corner and he shared his treasure around.

Our primary goal was Agadir, a city known among van travelers and hippies as a gathering place, famous for its beaches and the nearby souk—an open market where glass Venetian trade beads, hash, and marijuana could be bought. Heading west, the coast was edged with sand dunes and the hills were covered in a blanket of green, red, white, yellow, and purple—flowers both wild and cultivated, including fields of bright red poppies. In the rocky stretches, young boys tended flocks of sheep and goats. Local villagers rode sidesaddle, their heels beating a constant rhythm on their donkeys' flanks, urging the beasts forward under the weight of rider and bundles of fodder or kindling. South of Casablanca, we passed camels in the fields. The beasts pulled plows or carts filled with branches or packs of supplies. In the late afternoon sun, they grazed peacefully, their work done. Mother camels nursed their babies and once we even saw a pure white baby camel! Spring had arrived in North Africa.

It took us three days to travel the approximately 200 miles to Agadir. The city had been almost destroyed by an earthquake in 1960, and new construction was creating a tourist mecca with modern hotels, vacation homes, and a modern municipal campground. We stopped to ask questions at their office, but the abrupt and unfriendly manager waved us away.

"Full up!" he shouted. "No room."

Via networking in Spain, Tom knew the coast was lined with free camping opportunities, but we were nervous about the persistent rumors of hepatitis the previous summer when approximately 3,000 people had camped on the undeveloped beaches.

Groups of single travelers in tents, young couples in vans, and families from Britain in trailers were strung out for several miles along the beaches north and south of Agadir. We found a spot where only four other campers parked along a stretch protected by sand dunes from the blast of ocean wind. The next day, Tom and I enjoyed our type of Zen. We walked along the shore holding hands, ran through the cold winds to the blue water, then sprinted back to the van and bundled up in beach towels while gulls wheeled overhead. Tom pulled out his skimboard and skidded along the wet sand. I sat in a beach chair and read. In the evening, our chairs side by side in the sand, we bundled together in blankets, and watched the moon's reflection on the obsidian sea.

After a few days of this, we were ready to visit the renowned native souk at Inezgane. We entered the gigantic, dusty area through a gate in the surrounding dried mud walls. The packed dirt space, larger than a football field, was congested with masses of people, both sellers and buyers. Stalls constructed of canvas or blankets on poles were heaped with oranges, tomatoes, peppers, lemons, and mounds of fresh coriander, mint, ginger, chilies, and spice mixtures. Other stalls displayed rugs, caftans, shawls, and fabric. Arab men dressed in djellabas and turbans squatted in patches of shade, surrounded by piles of silver jewelry, containers of trinkets and colorful glass beads, bundles of raw sheep's wool, or roll-up reed mats. Camels and donkeys stood among the stalls, waiting for the end of the day when they would be reloaded with the unsold goods. The inside of the surrounding wall was lined with craftsmen's shops, the air filled with the clang of hammers and the smoke of charcoal fires. Colorful awnings protected cafés where men relaxed to sip mint tea and nibble on toasted nuts.

Waiting my turn to buy spices at the souk in Inezgame, Morocco.

Groups of men and ragged children gathered in circles and watched con artists, dancers, and magicians perform. Buyers, sellers, and tourists rubbed shoulders—hippies in tie-dyed T-shirts, English tourists in wide-brimmed hats, local women totally covered by long robes and veils, turbaned men in baggy trousers, and Berbers wrapped in swaths of indigo fabric, their skin burnished blue from the dye. Water sellers moved through the crowd, brass cups strapped around their chests and a skin bag full of cool water slung over their shoulders, the tinkle of their bells calling to thirsty shoppers. Tom, with his bushy head of unshorn curls, and I, in my blue California caftan, mingled with the crowd, enveloped by the bright colors, the constant movement, the sparkle of dust motes in the sunny air, and the odors of spices and camel dung.

We looked at djellabas and rugs, we bought lemons and herbs, and we fingered piles of ancient Venetian glass beads. Known as Goulimine beads, the multicolored glass beads were used as currency during the heyday of the slave trade and had recently become prized by jewelry makers. The souk was both overwhelming and glorious.

On a seldom trafficked roadway in Morocco.

But Tom and I weren't fond of over-touristy places. We wanted to attempt a seldom trafficked highway that veered inland through an arid valley skirted on one side by the snow-capped peaks of the Haute Atlas. The rocky foothills on the south side of the valley held back the endless sand of the Sahara Desert. For us, this type of geography whispered of home, but the California illusion was broken by herds of grazing camels and walled villages. When we turned toward the Atlas Mountains, the road twisted upward, steep and rough, until we lost the pavement altogether. At the top of the pass, the high slopes gleamed with pristine snow.

In this wild country, we dared not drive after dark. As the shadows grew longer, Tom pulled onto a wide, level spot next to the road. It was not ideal, but it would do. At dusk, we were surprised when a familiar van joined us and we recognized a couple we had first met in Barcelona. The world of the van traveler in 1972 was a small one, and western company was always a welcome diversion.

The next morning, we drove down the far slope of the Atlas Mountains, past countless boys selling pretty salt rocks and lavender crystalline geodes, their treasures spread on blankets on the ground. Here, we practiced our bargaining skills away from the pressure of the market. Tom bartered with a teenager who squatted next to his goods. He traded a bottle of Spanish hair tonic for a split geode. Later he purchased a larger geode in exchange for his short-bristle hairbrush which could no longer cope with his overgrown hair. I was fascinated with the red-orange salt rocks, each round nugget of stone the size and shape of a pea. I bought a bag of them for a few coins and knew they would bring me pleasurable memories whenever I held them in my hand.

More confident in our bargaining skills, we bartered again with a young man selling beads and silver bangles. Tom scrounged up a few items from our roof storage and I unearthed a couple of seldom-worn shirts. But nothing would suit this seller except money, and we could not agree on a price. Rather disappointed by our lack of success with the bangle seller, we were eager to try our skills at another city souk.

In Marrakesh, at the municipal campground, we were elated to find full facilities (Showers! Toilets! Electrical outlets! A water faucet at each campsite. Wow!) and to find friends (travelers we had met in Spain and in Agadir). Tom helped one of them with car repairs while I did household chores. On the second day, he and I headed downtown.

The market area, like all we visited in Morocco, offered a plethora of produce, crowds of people, drummers and con artists, nighttime food stalls, and water sellers dressed in red. In the adjoining Medina (the old Arab business section), restaurants served a tempting array of meat and vegetables on skewers, tagine (a flavorful stew served over couscous), and round wheat bread. Rows of djellabas in dark, somber colors hung like banners from the awnings of women's clothing stores. Inside, next to stacks of the long, robe-like garments, shopkeepers displayed the gaily hued, embroidered caftans women wore at home. At one boutique, I bought my djellaba, a deep purple robe with a detachable hood, and wore it for the rest of the afternoon.

Daily, the food and excitement of the market streets tempted us back.

One afternoon we sipped mint tea and watched the unlicensed vendors scurry to avoid ever-vigilant police. They carried all their goods—silk scarves, embroidered blouses, or other light items—gathered up in a square of black plastic. When no police were around, they opened the bundle on the ground, fluffed up the scarves, and called to women who immediately came over to buy the items. When an officer approached, the vendors quickly gathered up the plastic by the four corners and sauntered off, disappearing into the maze of alleys. Minutes after the policeman turned a corner, the vendors returned.

Later we entered a shop where the walls were hung with carpets. More rugs were stacked in the center of the room. A kilim, woven of natural wool and scattered with brown, white, and yellow squares, hung on one wall. I nudged Tom and nodded my head toward the carpet.

"What?" he said.

Without hesitating, I pointed. "The big one on the wall with the yellow spots." He smiled and we stepped closer for a better look. That was a mistake. The proprietor, who had probably watched us from the moment we crossed the threshold, materialized by our side.

"You like it," he said in a syrupy voice. "I can give you a good price."

Though we played along for a while, we knew our initial enthusiasm had ruined any chance the kilim could be bought for a reasonable price.

As we left the store, I said to Tom, "I really want that rug! It's so beautiful. If only we hadn't given ourselves away! Do you suppose if we came back tomorrow, he'd remember us?"

"I'm sure he'd remember you," Tom said. "Beautiful blondes are rare in Marrakesh." He grinned. "I have a better idea. Craig owes me a favor for helping with his car repair. And he told me he's a good haggler."

"Would he come into town with us and help?" I asked.

"I think he'd consider it a lark."

We returned to the medina with Craig, a single, bearded, and scruffy guy from Massachusetts, who in no way resembled a rich tourist. We showed him the shop, then hurried away to wait at a tea stall around the corner. Craig was careful not to notice the kilim we had described to him until he had already discussed several others with the salesman. After about an hour of back-and-forth Arab bargaining on our behalf, he got the rug for less than the maximum price we had agreed to pay. He proudly held out the bundle. I gave him a big hug before I peeked inside the paper and rubbed the scratchy wool between my fingers.

Chapter 10

The Crossing

The days slipped by. North Africa invigorated us, but we were long overdue in Rome. We agreed to drive straight through Algeria to Tunisia and catch the ferry to Sicily.

Our last night in North Africa, camped next to the road in mountainous country near the border between Algeria and Tunisia, heavy rain beat on the Turtle's roof. We awoke to gray and foreboding weather, icy sleet coating our windshield. By the time we arrived in Tunis at midday, wind from the sea had pushed the swollen rain clouds across the sky to reveal patches of azure. We ate lunch surrounded by the white, sun-gilded columns of Carthage. Just beyond the toppled ruins, the cerulean Mediterranean was tossed by winds, the waves frosted with sparkling whitecaps.

At the shipping office, the Tunisian ticket agent informed us a ship to Sicily was scheduled to sail that evening. He described the drive-on ferry as modern, elegant, and offering dinner service. My heart soared.

I was ready to experience the rare pleasure of a cruise and a restaurant meal. The agent apologized profusely when he told us the only cabins still available were single-sex dormitory style.

"Of course," he said, "you can wait five days for the next crossing."

Tom and I put our heads together and consulted. "What do you think?" he asked.

"We've already seen Carthage. There will be plenty more Greek ruins in Sicily and Roman ruins in Italy."

"We're low on cash," Tom said. "I'd rather have my mom wire money to Rome than here." He paused. "But what about the cabins? You OK with separate dormitory rooms?"

I hated the idea of a cabin of strangers. "Can't we sleep in the van?" I asked.

"They won't like it," Tom said. "But we can probably get away with it. We should have full access to the van and after dinner we can go down and sneak in. No lights, but we could sleep in our own bed. Actually, the security aspect suits me."

"If they find us and make us go to the cabin, it's only for one night. Let's try," I said.

We paid the $106 fare for two adults and one car, gathered up our tickets, and listened to the instructions from the agent. "You need to be at the dock, right down to the left of this building, no later than 6:00 p.m. There will be a line of cars, so you won't miss it. Sailing is scheduled for 8:30 p.m. Dinner is served until 10:00 p.m. It isn't included in the fare, but you can pay with either Tunisian *dinar* or Italian *lire*. You'll be in Trapani, Sicily, in time for breakfast, but you can get coffee and bread in the dining room if you get up early."

When we returned to the dock at 6:00 p.m., a queue of cars and vans curved up to a big steel gate at the side of the terminal building, which blocked any view of the quayside. We relaxed and nibbled on crackers while we waited for the line to begin moving. An indolent hour crept by and turned into an hour and a half. The line of cars remained immobile. Curious drivers wandered up and down the line, asking each other questions and speculating on the cause of the delay.

We were a mixed group of travelers. Dusky-complexioned, Arab men with piercing eyes sauntered by in their long, brown djellabas, their women at home or patiently waiting in the car. Young Italians in dark sunglasses and silk shirts talked among themselves in quick strident voices. They moved on to gather with a group of American and French hippies with long hair, beads, and loosely woven shirts. A few older tourists leaned against dusty, European sedans, but it was an overwhelmingly under-thirty crowd. We were all eager, adventurous travelers, otherwise we wouldn't have been in Tunis in line for a ferry to Sicily, an island known for Greek ruins, volcanos, and the Mafia.

Tom checked his watch constantly. I rummaged through our seriously depleted stores for nibbles to quiet our rumbling stomachs. No sooner did Tom decide to march to the gate and insist on information, than the line began to creep forward. In the gathering darkness, we inched toward the quay. Why was the line moving so slowly? How could driving up the ramp of a sleek, new ferry be such a tediously slow process? It was already after the scheduled departure time and we had barely reached the gate.

When we rounded the end of the terminal building, we were shocked by the sight revealed. Clearly outlined against the night sky was a medium-sized ship, but it was not a ferry. What we saw was a conventional bulk-cargo passenger freighter, not unlike the SS *Donizetti* but much smaller. Passengers struggled up the steep gangway. Aghast, we watched as the ship's boom worked ponderously to lift a weathered, gray sedan with Italian license plates high above the heads of a couple of shouting longshoremen. The car was secured inadequately in the boom's sling and no rope lines were attached to guide the vehicle and curb its tendency to pivot. The dusty sedan hung precariously in the sea air, spinning and twirling as if in a dance.

"Oh, my God!" Tom's face mirrored his distress as he sprang into action. "We have to secure the van," he said. "You know what to do!"

Only two cars waited ahead of us. There was no time for an orderly process. Tom first removed his stash of precious tools from the hidden floor storage and dumped them in a heap in the middle of the van, holding on to one precious wrench, which he used to undo the bolts that held the plywood barrier. I grabbed our daypacks and stuffed in our overnight necessities, a change of clothes for us both, our passports, and the tickets. I grabbed the two oranges and a hunk of cheese from the now empty refrigerator and turned it off. Tom squeezed by me with the plywood barrier, locked it in place between the front seats, and tightened the six bolts with his wrench.

"Lock the side door and get out," he said.

I flipped the lever to lock the side door from the inside, crawled up onto the bed platform, and backed my way to the open rear window, dragging the backpacks with me. Dressed for a nice dinner on the ship, I ignored my mini-skirt which slid up as I maneuvered out, feet and rear end first, and dropped to the ground. Tom followed, also feet first. He locked the rear window with a padlock from the outside and carefully put the padlock key and his precious wrench in his pocket.

It looked as if we would be the next car to be loaded, but the longshoreman in charge waved us to one side and motioned the car behind us to move forward.

"He doesn't know what to do with us," Tom said. "These guys have never loaded cars before and they don't know their asses from a hot rock." This was typical language for Tom when he was frustrated, a sure indication things were not going well.

The longshoremen continued to load the other, smaller cars from the line behind us, lifting them up and over the ship's rail until the hold was full. Our van and an English travel-trailer still waited. We stood with the English couple, their sedan the last to enter the hold, and watched as their caravan was lifted and set on the open deck. Now it was our turn. There was only a wedge of space left between the caravan and the ship's rail. Tom went over to the group of longshoremen and hovered nearby to make sure the van was properly in the sling. I looked at my watch. It was after midnight.

Tom returned to my side and I gripped his hand. As our home was lifted, I heard a telltale clang of metal falling. Damn! I had left our hot water pot hanging from its hook over the sink and now I knew it had fallen splashing on the floor. Luckily, Tom was too preoccupied to hear the noise. The longshoremen bounced the van up and down hoping it would slip into the tiny space left, but it was similar to trying to fit a jigsaw puzzle piece into the wrong spot.

"Bring it back down! I can take off the spare tire on the front," Tom yelled. The head longshoreman nodded and the van swung out again and landed intact on the dock. Tom scrambled inside through the rear window. In less than a minute, he backed out with the lug wrench and ran to the front of the car to unfasten the spare tire.

Tom would be in a foul mood and the water on the floor of the van would exacerbate his displeasure. I was often forgetful about removing the water pot from its hook before we started driving and it always made him snappish. Perhaps there was time for me to wipe it up. I stepped onto the bumper.

"Let me help!" I heard a longshoreman offer and felt his hands on my rear end, pushing me in, but I didn't care. I was on a mission. I grabbed a towel, mopped up the puddle, and returned to the dock just as Tom came back, rolling the spare tire ahead of him. He stuffed the tire and the lug wrench into the van, locked it up again, closed the rear window, and padlocked it a second time. We watched as our green home lifted into the air, swung over the bulwark, and was nudged into the sliver of space remaining.

Tom and I were the last passengers to board.

The captain released a loud blast from the ship's funnel and the vessel moved away from the dock. We were thirsty and exhausted. I desperately needed a cup of hot tea and Tom wanted a beer. We peered longingly at the rows of bottles and glasses behind the locked glass doors of the ship's bar and nibbled the cheese and oranges in my bag. We located a steward, a young man in a stained white jacket, who brought us a glass of water and showed us how to find our cabins. Sleeping in our comfortable van was no longer an option.

In my assigned cabin, all was dark except for a dim nightlight that revealed a sink and six bunks, two unoccupied. There was no sound except for the breathing of the four, unknown, sleeping women and the slap of the waves against the hull. I climbed up to the vacant top bunk and collapsed on the thin mattress. I could feel the up-and-down movement of the ship as I fell asleep in my clothes.

I awoke to an empty cabin. I pulled on my jeans and T-shirt, wadded the dress I had slept in into the bag, and climbed the companionway to the lounge. Tom was already there, looking tired and unhappy. All the seats were taken by exhausted passengers and more travelers sat on their backpacks and leaned against the walls. Tom rose when I approached and gave me his chair. Perched on its padded arm, he asked, "You OK? How'd you sleep?"

"I'll live. My cabinmates were asleep when I arrived and gone when I woke up."

"I had more than enough of my bunkmates," Tom said. "They drank arak, smoked and talked most of the night. One guy was seasick and kept jumping up and running to the head."

"Gross! I was lucky, I guess."

"I hope I never meet those guys again! I wasn't feeling so good myself and the head was simply disgusting."

I looked around tentatively, gauging the status of things. "Is there any coffee or tea? Or breakfast?"

Tom made a face and shook his head. "Not likely," he said. "This ship has nothing. It was thrown into service at the last minute because of a major mechanical snafu with the ferry. There was coffee earlier, but they ran out. Now they only have water, club soda, and coke."

"If we'd left on time, we'd be in Sicily by now," I said. "Have you been able to find out anything about when we'll arrive in Trapani?"

"I was able to locate a first officer and he said his best guess was late morning."

I remained in the lounge, while Tom wandered out on deck to get more information. He returned periodically, brought us a club soda to share, but never more news. At 10:00 a.m., we passed the breakwater and entered the harbor. When the Italian officials came aboard, they collected passports and left again, their arms loaded with documents. An hour passed. People were restless and angry. Shortly before noon, the officials returned and handed back our stamped passports. Finally, we were free to go ashore.

Our green Turtle waited on the dock, crusted with dried salt spray and marked by only one new dent. We couldn't wait to drive away from the port. We needed two things—food and sleep. At a corner market we bought bread, eggs, and milk, then drove into the country where Tom found a free campsite on a loop of narrow farm road. I scrambled six eggs which we gobbled up, our first meal in more than twenty-four hours. The last bite barely swallowed, we dumped our plates in the sink and collapsed onto our wonderful bed. We did not wake up until the next morning.

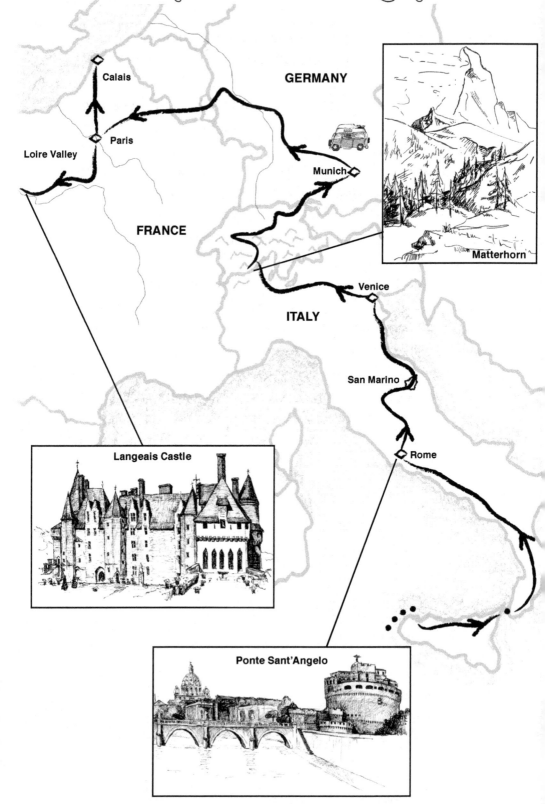

Italy to France, April to July 1972

GERMANY

Calais

Paris

Loire Valley

FRANCE

Munich

Matterhorn

Venice

ITALY

San Marino

Rome

Langeais Castle

Ponte Sant'Angelo

Chapter 11

For Richer or Poorer

We awoke to a bright and sunny day. The camping spot we had found in our sleep-deprived stupor was near a small bridge over an irrigation ditch. Fields and farmland stretched out on both sides.

No sooner had we set the hot water pot on the stove than a dusty Volkswagen bug pulled up behind us. Three men emerged from the car and two of them went to the bridge where they checked a gauge that hung down into the flowing water. The third man, a young, stocky blond who perfectly fit our visual concept of a Sicilian, came to the open side door of our van.

"Hello," he said. "Americans?"

Tom stepped down from the van. "Yes, Americans. California." We had found almost everyone we met, even country people, knew of California, the home of Disneyland and Hollywood.

"*La mia terra. La mia fattoria.*" He swung his arm in an arc toward the fields on one side of the road and structures in the distance. "*Ben venuto.*"

Tom smiled and stuck out his hand, which the Sicilian took firmly in both of his. "Sorry. No *Italiano*," Tom said. "*Español? Un poco.*" He pointed at me. "*Mi mujer, Katie . . . esposa.*" He touched the wedding ring on his finger, then put his hand on his chest. "*Tomas*," he said.

The farmer touched his own chest. "*Aberto.*" It was obvious we had no language in common, but his broad smile spoke volumes. He peered into the open door of the van and I smiled back. "*Per favore. È la tua casa?*" he said.

I understood only the one word—*casa*—and invited him inside with a gesture. He stepped up into the microbus and looked around with curiosity. I pointed out our amenities, hoping my limited Spanish would sound close enough to Italian he would understand. "*Estufa. Lavabo. Agua.* Bed for *dormir.* Closet . . . *para ropa.*"

When he had seen everything, Aberto stepped outside again. "*Grazie.*" He looked back and forth between Tom and me. "*No bambini?*" he asked. We could understand this and would soon learn this was one of the first questions most Italians asked.

Tom laughed and shook his head. "No bambini." He pointed again to his fancy gold wedding band. "*Solo ocho meses.*" Tom held up eight fingers to show the number of months we had been married.

Aberto glanced at my flat abdomen, smiled, and pointed to himself again. "*Sì, a me, otto mesi,*" he said. He held up eight fingers and pointed to the ring on his left hand. "*La mia donna. Con il bambino. . . presto.*"

The three of us nodded and smiled to indicate we understood each other. I spread my arms to encompass our tiny home. "Very *pequeño*, too small . . . *para un bambino*," I said. Aberto seemed to understand my mash up of English and Spanish because he nodded again and laughed.

The other two men finished checking the gauge and the irrigation ditch. They came over and stood by the van door as well. Aberto spoke to them in Italian and they smiled and stretched out their hands to say hello.

"Bye, bye," Aberto said as they left.

Later, as we sipped our morning coffee and tea, Aberto returned, this time with a pretty young woman with a swollen belly. Tom and I stepped out of the van to greet the couple.

"*Rosalia,*" Aberto said, his arm around the woman's waist. He gently touched his wife's abdomen and added, "*Bambino.*"

The young woman smiled shyly and offered us a bottle of milk with one hand, four eggs cradled in the other. Her husband spoke for her. "*Per te. Un regalo.*" He made the hand gestures to indicate milking a cow, then grinned and pointed to the eggs. "*Uova. Cluck. Cluck. Polli?*"

"*Si. Grazie.*" Tom assured him we had understood. "*Pollo en Español.* Chicken in English."

Aberto said a few words quickly to his wife in Italian. She went back to the car and returned with a photo album, which she offered for us to look at. "*Foto del matrimonio,*" Aberto told us.

We were honored they wanted to share their wedding pictures and looked through the photos—a beautiful Rosalia with flowers in her hair and Aberto in a black suit beside her, the couple on the stairs in front of a church, and several shots of older family members seated at a long table under a grape arbor. The album continued with countless pictures of guests dancing or raising glasses of wine in a toast. After they left, Tom and I felt lightheaded with the pleasure of connecting with local people.

"Our broken Spanish isn't much help," Tom said. "But we managed to communicate."

"A smile works magic," I agreed. "And hand gestures are great, too!" We both laughed at the memory of Aberto tugging invisible cow teats with his hands.

As a student of art history, I wanted to see the famous Greek ruins of Sicily. For several days we hopped from one magnificent Greek ruin to another, ending at an ancient Roman stone quarry turned into a garden of ferns, dripping water, and abandoned grottos.

Mount Etna was on the top of Tom's must-see list. On the lower slopes of the volcano, we spent a night surrounded by congealed lava from the most recent eruption less than a year before. In the morning, at an observation area, we viewed the two cinder cones that had formed during eruptions in the early twentieth century. Snow fields covered the high slopes of Etna and the wind was frigid, so we bundled up before we walked to the edge of the fissure and looked into the bottomless pit, gazing into the heart of the earth. I stepped back immediately, reacting to uneasiness deep in my stomach. But Tom moved closer. He climbed down to a ledge near the precarious edge of the chasm and dropped stones into the volcano, trying to hear them hit bottom. My husband delighted in cliffs and unbarricaded, high edges as much as I feared them.

"Amazing," he said when he rejoined me.

"From now on if you do something like that, please give me the keys to the car first."

"What?" He was mystified.

"If I'm left alone in a remote, godforsaken place with you in pieces hundreds of feet below, I want to be able to get in the car and go for help. Or at least sit comfortably and grieve."

"OK. But you might need to remind me," he said.

From then on, I had more than one occasion to ask for the keys while Tom stepped to the edge of a cliff in the middle of nowhere.

Totally unlike the ship we had taken from Tunis, the modern ferry from Messina transported train cars, autos, and passengers. We landed on the tip of the Italian boot only thirty minutes after boarding and drove north on the Italian coast to Scilla. The old town clung to a cliff overlooking the sea, a crescent of beach below. In the falling light of dusk, we sauntered along the sandy shore, Tom's arm wrapped around my shoulders. A bride and groom walked the other way, hand in hand, the young woman, still in her white dress, carrying her pretty shoes in one hand.

Near the water's edge, a shrine perched among the rocks. In front of the miniature chapel, the bride had left her wedding bouquet as an offering to a statue of the Virgin. Was it a prayer for a long and happy marriage?

"Let's put an offering in the shrine, too," I said.

"Prayers to the Virgin are like whistling into a gale," Tom said.

I searched among the rocks and tide pools, looking for a worthy gift. "Not a prayer . . . more a token of thanks for our happiness together."

"How about this?" Tom bent down and lifted up a strand of leafy seaweed with a mussel shell attached to the base. He tied it into a circle, making a kind of bracelet, which he gave to me. "A token of my love," he said. "Come on. I know how to do this." We held hands and stood in front of the shrine. "Holy Mary, Mother of God. Thanks." He crossed himself Catholic style and released my hand. "Your turn."

Laying the circlet of seaweed next to the bridal bouquet, I whispered, "Thanks for Tom's love. And for our year of travel together."

The next morning, Tom left the older roads, which we preferred, for the new autostrada. It was time to head to Rome as fast as possible and telephone Tom's mother. We needed money. The autostrada in southern Italy was still under construction. The traffic was light and there were few toll stops.

I relaxed, reading in our Michelin guidebook about Rome. Unexpectedly, I felt the van slow and looked up. Two Italian police officers stood directly in our lane and waved us to the side of the road. "What's going on?" I asked.

"Don't worry. I've got it," Tom said and jumped out of the car.

One of the policemen let out a stream of Italian. I could understand none of his tirade except the words, "Three thousand lire!" repeated several times at various intervals.

Tom shook his head and displayed a puzzled expression. He tried broken Spanish and a long English explanation of ignorance as to what he had done wrong. He came across as splendidly dumb. I sat in the cab, ignorant of what had happened and watched the drama unfold.

The policeman again rattled off Italian and jabbed his finger at his ticket receipt book.

He looked at our car license plate and exclaimed, "California! *Si, si* . . . California." He pointed again at his ticket book and pushed it toward Tom, pointing at what was written there.

Tom nodded his head as if he understood. "Ah . . . turistas solo." He pointed at the ticket book entry and repeated in his mangled Spanish. "California. Turista." Then as if puzzling it out, "California, turista. Solo para turistas?" He shook his head as if in disbelief and muttered, "Solo for turistas."

After a few moments of this, the policeman became agitated. He conferred with his partner and waved Tom to get in the car. With hand motions he indicated we could drive on. "*Partire! Andare immediatamente.*"

Tom did not hesitate to follow his motioned instructions. "What was that all about?" I asked as we pulled back onto the autostrada.

"Quick. Look behind," Tom said. "Another police car pulled over. Probably a higher-ranking cop. I think our two guys were afraid I'd make too much fuss about tourist-only tickets. They wanted me out of there."

I turned around and saw the second car by the side of the road. Two new policemen had joined our officers who stood at attention, listening to what appeared to be a serious discourse. "But why did they pull us over in the first place?" I asked.

"There was a 'no passing' sign. We drove by another one earlier, right when I was passing the truck." Suddenly, I understood. "The last ticket in the book, the one the officer showed me, was also for a car with California plates," Tom explained. "It gave me the idea to pretend I thought the fee was a scam only for tourists."

We had been told fines in Italy were generally collected in cash at the traffic stop, so we felt lucky to have been let go. A fine of 3,000 lire would have seriously depleted our almost empty wallet.

On Saturday morning, a month later than we had expected, we drove into Rome with a few lire notes left. Because the next day would be Sunday and government offices would be closed, we went to the Ufficio dell'educazione where, as a teacher, I received free passes to all national museums and historical sites for both of us. At the main postal office, we claimed a thick rubber-banded stack of letters from home—several from each of our parents, one from my sister Una, and even a letter from one of my teacher friends. Thrilled to have California news, we walked to the nearby Spanish Steps to read our letters. We always read letters from home out loud, taking turns. After reading the first few, we moved to a café and continued as we slurped long strands of buttery, garlicy, clam pasta. The next day, Sunday, would be better for telephoning Tom's mom, so we set off toward Saint Peter's Square.

Tom and I were excited to be in Rome, a first for us both. Tom, raised a Catholic, had been a tentative candidate for priestly orders and attended a seminary as a preteen. His great-uncle, the monsignor who had helped us arrange our wedding, had been assigned to the Vatican as a young man. Naturally, in spite of Tom's change in religious perspective, Rome was significant to his boyhood. For me, Rome was the home of an abundance of classical and renaissance art, all of which I had studied in my university classes.

At my insistence, we went to Saint Peter's Basilica to view Michelangelo's *Pietá*, a sculpture of Carrara marble created in 1499. After viewing countless slides of the statue in art history classes, I found the real thing almost a let-down. On a raised stone platform set back into an alcove, the real Pieta was cordoned off by a velvet rope. We could not walk around it to view the back and the work was so high above eye level, Christ's face was obscured. Nevertheless, I was thrilled to study an actual Michelangelo. We could not know that in less than a month, a vandal would smash into the sculpture with a sharp geologist's hammer, severely damaging the Virgin's arm and face. Though painstaking restoration followed, from then on additional safety precautions made viewing it even more difficult.

Oblivious to our great luck to see the *Pietá* in pristine condition, we climbed to the top of the Basilica's dome. Promised no unprotected precipices, I followed Tom up the long curving ramp to a snack shop and restrooms on the roof. On one side, Saint Peter's Square stretched out below, the people like toys. On the other side, we looked into the cool, tree-shaded garden of the Pope's residence. From the balcony at the base of the giant dome, we viewed the interior of the church, the stunning marble patterns on the distant floor of the Basilica and the arched mosaics of cherubs on the ceiling above.

Our first night in Rome, we slept in our van near the Tiber River, on a quiet street temporarily closed to through-traffic because of repair work. In spite of construction barriers and parked work vehicles, Tom found a tree-shaded spot away from pedestrian looky-loos. While we waited for our money to arrive, we became experienced "street camp-ers" in Rome. Public fountains offered water; blue chemicals added to our infamous bucket kept the contents odorless until we could find a public latrine. Though our locations were occasionally chosen because of their convenience to our morning plans, the riverbank site became our favorite place to bed down for the night.

On our first Sunday morning in Rome, we moved to Saint Peter's Square as soon as we woke up. After breakfast, I stood next to the open door of the van, brushing my hair in the center of one of the most famous locations in the world. Tom headed off through the gathering crowds to find the public latrines, our green bucket hang-ing nonchalantly from one hand. I watched horrified as he suddenly swung the bucket in a complete circle up and over his head. Not a drop spilled. He turned back with a grin to make sure I had witnessed this maneuver.

Promptly at noon, Pope Paul VI emerged on his balcony and spoke. We glimpsed the white dot of his vestments in the distance, and with our binoculars, he became a recognizable human figure. As much as I was thrilled to see the Pietá, Tom was thrilled to see the Pope. He couldn't wait to tell his parents he had been among the thousands who received the Pope's blessing.

The central train station was the best place to make an international call home. Once Tom had talked to his mother, we located the station's public shower and bathing facilities. For the low fee of 80 cents each, we delighted in our first real shower since Lisbon! Thirty seconds under an icy trickle of water in a winter campground and the sponge-baths in the van did not compare to standing under a lavish shower of hot water in a spotless, private, tiled room. We came out feeling reinvigorated, clean to the roots of our hair and between each toe. We were ready to experience Rome. Though we would have to be careful with spending for a few days, we expected our money to arrive no later than Thursday.

We hiked all over the ancient classical area of the city, visited countless churches, and one night slept in the middle of Saint Peter's Square surrounded by lighted fountains and colonnades. At the Sistine Chapel, we stood in wonder with a half-dozen other tourists. We studied the ceiling with binoculars and read in our guidebook about the paintings. Tuesday night, we slept in a vacant lot in the nearby town of Tivoli and spent the day in the gardens of the Villa d'Este.

We returned to Rome feeling romantic and drove around the city, enchanted by the magical glow of lights on the city's fountains and classical ruins. We each tossed a coin over our right shoulder into the Trevi Fountain and wished for a return to Rome one day. On our way back to our favored camp spot next to the Tiber River, we passed through a district where we saw several ladies in heavy makeup and short skirts loitering on a corner.

"Ladies of the night!" Tom said.

Later, in our cozy home, I was inspired. "I will be your lady of the night," I whispered as I responded to my husband's ardent embrace.

Thursday morning, we went to the American Express office to see if our money had arrived. We had given it four days, but there was no money waiting. We walked around a district of expensive shops and every few hours returned to the American Express office, but each time we were disappointed. Friday, we hiked the city again and visited museums with my free teacher's pass. No money that day at the American Express. Saturday, we wandered around the gardens above the Spanish Steps and window-shopped. Still, no money. The American Express would not be open again until Tuesday because of a Monday holiday. In spite of dwindling funds, we wanted to spend the weekend at Ostia, near the sea, but first we placed another call to Tom's mother. Yes, she had sent the money. Surely it would be in Rome by Tuesday.

At the Ostia campground, we relaxed, filled our water tanks, scrubbed our bodies in real showers, and checked out the well-stocked camp store, though we dared buy only an ice cream bar each. On Tuesday morning, we telephoned the American Express and asked if our money had arrived. Nothing yet. Unable to remain at the campground, we sadly returned to our spot on the Tiber River. It would be our home base until money arrived.

Our emergency pantry was almost empty. We ate the last package of dry soup and opened the remaining can of processed, Spanish cheese. We had a couple of cans of potted meat and tuna remaining, a handful of Spanish soup pasta, and half a bag of rice. Eating meals concocted from these few items when we were surrounded by the delectable food of Italy was beyond depressing. Each day, when we walked around town, I lusted after wedges of cheese and pink, veal cutlets displayed in shop windows.

We bought fresh food one meal at a time. Breakfast in the van was simple, usually bread with jam or Spanish cheese. When the money wasn't at the American Express office in the morning, lunch was also meager. The afternoon would be filled with daydreams of a restaurant dinner if the money arrived before the office closed for the day. When there was no money, we counted our lire and bought only enough to augment what was left in the pantry—four eggs for an omelet, a small loaf of bread, a tomato, a pint bottle of milk, and a couple of mushrooms to turn our can of tuna into a casserole. We tramped the streets of Rome, peered into the windows of shops, and sat on the Spanish Steps people watching. We strolled past restaurants, breathed in the aromas of garlic and baking bread, and occasionally read menus, marking our map for a later return. We visited museums and art galleries and spent hours in the gardens above the Spanish Steps. Each evening, we walked back to our site by the Tiber River.

One morning, midweek, I rummaged through the glove compartment in search of a pen. I discovered, stuffed in the corner, a wrinkled envelope. What I found inside cheered an otherwise bleak morning. "Look! French francs!" I handed it to Tom who counted the bills. "Remember when we left Carcassonne," I said, "we had money left over and we saved it for when we were in France again. How much is it?"

"About eleven dollars' worth," Tom said. "Get dressed quick. We can exchange these francs for lire. We should have a slice of pizza for lunch to celebrate." At the American Express where we changed the bills, Tom separated a couple of lire and put them in his shirt pocket. "If the money doesn't arrive by this afternoon, I'll use this money to call my mom again."

We had no idea how long our windfall needed to last, so we didn't squander it. We called California again and asked Tom's mother to send more money and put in a loss claim at the bank for the previous amount. We went to the American Embassy to ask what else we should do. They were concerned and one officer there even offered to loan us twenty dollars' worth of lire if we totally ran out of cash.

We waited, careful with each centesimo. The Spanish cheese was finished. All our tanks were almost empty—gasoline, butane, and water. I carefully rationed the butane and Tom mandated the refrigerator must remain off for the duration. I served fried bread garnished with raw vegetables or a bowl of tiny, quick-cooking pasta topped with chopped tomatoes and a few herbs. We did not dare to move the car, and we spent our nights on the street by the Tiber River.

Soon, we missed the processed Spanish cheese and longed for meat. Each night, we wrapped our arms around each other and dreamed of food. Each morning, Tom carried our green bucket to the banks of the Tiber and tossed the contents over the embankment where it oozed among the Roman trash and garbage littered there. We hoped for a heavy rain to carry it away.

On Saturday morning, totally out of cash, we returned to the American Express office. If the money wasn't there, we would need to take up the kind offer of a loan from the embassy official.

The money had arrived! We were beside ourselves with joy. First lunch in a restaurant. Pasta with cheese and cream. Succulent veal, coated in a wine sauce and sprinkled with capers. A glass of wine each. Chocolate gelato! Our shopping list was long, and once we were stuffed, we returned to the food shops we had scouted out. Fresh fruits and vegetables, sausage, veal, cream, canned goods, fresh herbs. I would cook again! After the ultimate luxury—another hot shower at the train station—we returned to the Ostia campground with all our goodies, eager for a few stress-free days.

We exchanged our blue gas-tank for a new one and I cooked our first substantial meal in a week—veal and fresh pasta with mushrooms and tiny baby peas. We would have ice cream bars from the camp shop every day, maybe two a day.

Chapter 12

European Grand Tour

From Rome we headed to Naples and a visit with an American military couple who were friends of our Marrakesh carpet buyer, Craig. Whenever possible, we visited people who lived locally, sometimes friends of fellow travelers but more often the travelers themselves, now back home. These visits gave us insight into local life and if the friends were in the American military, the added perk of a trip to the PX.

We continued south to Salerno, then turned north to drive the sinuous coastal road around the rocky Amalfi peninsula. Each tight bend and hairpin turn revealed a stunning vista of the Mediterranean. Occasionally the two-lane road dipped down to a fishing village, only to turn again, cross a narrow gorge, and climb up the steep hills, their rocky escarpments dropping directly into the sea. As dusk turned the sea purple, Tom found a spot at an overlook wide enough to provide safe parking. Below us nestled a sandy cove and village. Across the road, a fancy hotel built of native stone was fronted by a patio lined with the bright colors of potted flowers. As the sky darkened and the village lights blinked on, we sat in the cab of the van, sipping wine.

"It couldn't be more beautiful." Tom reached across the aisle and squeezed my fingers. "I keep saying to myself, 'This is the experience of a lifetime.'"

We gazed at the silver streak of moonlight on the nighttime sea. The crash of the waves against the rocks below was familiar and calming, recalling memories of childhood. Happier and more content with our relationship each day, I savored the romantic setting. Even Tom seemed swept away. He moved to the back of the van and held out his arms. "Come here," he said. "There's only one way to make this evening more perfect."

The next afternoon, the final turn of the Amalfi road revealed a view of Mount Vesuvius in the distance. We arrived at the ruins of Pompeii as cool evening breezes stirred the dust of the ancient streets, a perfect time to stroll where Roman carts and chariots had worn deep grooves into the stone pavement. We could only imagine the terror of the townspeople as ash rained down on them from the mountain above.

Our days in Italy were a journey through the centuries from ancient Pompeii to medieval Assisi, the home of Saint Francis, to Perugia and Siena and finally Florence where we camped overnight at the Piazza Michelangelo overlooking the Arno River. The giant replica of *David* towered above us and city lights glittered below.

We stopped for a picnic and a visa stamp at the tiny kingdom of San Marino, drove to Ravenna for Byzantine mosaics, and on to Venice, where we lingered. Each morning, we loaded our daypacks and took a local bus from the campground to the nearest water-bus station. We explored the car-free streets and alleyways, rode the water taxi in the gray light of a rainy dusk, and toured the Doge's Palace. We relaxed at a café in Saint Mark's Square, sipped glasses of wine, and watched passing pedestrians. We lounged on the boat quay to soak up the view of the sparkling waters of the lagoon and the ferry boats bobbing back and forth between the monastery on San Giorgio and the island of La Giudecca. We ate dinner

A picnic in San Marino.

in a restaurant tucked behind the Doge's Palace, where we devoured with gusto a platter heaped with fried seafood (fritto misto—shrimp, squid, sardines, oysters, and finger-size, whole Adriatic fish, all fried in a light golden batter), a meal too complex for my tiny kitchen.

After Venice, we headed north toward the Swiss Alps.

Though Tom was anxious to get to what he called Volkswagen Land, he was willing to indulge my Heidi dreams. As a child, I had favored books about orphans who, after the loss of their parents, experienced hardship and adventure only to find loving adults in an unexpected way. Variations on this theme included *The Boxcar Children* by Gertrude Warner, *Mistress Masham's Repose* by T.H. White, and *Nancy and Plum* by Betty Macdonald. Closest to my heart was *Heidi*. Written by Johanna Spyri in 1880, *Heidi* was given to me by my grandmother who had read it herself as a young girl in Germany. Perhaps my devotion to this book was tied to my love for my grandmother. I was eager to walk in Heidi's footsteps. I wanted to experience things described in my favorite childhood book:

- see a Swiss chalet
- hike an Alpine trail
- frolic with goats (or at least watch goats romp in a mountain pasture)

Besides that, we both wanted to see the famous Matterhorn. The 1959 Disney movie, *The Third Man on the Mountain*, about a boy who conquers the mountain that killed his father, was a mutual favorite and we had often ridden on the Disneyland ride the movie inspired. We crossed the Italian Alps on the Simplon Pass and the famous mountain was not far off our route. The mountain road ended in the town of Brig, where the streets were lined with chalets, their balconies spilling brightly colored flowers. The first item on my Swiss list was already accomplished.

We camped in a vacant lot behind the main street and woke to find the village lightly frosted with newly fallen snow. We stuffed a simple picnic in our daypack, along with a few of my art supplies, and caught the cog railway up to Zermatt at the base of the famous peak.

From the train station, we climbed uphill amidst drifting snowflakes through the village to a vista point. At the lookout, shifting, misty gray clouds partially obscured the ghost of the mountain's shape. The snow had stopped, so we hiked further on the steep trail, across green slopes sprinkled with patches of Alpine flowers. A few shady spots still held coverlets of snow. We ate our picnic of bread and cheese on boulders protected from the wind by a curve in the trail. With renewed energy, we reached another vista point near the base of the Matterhorn, its snow cliffs a solid foundation for the starkly angled peak partially obscured by swirling mists. Tom photographed the breathtaking sight while I did a fast sketch, then we returned back down the mountain, pleased to tick off the second item on my Swiss list. As we hiked, the sky slowly cleared until the Matterhorn emerged in all its glory. With the blue-sky background, swirls of white snow blew in feathering spumes off the south face creating an ethereal cloud.

On the train ride from Zermatt back to Brig, we saw goats grazing on a mountainside and a young goatherd watching over the flock. All three items on my list, and the Matterhorn, had been ticked off the first day!

Every road in Switzerland offered stunning vistas—green pastoral valleys, forested slopes, meadows with cows and goats, and more Swiss

Covered bridge in Lucerne, Switzerland.

chalets than one could count, each with distinctive wooden trim, rushing rivers, and wide, blue lakes dotted with sailboats. We spent a string of days passing from Interlaken, bookended by two glacial lakes, to Bern with its famous bear pit and clock tower, to Lucerne with its covered pedestrian bridge, and finally Zurich for another stack of letters. More excited than usual to get mail, we anticipated news about summer plans.

In Rome, a letter from my mother had described a trip she and my father had taken to Baja California in their Westfalia camper. They had taken their grandchildren, Mike and Michelle, with them. My mother made camping with children sound like a pleasant adventure. The letter set Tom and I thinking. Wouldn't it be great to have my niece and nephew join us in the summer for their school vacation? The kids could bring a pup tent to sleep in. We thought England would be the perfect place to share with children. We asked my parents if they would be willing to pay the two children's airfare. If so, Tom and I would cover all their expenses while the kids were with us. In Zurich, a letter from my parents confirmed that they had bought air tickets for Mike and Michelle. We would have a little family for the summer! All we had to do was get to London in time to meet the kids at Heathrow Airport.

We stopped in Germany, "the land of the Volkswagen," only long enough for Tom to finish his list of car maintenance projects. In Munich, we found a large vacant lot next to an auto junkyard that would be our free campsite for the next week.

During the first day, Tom went off on foot and by bus to scout out auto-parts stores for what he needed, while I stayed home to watch over our van, do laundry, write letters, and read. He spent most of the second day under the van. He pulled the engine, repaired a forward seal leak, installed a new clutch and pressure plate, renewed a few gaskets, and returned the engine to the car. I watched, amazed by what this man could do. In my family, we joked that my father couldn't even change a lightbulb! What I had learned about using a screwdriver and a hammer, I had learned from my mother and from the half-semester in high school when the girls took shop while the boys learned to cook and sew. How had I gotten so lucky to find a man who could fix anything?

Driving back and forth, looking for a VW mechanic to do a major repair, we saw most of Munich, which was busy preparing for the upcoming Olympics—block after block of new apartments, roads under construction, and city historical sites newly refurbished. But we couldn't find anyone able to tackle the job for two weeks, so Tom decided he would install a new steering box, torsion bars, and a new muffler himself, even though he had never done it before. Back in our vacant lot campsite, he set out his tools, including a few new acquisitions, and slid under the van.

The first evening, when he was only half-finished with the project, Tom sat in the cab of the van while I finished dinner. He sipped on a beer and fiddled with the radio dials. We had not had the radio on for the last several months as station call numbers changed constantly and the programing was unintelligible to us.

"What're you hoping to find?" I asked. Nothing but a garble of German came from the radio, and I found it irritating.

"I don't know," he said. "Maybe the BBC." Suddenly a short burst of English came from the speakers. "Listen," he said. Tom tweaked the dials to bring the station in more clearly and the van was filled with the sound of Neil Diamond crooning "Song Sung Blue."

The music made me feel dreamy.

When the song ended a distinctly American voice announced, "This is the Voice of the American Armed Forces Radio."

"Wow!" Tom said. "We used to listen to Armed Forces Radio on the ship when we were in Saigon. I forgot all about it. Of course, they're in Germany with all the U.S. bases here." He looked up with a smile, suddenly more relaxed. "We're going to love it. Music for you and news for me."

American Armed Forces Radio became our companion while we were in northern Europe. We caught up on the latest news, learned new songs from the hit parade, and best of all, one night heard an old episode from the radio version of *Gunsmoke*, which we had both listened to as kids. The programs brought us a touch of home.

When all the car work was finished, we allowed ourselves a special afternoon exploring old-town Munich. The Marienplatz, embraced by the neo-Gothic town hall, an arcade of beautiful shops, and rows of flower-filled planters, was a haven for pedestrian shoppers. We waited to hear the chime of the Glockenspiel and watched the life-size, wooden figures of sixteenth-century ladies and gentlemen prance below the big clock. By the time the golden rooster at the top of the tower chirped three times to signal the end of the display, we were hungry. Down the main street, we found the Augustiner-Keller, a popular beer hall known for its Bavarian cuisine. I was eager to taste food my grandmother had told me about, dishes from her fond memories of life before the Nazis.

The hall was well lit and noisy, filled with people raising steins of frothy beer. We sat at one of the long wooden tables and ordered

Leberknödelsuppe (a rich, clear broth afloat with delicate dumplings made from ground liver and herbs), *Brotsuppe* (sweet and sour bread soup made with black and white bread, apples, wine, and raisins), and *Bratwurst mit Kraut* (sausage and sauerkraut). A young couple from Canada ate near us and we overheard them speaking English. Beer loosened our tongues and the evening melted away.

With my half-Jewish heritage, I couldn't leave the area without a stop at the Holocaust monument at Dachau. The somber exhibits emotionally drained us—the rows of photographs, the reconstructed barracks, the memorial erected by survivors in memory of their lost friends, the three chapels at the far end of the grounds, the glass-encased, striped prison garb, and the crematorium. A powerful movie traced the history of the camp from the first political prison to its use as a work camp for tens of thousands of Jews, Gypsies and Slavs, through final liberation by the U.S. Army. I left the movie in tears. It had been impossible not to imagine how, with less luck, my father, his siblings, and his mother might have been brought here. Years later I would learn a cousin had been murdered here, but as we walked around Dachau, I already knew that if I had been born in Germany rather than California, my father's Jewish blood, passed down to me, would have made my own death during the Holocaust a possibility. It was a sobering idea—one that made me uneasy in Germany.

We hurried on toward Paris and our date in London, grabbing tidbits of German culture along the way. In Luxembourg, Tom took the engine out of the van (yes again!) to search for the cause of a mysterious knocking. While I did laundry, he refinished all the woodwork inside the van. After three days, we resumed our dash to Paris with clean clothes and the interior of our home glistening with fresh varnish.

Arriving in Paris at dusk, we headed for the Champs de Elysee to see the evening lighting illuminate the boulevard. Near the Place de la Concorde, a tour bus ahead of us in the traffic pulled over. Tom parked behind the bus as the tourists stepped to the sidewalk with their guide.

Half-timber building in the Rhine River Valley, Germany.

Quietly, the darkness adding to our stealth, we eased near the group and listened to the guide's English descriptions. When the bus proceeded, we followed carefully in its wake, through the darkened streets of Paris to the Louvre, Notre Dame, and Les Invalides. At one point, the guide noticed us. He was obviously unhappy with a pair of freeloaders who stopped every time the bus stopped and listened to his spiel, but there was little he could do to discourage us from following along. The tour ended at the parking area directly under the iconic Eiffel Tower. As the tour bus pulled away, Tom and I exchanged glances. The campground was on the other side of the city, we were exhausted, the area was deserted, and the symbol of Paris towered above.

"Let's sleep here," Tom said. "There's no one around. We can stay until they tell us to leave." What a romantic idea! We opened the bed and snuggled together before falling into tired dreams.

The next morning, after being awakened by the two French gendarmes, I navigated Tom to the Bois de Boulogne campground, the memory of sleeping under the Eiffel Tower safe in my heart. It was the perfect start for a lover's tour of Paris.

We learned to use the Metro and enjoyed the ease of traveling underground, but mostly we walked, the best way to soak up the sights and smells. We strolled hand in hand along the quays, thumbed through books at the stalls on the riverbank, and searched the lively streets of the Latin Quarter for a bakery to buy croissants. We wandered around the Luxembourg Gardens and the Tuileries and inhaled the sweet scent of the spring flowers bursting into bloom. At the Museum of Impressionist Painters near the Tuileries (the d'Orsay was not yet a museum), Tom learned to distinguish the styles of various painters. We circumnavigated the Isle de la Cité and its centerpiece, the cathedral of Notre Dame, where we studied the frightening gargoyles, marveled at the impressive flying buttresses, and contemplated the sculpture and high columns of its dark, quiet interior. On the tip of the Isle de la Cité, we discovered a starkly modern memorial to French Jews who died in concentration camps. Best of all, we were able to go inside the Saint Chappelle, built in the eleventh century with walls almost entirely of stained glass. Sunlight streamed through the tall, multicolored windows, and a kaleidoscope of hues turned the king's chapel into an airy confection.

We admired Napoleon's Tomb, and for Tom, visited the Musée de l'Armée, touted as "the best military museum in Europe." For me, the nearby Rodin Museum was the highlight of our days in Paris. The sculpture garden basked in afternoon light. "Just like us," I whispered as we stood in front of my favorite piece, *The Kiss*. I pulled Tom to join me on a nearby bench and laughing, we duplicated the statue's pose.

We took the Metro to the Arc de Triomphe and tramped the length of the Avenue des Champs-Élysées and from there, across the Seine to the foot of the Eiffel Tower, where we ate a picnic on the grass of the Champs de Mars. Revived by our bread and cheese, we crossed over to the Louvre and spent three hours in the museum, a time both too long and not long enough.

On our final day, we hiked from the Metro Station at the base of Montmartre up to the Sacré-Cœur and explored the narrow streets behind the church, poked into the art shops, and looked over the shoulders of the artists who spent their days doing charcoal portraits of grinning tourists. Later, we found a working-class restaurant housed in an old post office with an atmosphere of dark wood and serious food. I ordered lamb stew and Tom ordered *tartare de filet de boeuf*. He had learned to appreciate this dish of raw ground beef, seasoned with onion, salt, pepper, and topped with a raw egg yolk, at my mother's table. She made it often, buying the best sirloin from a local butcher who ground it while she watched. My father, who called it by the German word for chopped meat, *gehacktes*, loved to pile the concoction on top of toasted California sourdough bread. Tom relished each bite of his mound of ground steak.

"As delicious as your mom makes it," he pronounced.

After a quick stop at Versailles, we drove into the French countryside, through bright yellow fields planted with rape, a crop grown to make canola oil from its seeds. We camped on a back road, the Gothic spires of the Chartres Cathedral rising in the distance, tall gray shapes against a starry sky. We planned to hike to the cathedral the next morning, but Tom awoke in the middle of the night with an uncomfortable case of tummy trouble that kept him running to our green bucket. It was obvious the working-class restaurant wasn't as careful handling raw meat as my mother. Poor Tom spent most of the day sleeping and reading between unpleasant belly cramps, while I watched the shadows of the cathedral's twin spires march across the field. Around 6:00 p.m., when the dark shadows stretched out in long fingers, Tom felt well enough to take me into town for a quick look.

His illness past, Tom was ready to take to the road again, and I was determined to share with my husband the castles of the Loire Valley, which I remembered as a highlight of my earlier family trip. It was already the first of July and the kids were due in London in two weeks. Luckily Tom loved to drive. We visited a rapid succession of chateaux—Blois to Chambord, Chenonceau to Amboise and Langeais, and back up the river valley north to Calais. One night we shared a field with a group of Gypsies in their horse-drawn, wooden caravans. One afternoon we relaxed for an hour in a rented rowboat on the Cher River. Finally, we made a quick connection at the Calais ferry and crossed the English Channel at twilight on the third day.

Castle in Wales

End of the World

Edinburgh

ENGLAND

London

Amsterdam

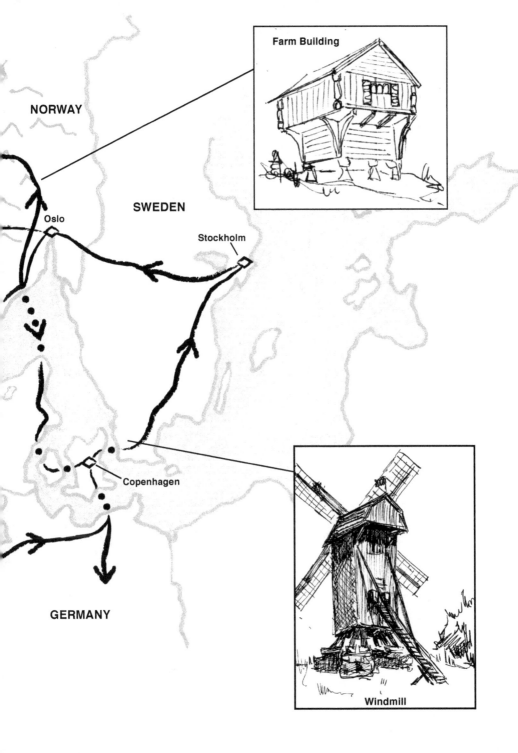

Farm Building

NORWAY

SWEDEN

Oslo

Stockholm

Copenhagen

Windmill

GERMANY

England to Germany, July to October 1972

Chapter 13

Experimental Family

A s our ferry approached the headlands of Britain, we stood at the rail and Tom warbled the World War II Glen Miller favorite, "The White Cliffs of Dover." His mellow voice drifted over the water as he sang about bluebirds, while white seagulls wheeled overhead.

Tom and I were immediately at ease in England—they spoke our language! We had managed in Europe with our high school Spanish and French, augmented by gestures and smiles, but it was a relief to be understood by everyone and to understand almost everything said to us, though we sometimes struggled with regional dialects.

In Dover, we discovered a self-service, coin laundromat, a rarer luxury than a hot shower! By noon, with a cardboard box of clean clothes stashed in the van, we entered the darkness of the cinema. Appropriately, *Mary Queen of Scots*, a recently released movie with Vanessa Redgrave, was playing. After the movie, we drove up to the top of the White Cliffs. Far below, the Channel stretched all the way to France just as it had 400 years before when Mary arrived, and in 1944, when Allied soldiers crossed with fear and exhilaration on D-day.

The village of Chigwell boasted a campground with showers, a pool, a playground, and a camp store. When Mike and Michelle were with us, we intended to stay in regular campgrounds so they could pitch their tent and we would have showers and a camp store to make life easy. Commuting into London was simple from the camp—a twenty-minute walk to the tube station, then a forty-minute ride on the underground to Victoria Station in central London.

While we waited for the kids, we rewarded ourselves with a metropolitan holiday. We dressed our best, entered cool, dark cinemas for the rare treat of English-language movies, and indulged in restaurant meals, including a lunch at a neighborhood English pub. We stood at the high counter workingman style and munched on pickled herring, hot Cornish pasties, and sausage rolls. I insisted on trying a Scotch egg but was disappointed to find it dry and tasteless. Tom sipped the ale appreciatively, but we agreed our picnic lunches in France were better.

Satiated with movies and good food, we were ready to meet my father's sister, Edith, who had immigrated to England when she fled Nazi Germany in 1936. By the time World War II was over, she was married with two children and London was her home. Nervous and excited to meet her for the first time, I entered my aunt's flat in West Kensington. Without hesitation, Edith and I embraced. "You look so much like Grandmother!" I brushed away tears. Edith shared her mother's stature (4 foot, 11 inches), and her gestures and features made me feel I was in the presence of my beloved grandmother.

Edith held me at arm's length and studied my face. "You definitely have good looks from my brother," she said. "All the girls were crazy for him." I felt proud to be my father's daughter. Edith hugged me again. "You know my mother always wrote you were her favorite. She lost her darling Hazel, my daughter, and my son Mike, too, when she received her U.S. visa in 1943 and had to leave England. But you were waiting for her, a newborn baby she could nuzzle and pamper. She always felt you were the best thing about her life in California."

More tears streamed down my cheeks. "I'll always remember Grandmother Clara as the best part of my childhood. I miss her so much! I can't believe it's been five years since she passed away."

Edith had prepared a simple dinner in her kitchen, and we sat around the table and talked until late. During the course of the evening, I was constantly on the edge of tears as Edith's gestures and the tone of her voice reminded me of my grandmother. By the end of the evening, I knew she had also inherited her mother's strong and feisty personality.

On Sunday, we took the train to Hemel Hempstead for dinner with a British family we had met in Paris. They showed us their village, including a canal-side country pub and took us home for a traditional, midday supper of roast beef (gray and overcooked the English way), with Yorkshire pudding (yummy). Later, we watched a game of cricket on the village green, then returned to their house for a light tea of Scottish shortbread and strawberries.

Monday was the big day—Mike and Michelle were arriving. We started out for Heathrow Airport before 8:00 a.m., a trip from one side of London to the other that took two hours via train and tube. We didn't bother to find a pay phone and check on the latest flight information (no cell phones or airline apps) and fully expected to have our rented kiddos in our arms at the appointed time. At the airline desk, we learned the plane carrying ten-year-old Mike and nine-year-old Michelle had turned back to Los Angeles due to engine trouble only an hour into the flight. The children would not arrive in London until late afternoon. We found a comfortable bench and settled in at the airport, anxious about the children alone on a plane having difficulties. When their flight finally landed, we waited at the arrivals' ramp expecting to greet our two young charges under the close supervision of an airline stewardess. We watched as streams of passengers from the flight exited. But no Mike and Michelle! Had the two children gotten lost during the delay? We were about to report our missing niece and nephew, when suddenly, there they were, at the top of the ramp, holding hands, their small suitcases at their feet, no airline personnel in sight. They looked lost and puzzled.

We waved and hollered, they ran to us, and we gathered them into our arms. "What took you so long to get through immigration?" we asked. "What happened to the stewardess who was supposed to be with you?"

Mike looked sheepish. "She told us to wait for her, but I thought I could find you OK."

"We got lost," Michelle piped up. "But a nice man showed us where to get our passports stamped."

"I got us through OK," Mike said. He was only fourteen months older than his sister, but he took his responsibilities seriously. He squared his shoulders and grasped his sister's hand again. She looked up and nodded her support. "The flight was terribly long," Mike said, "and when we turned back to LA, I saw fuel pouring out of the wing."

Michelle had more information. "The stewardess, a different one, took us to the fancy upstairs part of the plane when we were going back to LA. She said it was safer up there."

"It was cool upstairs. First class. And we had free cokes," Mike said.

I gathered them into my arms again. These two children were dear to me. "I'm so glad you made it," I told them. "We're going to have a lot of fun."

Tom picked up their dropped luggage and returned with all three pieces—two suitcases and a duffel bag with their tent, sleeping bags, air mattresses, and a few toys and books. "Come on," he said, "let's go to the tube. It's been a long day."

Michelle looked up at me. "What tube? What's that?"

"The subway," I explained. "An underground train."

During most of the ride back to the campground, the children chattered away and we told them all the things we planned for the summer.

After a while, Michelle leaned against my shoulder and fell asleep. Mike, too excited to close his eyes, gazed out the window as the lighted stations zipped by. When the train stopped in Chigwell, I jumped up, totally forgetting about Michelle who flopped sideways on the wooden bench and awoke with a start. "Are we here?" she asked, blinking, her new eyeglasses perched precariously on the end of her nose. I felt terrible. A mother would not have forgotten her sleeping child. I grabbed Michelle's arm and together we jumped off as a recorded voice repeated, "Mind the gap."

Tom and the kids set up the tent and a newly purchased, English wind protector while I made dinner. We fell into our bed and sleeping bags after 10:00 p.m.

Before long, we established our new routine. We got up early or late, depending on when we went to bed the night before. I fixed breakfast and we headed out to sightsee on foot or by car. Lunch was usually picnic style either in a park or along the road. A home-cooked dinner came at the end of a day of sightseeing. Nights we tried to find a place with a playground so the children could work off their pent-up energy after hours on the road. With four of us eating three meals a day and only the one tiny refrigerator, we shopped daily. The kids helped choose produce from the village grocer, bread at the bakery, and different English sausages and cheeses at the deli.

Mike and Michelle were easy travelers. They were polite, got along well together except for occasional older brother teasing, and were well trained by their mother to eat whatever was served. They were used to camping trips in Baja, Mexico, with their grandparents in a Westfalia. With a grandmother and an aunt who had been teachers and a mother who was soon to be one, the children knew they were expected to learn about the places they visited. My mother had instructed them to write each day in notebooks she sent along and warned she would read the journals with them when they returned. The trip was not meant to be a vacation, they had been told, but a journey of discovery. This fit well with the way Tom and I traveled, trying to see as much as possible. Before the summer ended, Mike, Michelle, and I coined the name "Tommy's Tours" for our travels.

The two kids were curious about British accents and strange English words. We made a list of "Brit speak" definitions: lorry = truck; pram = baby buggy; lift = elevator; biscuit = cookie; chips = French fries; and crisps = potato chips. As we traveled, the list got longer and Mike and Michelle tried out their new vocabulary.

Our tourist choices were now influenced by the children. On the kids' first day in London, at their request, we went to the original Madame Tussauds Wax Museum. Opened in 1884, the London location had been the first and only Tussauds up until two years before, when a second location opened in Amsterdam. This museum would not have been on our list without the encouragement of the children, but we were all fascinated by the historical figures set in tableaux, the core of the exhibit at the time. Both kids were intrigued by the figures of Henry VIII and his six wives.

For several days we rushed around London, from one monument or event to the next, traveling exclusively by underground, double-decker bus and on foot. We saw the beautiful equestrian changing of the Horse Guards, stood at the front of the crowd with our noses pressed to the wrought iron gate to watch the changing of the Palace Guards, and visited the Tower of London, where Michelle admired the crown jewels. Mike lingered at the exhibit of Henry VIII's armor, marveling at how it expanded in size along with Henry's girth. The children learned a ditty about the Tudor monarch that pleased their sense of the macabre and helped them remember the fate of his wives—"divorced, beheaded, died, divorced, beheaded, survived."

In St. James Park, we picnicked on the grass and watched the water birds weave circles in the lake. The children fed the pigeons in Trafalgar Square, imitating the Banks children in *Mary Poppins*, and posed for photos on the lion statues. We squatted on the pavement of Piccadilly

Circus and munched on fish and chips served wrapped in newspaper, traffic whizzing around us.

After their introduction to Henry VIII at the Tower, Mike and Michelle begged to visit Hampton Court, the king's favorite palace. They skipped down the garden paths where Henry had stepped and giggled at the sight of the big bed where he slept with his six wives. Best of all was the maze in the garden where the two children lost themselves for so long, Tom and I had to enter the labyrinth to search for them. At the well-preserved Tudor kitchen and banquet hall, I dreamed of cooking meals in such an enormous kitchen.

From the history of kings, we moved on to pilgrims and pirates. Our drive across England took us to Penzance and the tip of the Cornwall Peninsula. We crossed green rolling hills on narrow English roads, saw cows and thatched farm houses, and ate lunch in the shadow of Stonehenge. In Plymouth, the harbor from which the *Mayflower* sailed, we wandered the shore and collected sea glass and pebbles. We stayed two nights at a clifftop campground overlooking a long sandy beach, where Tom taught Mike and Michelle how to skimboard and we all swam in the chilly water. In the warmth of the late afternoon sun, we built a huge sandcastle that disappeared with the overnight tide. We drove to the western-most point of England, like many such places, known as Land's End, where the rolling, green hills stopped abruptly at rocky headlands. Tom parked near the edge of the cliff, the Atlantic directly below. Seagulls circled overhead, and out to sea, through the rising mists, we spotted scattered rocks, waves breaking in white foam against them, and a lone lighthouse.

Mike and Michelle pose with me at Land's End, England.

We had bought passes to the national heritage sites and the children, hooked on Henry VIII, wanted to go to all his castles. We headed for Falmouth and the defensive castle built there by Henry. Mike and Michelle led us around the ruins, up and down the narrow twisting stairs, from the basement to the roof, where we admired the cannons and the ramparts with their view of the surrounding sea. The exploration of ruined castles became a favorite pastime, a perfect combination of exercise and history.

For Tom, our driver, the English roads were frustratingly narrow and slow going. Country roads wove in and out of villages and left-hand-side driving added stress to his long days at the wheel. The children rode in the back without complaint for hours. Mike, who had a stomach susceptible to the curves, usually fell asleep across half the bench seat, while Michelle, who had no problems, read or looked out the window and counted cows and sheep. Tom usually listened to the BBC as he drove, and he discovered children's programing, including an afternoon read aloud show. Every Sunday at 3:00 p.m., we listened raptly to the story of *Elidor*, read by the author Alan Garner. Each new episode of the adventures of four ordinary English children in a troubled, magical land was a special Sunday treat.

My wish for my twenty-ninth birthday was to spend the day at Stratford–on–Avon and do a brass tomb rubbing, a popular activity in Britain. Tom made it happen—he got us to the area the evening before, made an appointment for me to do a rubbing the day after my birthday, and paid the fee. We found a campground with showers, and on my birthday morning, the bright sun promised a perfect day. Tom was definitely shaggy, and I felt guilty I hadn't cut his hair since Spain. After breakfast, I cornered him and removed at least three inches of his curly locks, then sent him to the showers. He returned looking civilized and the children cheered his new hairdo. With the entire family showered and wearing fresh clothes, we set off to tour Shakespeare's town. The day was completed with an extended picnic near a deer park. It was a beautiful birthday and I had the next day's treat ahead.

We arrived in plenty of time at the Saint James Church in Chipping Campden for my midmorning appointment. The church warden showed me the two tombs in the stone floor of the chancel, the brass tomb plates adorned with beautiful, three-quarter life-size effigies of the deceased occupants, a husband and wife dressed in elegant court robes from the early 1400s. The warden gave me pointers on how to do a successful rubbing. I taped the long sheets of thin paper to the floor but hesitated to make the first mark on the paper. Tom and the kids waited expectantly, unsure of their role.

"Let me work on this alone," I said. "You guys go explore the town for a couple of hours. I only have until noon so come back then."

"We'll bring you scones and cheddar cheese for lunch," Tom said. "Come on, kiddos. Let's leave Katie in peace."

Carefully, I rubbed the edges of the effigies with the side of a special square crayon. I reveled in the cool air and solitude, time on my own learning a new art skill. The two brass plaques were large and detailed. I was determined to finish the rubbings of both before my time was up. The church warden had cautioned me to go slowly, concentrating on one area at a time. It was far more exacting than the childhood pastime of rubbing a paper-covered coin with a crayon.

The cold stones bit into my knees and I folded up my sweater to pad them. First the lady, next her husband. I was in the process of removing the tape from the floor and carefully rolling up the rubbings, when the warden returned. I had not looked up the entire time, but when I did, I saw Tom and the children seated quietly in the rear pew. Tom read in the dim light, Mike snoozed against his shoulder, and Michelle wiggled her fingers in greeting.

After a fine meal of scones and cheese, we turned west again toward Wales, our route partially dictated by the list of national heritage sites free with our passes—the Elizabethan Manor of Snowshill, the Norman Abbey of Tewkesbury, a medieval merchant's home, and the castle in Monmouth. We ate one lunchtime picnic by a narrow canal with a hand-operated drawbridge, then tramped the trails in Brecon Beacons National Park, a wild country of waterfalls and rushing streams. We drove the roads of the coal mining districts, from their soot-blackened villages to the rugged coastline, where we found more castle ruins.

The evening before Mike's eleventh birthday, Tom asked a farmer for permission to spend the night in his field near a rushing stream. It had been a warm, sunny day, and after their tent was pitched, the children splashed in the stream to cool off while I prepared dinner. We were in vacation heaven on our way to Scotland to see bagpipes and kilts.

Mike and Michelle enjoy the waterfalls at Brecon Beacons National Park, Wales.

Chapter 14

Four Peas in a Pod

In the middle of the night, the weather changed. Rain splattered on our camper roof and against the children's tent. Not long after dawn, I heard the sound of the van's sliding side door. Michelle stood outside, a book in one hand, and peeked inside at us. "Can I come inside?" she said. "We're surrounded by sheep. They're nibbling on our tent."

Tom and I looked out at the sodden landscape. Mike stood behind his sister, rubbing his eyes. "My sleeping bag is getting wet," he said. "And I have to pee. Can I use the bucket?"

I waved them inside. "Sure. Don't stand out there in the rain. Come in and join us." I flipped open our blankets. "Come on up here and get warm. I'll fix breakfast in a minute."

Both kids used the bucket, something they had gotten familiar with during our long days on the road, and crawled in between Tom and me. I gave Mike a big hug. "Happy birthday, kiddo!"

He grinned. "Great start for my day," he said.

"It'll get better," I promised. "We'll drive until we escape the rain. And what do you say about dinner tonight? I'll cook anything you want."

Tom got out of bed with a grunt, started to heat water on the stove, pulled on a pair of jeans, and shoved his feet into his shoes. "I'll take down the tent," he said. "Make up the bed. We have to spread out the wet tent across the back. I hope it'll dry by tonight."

Barely warm, we scrambled out of bed, straightened the blankets, and folded the bed up for the day. Tom tossed in the sleeping bags, followed by the bright yellow, fleece mouse pillow Michelle slept with. Mike jumped out to help him dismantle the tent. Soon, we all sat at our table, sipping hot chocolate, surrounded by damp camping gear.

The day did not get better. In the first village, I shopped for Mike's special birthday dinner, but for the rest of the day we drove through rain. When we found the expressway, we headed directly for the Lake District, hoping to find sun when we arrived. But the rain continued to fall. At 7:00 p.m., we reached the first lake. The only campground on the south side of the lake cost $3.75 per night, twice what we usually spent. I cooked Mike's requested birthday meal while the rain drummed on the roof of the van. Even if we found a campground, the ground would be soggy and another night in their damp pup tent would be uncomfortable for the kids.

"Let's put the kids in our bed for now," Tom suggested after we cleaned up the dinner dishes. "I'll drive a while longer. Surely we'll find a better camp." He opened our bed and I helped Mike and Michelle find their pajamas in the mess. Soon, the kids were comfortably snuggled under our blankets. Tom started the car and I climbed into my navigator's seat up front.

The night was dark, the stars and moon covered by clouds, and rain continued to pour down. We drove in silence. We didn't want to wake the children, and we had nothing good to say. After two more hours, we were twenty miles south of the Scottish border and had found no campgrounds anywhere along our route. Exhausted, Tom pulled off the expressway and into a vacant lot. It was after midnight.

"Tomorrow will be better," I whispered. "It's bound to stop raining."

Tom grunted. "It's England, not California. Don't count on it."

We stretched Mike's mostly dry sleeping bag across the two front seats with the bucket ottoman filling the gap. Gently we moved him to the makeshift bed and covered him with his sister's sleeping bag. We pushed Michelle over to one side of our double bed and crawled in, too tired to even say goodnight.

Before dawn, Tom needed to pee, and with the bucket hidden under Mike, he used the kitchen sink, only a foot from where the boy slept. Suddenly the newly minted eleven-year-old sat up and turned to look at his uncle. "You're splashing me!" he said with a big grin on his face. We were learning Mike had an interesting sense of humor.

The morning found us all groggy and wrinkled. Carlisle wasn't far and we stopped at a car park in the town to eat breakfast and wash our faces. The rain had stopped, though heaps of gray clouds bunched across the sky. To stretch our legs, we walked around the ramparts of Carlisle Castle. Looking down from the defensive wall, we spied a man in a kilt practicing his bagpipe in a roofless courtyard below. The gloomy, droning sound of the pipe reverberated off the surrounding stones, matching our mood.

We drove into Scotland for another wet day with little to see beyond green hills covered with grazing sheep. At a mill town, the village green had been converted into an inexpensive camping spot, and Tom decided to quit early. Thinking positively, Tom and the children set up the tent. But while we ate dinner, it began to rain again.

"It's only a summer shower. It'll stop soon," Tom said as he tucked Mike and Michelle into their sleeping bags. The children looked skeptical but were too tired to argue.

It soon became obvious Tom's prophecy would not be fulfilled. The rain continued and threatened to inundate the tent. In they came for the second night in a row—Mike to his spot in the front cab and Michelle on the floor in the back, under the overhanging cantilever of our bed, the narrow, padded back of the bench seat making a passable mattress for her.

Even crowded together, we all slept soundly. When Michelle heard us fumbling to turn on the burner under the hot water kettle, she bounced up and asked, "Did you guys make love last night?"

I laughed. "No. We were too tired. But anyway, if we did, I wouldn't tell you!"

"But it's your honeymoon," she said. "Don't you make love every night?"

"No way," Tom said. "Only every other night."

"Not even," Mike piped up. "It's already been two nights."

Tom and I believed it best to be open with the kids, especially under such intimate circumstances. Whatever they asked, we tried to answer them honestly. I know we told them our travel adventure was making our marriage stronger and advised them never to marry anyone without first traveling together. I guess we must have also mentioned sex as a natural part of a relationship between a man and a woman, though it was meant to be private. The private part is what Michelle had forgotten.

The next morning in the mill town car park, the rain let up before Tom finished his first cup of coffee. Patches of blue peeked between the clouds. "We'll be in Edinburgh by noon," Tom said. "Let's get the soggy tent inside and get going."

This time, Tom's prophecy was correct. We were in Edinburgh by noon, ate lunch in a centrally located car park, and checked out the expensive gift shops on Princess Street.

From one of the iconic, red, British phone booths, Tom called the phone number our friend had given him in Panama. He expected to introduce himself to Mr. or Mrs. Gardner, Robert's parents, but it was Robert's voice that boomed over the line. He and Marie had separated at the end of their South American journey and Robert had returned to the Scottish capital to live with his parents and work at the zoo. The news seemed to contradict our belief that travel strengthened a relationship. Maybe travel also had the power to break relationships.

Robert's presence proved a blessing. He had a friend who offered to let us camp in the wooded backlot of his hotel and restaurant, and Robert's dad had a well-equipped workshop where Tom was invited to work on a special project.

The next three days were filled with activities—a tour of the city zoo, a spending spree at Robert's mum's favorite tartan shop, doctor and dentist visits, and a trip to the lumberyard and the hardware store. At English high tea at the Gardners' home, we stuffed ourselves with goodies. We might have stayed till midnight if I hadn't noticed Michelle's head nodding as she tried to stay awake.

Full of sausages, scones, and cheese pie, we returned to the backlot behind the hotel, ready to sleep. But the pup tent and windscreen had disappeared—all stolen. Luckily, their sleeping bags, Michelle's yellow mouse pillow, and the kids' two suitcases were in the van because, though we never imagined the theft of the little tent, we did worry about their things being stolen.

The reality of the loss of all our camping paraphernalia was too much to bear so late at night. Our little family was reduced to tears, swearing, and more tears. Finally, we pulled ourselves together. We all knew where to sleep after two rainy nights of practice. For the rest of the summer, Mike and Michelle slept inside with us. We were four peas in a pod. Despite the twenty-four-hours-a-day enforced intimacy, it was cozy.

The next day, I entertained the children at the Gardner's while Tom worked on his project, a storage box for our roof. Mike and Michelle had fallen behind in their journals, as had I, so we set to work writing. I wasn't as strict with them as my mother would have been. After they had completed a sentence or two, I allowed them to paste in ticket stubs and pages from tourist brochures. And I encouraged them to illustrate their journals with drawings. When he had brought his journal up-to-date, Mike went to the workshop. He loved helping Tom and often stood behind him when he worked on the car, handing him tools and learning about engines.

Tom's custom storage box turned out beautifully. With its two hasps and padlocks, the box effectively almost doubled our covered and secure storage. After Tom bolted it to the roof and stashed the items previously attached by bungee cords, the new box was only half full.

"Plenty of room for buying Persian rugs in Iran," he declared, "and for storing western toilet paper before we head to India."

When the Turtle was shipshape, we waved goodbye to our friends and headed nonstop for the southern ferry port. We had an appointment with an SAS flight out of Copenhagen in twelve days.

We made it to Belgium after a nonstop drive and a ferry crossing. None of us had bathed for two days and we were grubby and exhausted. In the gray light of dusk, Tom drove to a string of North Sea beach resorts and found a side street to park for the night. In the morning we realized we were only a block from a wide sandy beach. While I prepared breakfast, Tom and the children crossed the sand to the water. They returned eager to tell me what they had discovered.

"The beach is better than Laguna!" Michelle told me as she hopped into the car, her shoes in her hand. She grabbed a slice of the fried bread I had stacked on a plate.

I looked at her aghast. "No! Not possible. Not better than Laguna."

"There's lots and lots of sand," she said, "and only little-bitty waves. And you can walk way out into the water and not even get your clothes wet."

I looked at her damp and sandy feet. "You brought a lot of the beach back with you," I said.

Tom was outside toweling off Mike's feet. "Get back outside," he said. "You need to brush off the sand. I don't want to find sand in my bed later."

Michelle jumped back to the sidewalk. "Sorry." She quickly swiped at her feet with the towel and started to get back in the car. Mike grabbed her hand, pulled her to sit beside him on the edge of the door opening, and rubbed the towel between her toes and up her legs to her sandy knees.

Minutes later, we sat at the table and ate our first hot breakfast in several days, the sliding door open to catch the sea breeze.

The children and Tom were obviously bursting to tell me more.

"You can rent beach chairs and umbrellas," Mike said, "and they have cute changing houses, but you have to rent them, too."

Tom grinned at the kids and said, "Best of all, they rent—"

"Cycle carts!" Michelle shouted.

"Yep. Four-wheeled cycle carts. Just what I was about to say."

"Two people can pedal to make the cart go," Mike told me, "and two can ride in back. There's room for all four of us. Tom said we can rent one if you say it's OK." The children looked pleadingly at me while Tom leaned back and grinned, nodding his head.

"Of course, we can. If Tom says we can afford it, we'll go get a cart right after breakfast." The last week had been centered around the needs of the adults. It was time to do something fun with the kids. We ate quickly, stacked the dishes in the sink, and put the garbage in a nearby trash receptacle.

It was a glorious morning. The sunshine glinted off the white sand and the wood of the boardwalk was hot against our feet. The children chose a bright turquoise cart with white fringes swinging from its canvas roof. We pedaled along the boardwalk and into the surrounding streets. At first the adults were up front, Tom at the single-functioning steering wheel and I at the fake steering wheel, both of us pushing the pedals. The children sat in back, waving at pedestrians. But Mike and Michelle were not content to simply ride along—they wanted to pedal. I moved to the back and the kids took turns sitting with Tom, their short legs trying desperately to match his pace.

At the end of our time, the kids wanted to do more, but Tom was firm. "Enough pedaling for me. I need ice cream."

The cart was instantly forgotten and the children ran to a nearby ice cream stand to study the list of flavors. "How many scoops can we get?" Mike asked.

"Two for me," Tom said. "Two for you if you promise not to get sick."

"We won't," the kids said in unison.

Belgium was a delightful blur of canals and old buildings seen from the window of the van as Tom took us on quick city tours of Ghent and Brussels. In the late afternoon, searching for our next overnight spot, he drove down a side road that dead-ended suddenly. He struggled to turn the van around on the narrow lane, the stone wall of a brewery on one side and a line of high weeds and cattails on the other. The children sat quietly in back, sensing a tense situation, one of those times when Tom might become irritated. As he backed tentatively in the third phase of a U-turn, we suddenly felt the rear wheels slip and the car settled ominously.

"Everybody out!" Tom yelled. "If we land on the butane tanks, they could blow!" The children and I scrambled to obey.

A drainage ditch had lurked under the roadside vegetation and our wheels were now deep in mud. We stood to one side as Tom skillfully alternated the use of the accelerator, the clutch, and the brakes, hoping to help the wheels find traction in the grass and weeds. But the wheels spun and clumps of mud and reeds flew out behind. As the three of us watched, an invisible hand nudged the van backward and farther into the ditch. I heard muttered swear words, as Tom climbed out of the van and inspected the situation. He was obviously pissed by what he found.

"We need a tow," he said. "You can wait here or come with me." He turned on his heel and started down the road.

Before he had gotten two yards, a young man bounded over the low wall of the brewery. "I help?" he said in broken English. He pointed back to the gate. "Lorry. My lorry can help. Yes?" Tom nodded enthusiastically. Within minutes the fellow backed a large brewery truck out the gate and hitched his rear bumper to our front undercarriage, while Tom stood by to help. The young man looked at Tom and nodded toward the van. "No brakes," he said. "I pull." He motioned for Tom to get in the van. "You . . ." And he gestured the act of steering.

Within minutes, our van was safely delivered to the road, all four wheels again on dry land. We shook hands and thanked our savior. I climbed into the van, pulled out a bottle of sherry, poured the amber liquid into a glass, and offered it to the young man. He nodded his thanks and drank it in one gulp. As we drove down the road again, Tom smiled over at me and I breathed a sigh of relief. "That guy came in the nick of time," he said. "Bet he would have rather had a beer than a sherry. Me too! What a time to be out of beer."

The next morning, we entered the Netherlands, land of canals, windmills, wooden shoes, and bicycles. A Dutch couple at Chigwell had told us about a campground they described as "the best in Europe." As soon as the kids saw it, they begged us to stay for two nights. The grounds were large, an area of grass surrounded by hundreds of campsites, a playground, hot water in the showers, and a laundromat with dryers! A vast blue lake was dotted with vacationers in rented pedal boats. As soon as we parked in our spot, the kids ran off to the children's area. They returned after an hour, sweaty and hungry.

"It's the biggest playground I ever saw!" Mike told us. "There's even a trampoline."

Michelle, too out of breath to speak, nodded her head in agreement. "Tell about the tube," she managed to say.

"There's this big, big tube. Like a drainage pipe." Mike stretched his arms out as wide as they would go to indicate the size. "Bigger even than this. We could stand up inside it. Even older boys could. And when you walk inside the tube, your feet make it spin. The faster you walk, the faster it turns."

"The big boys were running," Michelle said. "It was scary, but fun, too."

This camp was a perfect place to rest, stretch out, and get chores done. The children spent hours at the playground. I did laundry, actual machines an almost forgotten luxury. Tom pulled out a small piece of plywood left from the box project. From the scrap, he built a platform to hold his volt meter, and attached it to the steering column so he could keep an eye on the car battery's voltage while he drove.

In the afternoon we trooped to the coin-operated showers—Michelle and I to the women's side and Tom and Mike to the men's. After we had showered and washed our hair, Michelle and I headed back to the van. On the way, we passed Tom running toward the showers, clad only in shorts and rubber flip-flops.

"We ran out of coins," he called to me as we passed. "Mike's in the shower covered in shampoo suds."

Both children were allowed to stay wrapped in their towels. After dinner, Mike sat at the table reading, while I cleaned up the remains of the meal, getting it ready for Tom to wash the dishes. Michelle was sitting in the front seat with him, reading out loud from our copy of *Bury My Heart at Wounded Knee*.

"Hey, Katie, look," I heard Mike say. "I have a pubic hair."

This statement took me by surprise and I glanced over. He sat with his towel spread open staring at his genitals. I stepped over to have a look. He was obviously not feeling shy. One tiny black hair lay on his pubis. "Wow," I said. "Pretty special for a boy who just turned eleven. It sure looks like a pube hair."

Mike laughed, his eyes glittering with humor. "Fooled you," he said. "It's an eyelash!" And he flicked it away with his thumb and forefinger.

"Cover it up, Mike," I said. But I couldn't help laughing, too. "You fooled me, kiddo."

A few minutes later, Michelle finished the chapter and Tom stepped back to wash the dishes. I moved to the driver's seat to make room for him in the kitchen.

"How's the reading going?" I asked Michelle.

"Good. Tom believes I can read good now." She smiled. "He didn't used to but he does now. Sometimes he asks me questions about the words to see if I understand what I've read."

"Do you understand all of it?" I asked. *Wounded Knee* was a difficult book.

"Well, there was a word in the last chapter I didn't understand," she said. "One of the Indian warriors made himself a tobacco pouch. It said he made it out of the privates of an enemy he'd killed. I don't understand what the privates are."

It was both a question and a challenge. I was pretty sure she had an idea but wanted it confirmed. Determined to stick to my belief in the value of honesty with the kids, I proceeded to explain as simply as possible what privates were and how a grown man's privates were big enough to hold tobacco. When I was finished, I looked over at Tom and he nodded with a grin.

Traveling in Holland with Mike and Michelle, I appreciated their willingness to try new foods. At a takeout shop, we ordered Dutch soft roll sandwiches called *broodje* and thick, potato fries slathered in curry sauce and mayonnaise. At another, we tried Indonesian *bami* and *nasi* balls (leftover stir-fried noodles or fried rice rolled into a ball, dipped in crumbs and fried) and *lumpia* (an egg-roll type snack). In one town, we crunched into *stroopwafel*, a waffle cookie sandwich filled with thick syrup. Near the coast, we ate the tender flesh of smoked eel. Later, at a cheese and sausage shop, the owner was pleased to have American children interested in his products and offered them free samples.

In Amsterdam, we camped in a vacant lot near a Volkswagen service center (for Tom) and a flea market (for the kids and me). Mike and Michelle knew little about World War II and the Holocaust, so I insisted we visit the Anne Frank House. Though crowded with tourists,

Mike, Michelle, and I nibble on smoked eel in the Netherlands. Yum!

the Secret Annex was an impressive monument to courage and optimism. Downstairs, the pictures of the Nazi occupation of Holland and the treatment of the Dutch Jews gave the children an introduction to Hitler's Jewish policy. We climbed the stairs to the Annex and walked into the bare rooms, unchanged since the police had arrested Anne, her family, and their friends.

"Imagine," I said, "being thirteen years old and living in these rooms with all those other people. For two years, no noise, no going out, always afraid the police would come."

They looked at me wide-eyed. Michelle hugged me silently while tears ran down her cheeks. Mike returned to study the two models showing the rooms as they had been with furniture, books, and dishes. In the cubicle where Anne slept, her picture collection remained pasted to the wall. Michelle reached out her delicate finger toward the display. I took her hand and squeezed it in understanding. Later, they were both subdued as they wrote in their notebooks and pasted down their ticket stubs to the Anne Frank House.

We strolled along the Amsterdam canals and ogled a jeweler while he polished a diamond. Tom led us into the old sailors' quarters to visit Our Lord in the Attic and the surrounding, notorious, red-light district.

The streets of the quarter were lined with bars and pornography shops, their windows displaying explicit pictures, sexual paraphernalia, and cheap Dutch souvenirs. Tom gave a carefully worded explanation of the use of dildos when Mike asked. Luckily, my nephew was more interested in their size and variety than their actual function. Michelle studied the revealing costumes and the exposed flesh of the prostitutes, forgetting she had been taught not to stare. The women, in silky robes or black fishnet stockings and leather stood in doorways and smiled at Tom who walked slightly ahead of his trailing family. A lady, wearing nothing but a scant pair of lacy red panties and red sequin disks pasted on her nipples, sat in a tiny room behind a picture window. She waved to Mike causing him to blush. One alley was lined with similar rooms, each glass-fronted display case for a prostitute. Tom spoke to one of the ladies of the night who stood yawning in her doorway and introduced Mike, who had inched up close to his uncle.

"See you in a few years?" she said as she shook Mike's hand. To his credit, he kept silent.

Michelle hung back with me, for once speechless. I have to admit, I was in awe myself. Of course, I knew Tom was familiar with red-light districts around the world, but I had never watched him in that milieu. He was at ease with the prostitute, which I found interesting but, strangely, not upsetting.

After our X-rated morning, we headed for a family-friendly tourist site.

Madurodam, a 1:25 scale model miniature that represented the Netherlands, was built in 1952 as a memorial to a young Dutch-Jewish soldier, George Maduro, who joined the Dutch resistance after the fall of Holland and died of typhus in Dachau in 1945. The large park featured tiny buildings, streets, harbors, and farmland that represented actual places in Holland. Countless coin-operated mechanizations made little people move and perform. Tom was drawn to the harbor with ships, the airport with planes that taxied down a miniature runway, the working railroad and streetcar system, and the canal boats going up and down in locks. I liked the everyday touches—an organ grinder who made music, a turning Ferris wheel complete with passengers, soldiers marching in formation, and a tiny replica of the cheese market of Gouda. The kids loved it all.

With only three days to get the children to Copenhagen, we began another cross-country dash. We drove northward along the ZuiderZee, across the windswept Enclosure Dike, and nonstop across Germany. The ferry to Denmark dropped us an hour south of the capital.

The next day began our twenty-four-hour countdown. In Copenhagen, we bought a duffel bag to replace the stolen one and filled it with the children's things, even the fist-sized, melted glass nugget Mike had found on the beach in England. Surrounded by gay music at the Tivoli Gardens, Mike and Michelle romped in the playground and rode a kids' roller coaster. While we all sat in the shade licking ice cream cones, Michelle asked about the Little Mermaid.

Tom studied our map of the city. "She's a ways from here, but I think we can get there before your bedtime."

The charming mermaid on her rock glinted in the light of the Nordic evening. We stood together, Tom's warm arm draped over my shoulder, the kids in front, leaning against our legs, as the sky turned to gold. The next day our summer together would end.

We arrived at the airport an hour before flight time (no long TSA lines in those days) and went to the SAS counter to check the children in. The woman at the desk studied their tickets for a moment, only to look up distressed.

"The flight will take off in ten minutes," she said. "They've already loaded! We have to hurry." She came out from behind the counter. "We have to run. Only one of you adults can come with me to get them on the plane. Which one will come?" She was agitated and kept looking at her watch.

"You go," Tom said. "They're your family."

It all happened quickly. Neither Tom nor I had time to realize we ought to question her headlong rush to the plane. The airline woman had already turned toward the gate. In our mind, she was the authority on plane departure. I grabbed the bulging duffel bag and each child picked up their suitcase. We rushed after the retreating woman who waved her arm at us to hurry. We literally ran through the airport, down the ramp, and into an airplane filled with seated passengers. The SAS woman found two seats for the kids and told them to sit. She and I stashed the luggage in the overhead compartment.

A stewardess came down the aisle. She turned to me and asked, "Are they going to Portland? Will a parent be meeting them there?"

I had little time to think, but I assumed Portland must be a layover and the plane would fly on from Oregon to LA. "No," I said. "They are going all the way to Los Angeles." I emphasized this firmly. "They are not to get off in Portland. Their mother will pick them up in Los Angeles."

The stewardess looked puzzled but nodded her agreement. "You have to leave now," she said. "We're about to take off."

I hugged the two children one last time and told them, "Don't get off the plane until you get to Los Angeles." They nodded. I turned to the airline woman who was already near the door of the plane, waving her hand for me to follow.

When we rejoined Tom, she admonished us. "You must stay at the airport until their flight is off the departure list. This is a rule for unaccompanied minors. In case there is a flight delay, you'll be here to help with the children."

Tom and I stood by the plate glass windows and looked out across the tarmac to the spot where I was sure the plane had been parked. Though it was gone, the kids' flight number remained on the departures board. We waited. Another fifteen minutes and their flight number remained lit.

"Maybe it's delayed out on the runway," I said. "The plane I put them on was right there." I pointed to the empty terminal ramp.

"Was it a 747?" Tom asked.

I had no idea. I didn't know one type of plane from another. I shrugged. "I don't know. It was all so hectic. What does a 747 look like?"

Tom was incredulous. "You know. The one with the second story. The big, wide, jumbo jet."

"I don't think it had an upstairs." Now I was worried. "Let's go ask at the desk about the flight," I suggested. "Maybe they forgot to take it off the list."

When we posed our question to the same woman who had led me to the plane, she looked blank. She examined the paperwork I handed her and checked her records. "Wait here," she said. "Wait here! I've made a mistake." She disappeared down a hallway.

This was not good. Now both Tom and I were seriously worried. In less than five minutes, she came back with her supervisor. "Follow me, please. Don't worry. Everything will be fine." He ushered us into his office.

As we sat down, Tom said, "It better be."

We were told the SAS employee had read the tickets incorrectly. She had looked at them too quickly and confused the flight numbers. She had put them on flight #1683 to Portland, Oregon, when they should have been on flight #1693 to Los Angeles, which was scheduled to leave any minute. The SAS supervisor was sorry. They had already notified the captain of the Portland plane. He promised the crew would take care of the children. In Portland, a stewardess would stay with them and get them on the first available flight to Los Angeles. Their arrival in LA would only be a couple of hours late. The supervisor said he would personally call the children's mother and let her know what had happened.

"Rest assured, we will get your niece and nephew safely to their mother."

None of this calmed me. Mike and Michelle were alone, flying over the North Pole. The airline had made this mistake—they could easily make another.

"That's not enough," I said, pushing down my anger and fear. "How could you make such a stupid error?" My hands shook as I stood up. "I want to talk to my sister myself when the children are with her. I need to hear from my sister that she has her children back safely. It's the only thing that will put my mind at ease."

Tom stood next to me. "We'll be back first thing tomorrow morning. We expect you to pay for a telephone call to California so my wife can talk directly to her sister. We want to hear from the children's mother that they are safe."

Back at camp, we collapsed from emotional exhaustion. I slept restlessly, waking each time a plane from the nearby airport flew over the campground. As promised, I was able to talk to my sister and she confirmed Mike and Michelle were home safe. Our summer together had ended with unexpected stress, but Tom and I both agreed we would do it again. We had loved our time with the kids and were now very sure we wanted a couple of our own in the future.

Chapter 15

Second Honeymoon

The excitement of the last twenty-four hours took a while to dissipate. A day in camp helped us relax, and after buckets and buckets of hand-done laundry, the box of clean clothes and linens stacked on our back seat gave us permission to tour Copenhagen.

As a belated anniversary treat, Tom took me to the cooking demonstrations at the Danish Agriculture and Food Council Tourist Center. For their hot meal demonstration at noon, a pretty blonde prepared a typical dinner of *frikadeller* (pork balls), stewed peas and carrots, and a rich cake filled with juicy, fresh plums. As Tom and I watched the instructor roll and slightly flatten the seasoned ground pork, then pan-fry the balls in butter, we were unaware Danish meatballs would one day be a favorite meal of our future children.

Delighted to relax, watch, and nibble, we stayed for a second demonstration. This time, the young woman made *smørrebrød*, open-faced sandwiches—first rye bread with a smear of butter and topped with pickled herring, then other thin slices of different breads topped with chicken salad, ham, sausage, or cheese. To finish, she scattered fresh vegetable decorations on top to make these knife-and-fork sandwiches both pretty and healthy. Tom and I loved the peppery taste of a garnish of watercress sprouts. We had seen these tiny sprouts rooted on wet cotton batting in small flats at the grocers. The gift shop sold packets of the seeds and growing trays, as well as deli items for smørrebrød. Naturally I left with a full shopping bag.

Wedding gift money sat in our bank account at home, and I was eager to spend it on Scandinavian designed dishes, cutlery, and table linens. Off we went to the three-story Den Permanente, a venue where artisans and manufacturers promoted Danish design. Founded in the 1930s, Den Permanente was a landmark until it closed in the 1980s when interest in Danish Modern waned. As I "oooed" and "ahhhed" over the furniture and housewares, Tom jotted down descriptions and prices in his tiny notebook. By the end of the day, we had a list of what we would buy after our tour of the rest of Scandinavia.

That evening, we did not worry about waking the children with sighs, sweet nothings, or the creak of the bed. Perhaps other campers noticed our green van had an unusual bounce to it, but we didn't care.

In Copenhagen, our excursions included the Royal Copenhagen China factory, the Resistance Museum dedicated to Denmark's World War II underground, the canals of Christianshavn (a lovely place to drift around in a rowboat), The Carlsberg Brewery, where Tom got tipsy on beer samples, and The Burmeister & Wain Museum, a leading designer and builder of diesel engines, including marine diesels, not a few of which Tom had repaired as a ship's engineer.

We crossed by ferry to Sweden where our entry was unexpectedly delayed by a suspicious customs inspector who was suddenly on high alert when he saw our Moroccan visa stamps. He rummaged through our medical supplies and food and asked us directly if we used drugs. I wonder, if we had been druggies, would we have answered truthfully?

As a child I had read *The Wonderful Adventures of Nils*, written by Swedish author Selma Lagerlöf in 1907 and given to me by my father who had read it translated into German when he was a child. Nils, a cruel and naughty farm boy, was bewitched by an elf. Suddenly, the nasty bully was only twelve inches tall. For one season, he traveled the length and breadth of Sweden on the back of a wild goose, learned valuable life lessons, and returned home a changed boy. More than anything, this book made me yearn to travel. I wanted to see Nils's Sweden.

We drove or stopped depending on our mood. We were enraptured by the beautiful scenery, ate well, and held each other close at night. The drive to Stockholm crossed a forested landscape dotted with lakes. One morning, we awoke to the rosy glow of sunrise reflecting off clear blue water. I couldn't resist a bath and splashed nude into the lake. The icy water enveloped me, an intimate touch that reached every inch of my body. I submerged until even my scalp tingled. My long hair floated in a fan around my head as I lay back and gazed up at the sky. Overhead, a flock of geese glided, their V-shape pattern black dashes against pale blue, and I imagined one of them carried the elf-like Nils on its back.

Tom followed me tentatively into the frigid water, dunked up to his waist, splashed his head and chest, and retreated. When I returned to the van, my white skin covered in raised goosebumps, he wrapped me in a dry towel. I twisted my wet hair into a knot on top of my head, the icy water dripping down my shoulders. "You're a crazy woman," Tom said. He hugged me tight and handed me a mug of sweet, hot tea.

We arrived in Sweden's capital two days before Tom's thirtieth birthday—Stockholm would be his birthday present. This city, modernized in the 1960s, boasted new contemporary housing complexes with their own sewage reclamation facilities, underground parking, wheelchair ramps, children's playgrounds, shops, and subway stations. Pedestrian bridges arched over the roadways and the outdoor spaces were landscaped and clean. No wonder the Swedish people were always smiling. Downtown, families strolled in the central plaza to soak up the afternoon sun. On the waterfront, we found a camping spot, centrally located but secluded, with a view of the busy harbor and an amusement park across the channel.

Some years before, Tom had read about the *Vasa* Museum in *National Geographic*. The *Vasa*, a Swedish warship, sank in the middle of Stockholm Harbor on its maiden voyage in 1628. Caught by a gust of wind, the top-heavy ship heeled, toppled, and sunk with crew, passengers, and visiting celebrants aboard unable to escape. After three hundred years underwater, it was rediscovered in the 1950s, and in 1961, salvage began. Thousands of artifacts— clothing, weapons, cannons, tools, coins, cutlery, food, drink, six of the ten sails, and the remains of at least fifteen people—were found. We spent a full day at the Vasa Museum, which included a gigantic room for the remains of the ship's hull, in surprisingly good condition due to the lack of wood-eating shipworms in the super-cold waters of the Baltic Sea. The sailing ship fascinated Tom, and we walked around it three times, enveloped in a fine mist, a combination of water and polyethylene, designed to keep the wooden structure from falling into dust as it dried.

The next morning, we lingered over Tom's birthday breakfast of dollar-size pancakes slathered with lingonberry jam.

"Do you remember the print we saw yesterday at the museum?" he asked.

I nodded. The large woodblock print of the *Vasa* after its long sleep at the bottom of the harbor depicted the sunken ship in shades of green that evoked the cold Baltic waters.

"I wish we'd bought it," he said. "I shouldn't have procrastinated yesterday."

"We can go back and get it today," I said. "For your birthday present." I was pleased my engineer was developing a taste for fine art. He seldom thought of buying anything for himself besides car parts and tools, so I pushed the purchase of the print.

With the *Vasa* woodblock rolled up and stashed in our roof-top storage, we drove south and west across the waist of Sweden, listening to the Voice of America radio. The news from the Berlin Olympic Games was not about sports. Palestinian terrorists had attacked the Israeli athletes, two Israelis had been killed and nine others were taken hostage. This was followed by a botched rescue effort by German police. A disaster all around, the events in Munich were distressing and we wondered how Germany would be changed when we returned in a few weeks.

Our first weekend in Norway, we called a couple about our age whom we had met in London, and they invited us to their home in a small town south of Oslo. Inga prepared open-faced sandwiches, and over lunch we talked of our travels and their daily life. On weekdays, Leif pedaled his bicycle to his law office, while Inga, who was expecting their first baby, walked to the nearby school where she was a teacher. Later, we drove together to a place where the North Sea, the end of the Oslo Fjord, and the land met, an area known as End of the Earth. Islets and peninsulas, formed of sea-worn, ochre granite, stretched like fingers into the sea. We four clambered over the rocks, led by Inga who was the most agile in spite of her swollen, expectant belly. The rocks, which had appeared to be devoid of vegetation, revealed a living coverlet of moss and miniscule flowers. At the end of the day, Leif suggested we park overnight in their driveway and Inga invited us to join them again for dinner the next evening.

While our friends were at work, Tom and I returned to the End of the Earth. At a fishing harbor we had passed the day before, we rented a rowboat. While I reclined in the bow snapping pictures of the scenery, Tom rowed under a small bridge and among the granite formations. The sun shone down, the water was calm, and a light breeze rippled the surface. In the lee of one of the rock islets, a fisherman pulled up his traps and dumped the catch into the bottom of his skiff. Silvery fish and a few crabs flapped and glistened against the ropes and fishing nets. Among the bounty was a large cod, a perfect gift for Inga.

Later, Tom and I took turns under the flow of warm water in the apartment shower. While I was toweling dry, I noticed an odd, black speck on my stomach, a few inches above my belly button. After I dressed, I pulled Tom to one side in the living room and carefully lifted my blouse. "Look at this. It looks like a big blackhead, but it doesn't hurt."

Tom peered closely at my abdomen and ran his finger gently over the spot. He shrugged and shook his head. "We should ask Inga to look at it," he whispered. We beckoned to her and I lifted my blouse again. Tom pointed to the spot. "What do you think it is?" he asked.

Inga took one look and laughed. "It's only a tick," she said. "Leif is good at getting those out." She waved him over and I lifted my blouse again. Within moments, the dapper lawyer was probing at my stomach with a pair of pointed tweezers. He grasped the tiny, black tick deep down by its neck and gently but firmly pulled. With an audible pop, the beast let go of my flesh and was cleanly removed. Inga swabbed the spot with alcohol and returned to dinner preparations.

We were determined to visit one of the famous Norwegian fjords along the North Sea coast. It would be a long drive northward and across the mountainous spine of Norway. We stopped once to visit a traditional church, covered from ground to steeple with wooden staves (long shingles) and painted inside with floral patterns, a wooden structure that still survived 800 years after it was built.

Our route gradually twisted higher and higher, past highland farms where women milked nanny goats and poured the warm, creamy liquid into silver cans. We continued upward on narrow, switchback roads, bypassing several tunnels. We stopped for the night at the top of a 4,000-foot pass and slept surrounded by rocks and snow, a starry sky arching overhead.

Our morning descent twisted past waterfalls and rushing rivers to the town of Odda on the southernmost toe of the Hardangerfjord. Near the harbor, attracted by tempting aromas and billows of steam, we found a dockside food truck. The fisherman owner sold us a whole smoked mackerel, as well as a liter can overflowing with freshly boiled shrimp, a lemon perched on top. A short way down the street, a bakery

Stave Church in Norway.

displayed loaves so fresh from the oven their steam vapor coated the window glass. Near their door, a cold storage box contained a selection of local cheeses and butter.

Unwilling to sit inside the van on a sunny day, we set up stools on the wharf as a luncheon "dinette." The inky water of the fjord stretched out behind us. We tore shrimp from their shells and dipped the succulent meat into melted butter with lemon, mopping up the juices with fresh bread. I looked across our table, a folding stool topped with my chopping block, and smiled at my handsome husband. He reached across with a scrap of paper towel and dabbed a drizzle of butter as it slid down my chin. Relaxed and smiling, he blotted his beard with the same bit of towel.

"We need to take a picture," I said. "It's so beautiful here."

Tom was eager to comply as I usually discouraged him from photographing me or our van saying, "I want to remember all the wonderful sights. I don't need pictures of myself." Suddenly I realized I might be wrong. Tom set up his camera on a low, stone wall, tripped the timer button, and rushed back to pose with a shrimp poised near his lips.

Our last few weeks had been a Scandinavian idyll, but it was time to direct our course toward Germany and from there eastward. We made quick stops at Oslo's Vigeland Sculpture Park and the Kon-Tiki Museum, then caught the ferry to Copenhagen where we retrieved mail, had money transferred, and purchased our "wedding gifts," an endeavor Tom had begun calling "Katie's shopping spree."

Tom and I enjoy a perfect lunch of shrimp near a Norwegian fjörd.

Another ferry crossing, followed by long hours on the Autobahn, brought us to Heidelberg, Germany—again the land of the Volkswagen— where Tom could indulge in his compulsion to do auto maintenance. At a riverbank campground, in spite of the constant gray drizzle, Tom crawled under the car.

While he worked, I watched barges going up and down the river. A white swan roamed the puddled campground in search of slugs. The wet weather turned my thoughts to soup. I pulled out the pressure cooker, cut up a hunk of beef I had purchased the day before, and added carrots, red cabbage, mushrooms and tiny pearl onions—it would be a dish fit for a German duke. If I couldn't help with the engine work, at least I could serve Tom a tasty, hot meal at the end of the day.

After dark, smudged with engine oil, he came to dinner with news that he had found a new crack in the engine block, as well as scored grooves on the bearings. Even the aroma of the bubbling soup could not lift his spirits.

"I'm going to buy a complete, rebuilt German Volkswagen engine," he told me. "One under warranty."

I sighed and wondered what I'd prepare for dinner the next day, making a mental list of what I needed to buy at a market on the way back from the VW dealer.

For three weeks, Germany would be our headquarters while we dealt with a long list of chores, errands, and must-do paperwork. Naturally, besides replacing the engine, Tom tackled a few home improvement projects. At my request, he built a wooden rack attached to the dashboard to hold my tray of watercress sprouts. He also built a new plywood lid for the roof storage box. (Did I mention the lid blew off along a fjord in Norway when he forgot to secure it?)

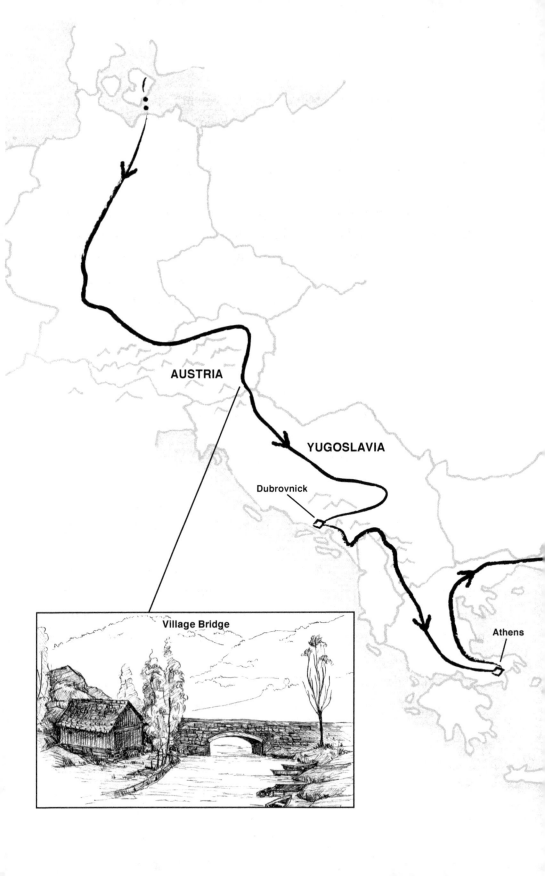

AUSTRIA

YUGOSLAVIA

Dubrovnick

Athens

Village Bridge

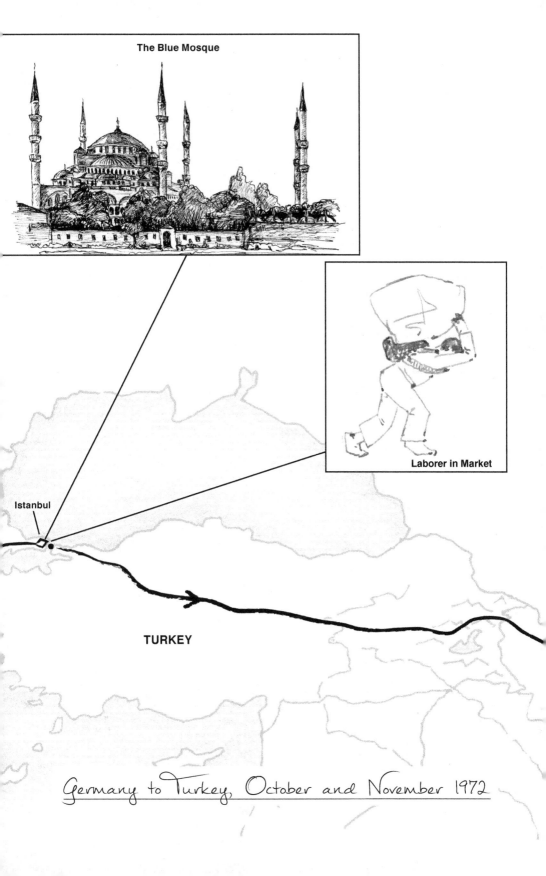

The Blue Mosque

Laborer in Market

Istanbul

TURKEY

Germany to Turkey, October and November 1972

Chapter 16

So Far to Travel

Finally, we headed east, skirting Munich, and did not stop until we were in Austria, aglow in autumn colors. Because we both loved *A Sound of Music*, we could not pass through Austria without stopping in Salzburg and Vienna.

Halfway between these two cities, we pulled off the Autobahn at Saint Florian for a picnic lunch, and Tom spotted a VW repair shop. (Does it ever end? No!) Monitoring every click and hum of the van, Tom had tried to take a compression check the day before, only to find the spark plugs frozen in place. At the auto shop, he requested a diagnostic check of our engine. The mechanic struggled with the spark plugs which remained stubbornly stuck for him, too. With little choice, Tom agreed to let the Austrian mechanic take out the engine the next morning and fix the problem. We would be stuck in Saint Florian overnight.

As we washed up after dinner, Tom realized he had not gotten the engine's purchase receipt stamped at the border in order to get a rebate of the German sales taxes. Always willing to do extra driving if it would save us money, he insisted on returning to the border. The trip to the nearest border and back to Saint Florian took until after midnight, but still, we were in front of the auto shop before it opened.

The shop had no waiting room, so I opted to stay in the van, high on the lift as the mechanics struggled with the repair. Tom spent the day on the ground, hovering over the workers, watching, guarding, and learning. Meanwhile, though I had to move slowly and gently six feet up on the lift, I read, sipped tea, and prepared lunch for Tom.

"Please let me know when they're about to lower the van," I called down to Tom after lunch. "I'm going to start a drawing." I worked in India ink, using a small, crow-quill pen with a flexible nib, a tool which necessitated constant dipping into the bottle of permanent, black India ink. A spill would be a disaster. In my art journal, I sketched a layout in pencil, then began the ink drawing using lines to form structures and crosshatching to fill in darker, shadowed areas.

Late in the afternoon, with new heads and spark plugs, we made it to the quarry town of Mauthausen, the location of a Nazi slave labor camp during World War II. Established in 1938, the camp worked and starved to death 120,000 prisoners in the granite pits. Again, as at Dachau, I felt deep in my gut a personal connection to the murdered Jews.

In Vienna, we got cholera shots (needed for Afghanistan and India) at the United States maintained public health service office, the head-quarters for clearing all Eastern European refugees. Then we were on our way to the Socialist Federal Republic of Yugoslavia, still a communist country under Tito, the velvet-fisted dictator who had ruled the nation since 1943. Tito suppressed nationalist sentiment among the various ethnic groups and promoted the spirit of brotherhood and unity between the six Yugoslav nations. The unified nation fell apart when he died in 1980, resulting in years of strife, civil war, ethnic cleansing, genocide, and the eventual formation of multiple, autonomous nations.

I had been to Yugoslavia when I was seventeen, on the summer trip with my parents and younger sister. When I traveled with my family, Tito had recently opened his country to international travelers for the first time since World War II. My first trip to Yugoslavia whetted my appetite for exotic places—the stone villages; the mosques with their slim minarets; the farm women in baggy, flowered, harem pants, their heads and necks wrapped in colorful scarves; carts pulled by donkeys and oxen; and the old, walled city of Dubrovnik. However, my most vivid memory of the trip was of my first, face-to-face experience with real poverty.

That summer, as my father drove through the rocky countryside, we passed a woman plodding along the road, a young girl by her side and an infant in her arms. She and her daughter were barefoot and dressed in rags, while the baby squalled in its thin wrappings. My father stopped the car and rolled down his window to speak to the woman. She stepped close to the car, and in a language even he could not understand, begged for food by motioning to her mouth and pulling open her bodice to show her empty breasts flaccid against the washboard of her ribs. I was shocked and moved to tears. My mother dug into our picnic supplies and handed her bread and two apples. In the back seat, I stripped off my brown dress, a garment I had grown to dislike over the last few weeks, and handed it to her through the window. I wrapped myself in my mother's shawl and, as we drove on, I turned to watch the woman strip off her rags and slip on the new dress.

By 1972, conditions in Yugoslavia were obviously much better, though most of the exotic sights remained. We traveled the main road south down the middle of the country, the same route taken by my father a dozen years before.

In narrow villages, tall stone houses faced the main road and chickens scratched in the dirt. It was nearly the end of October and acres of land held nothing but dried corn stalks, a few scattered pumpkins, and rows of cabbages the size of basketballs. One morning, we woke to

A snowy morning in Yugoslavia.

find the ground glistening with frost, the air icy, thick gray clouds overhead. Two mountain ranges stood between us and the Adriatic coast. We crossed the first through a narrow river gorge, gray and white limestone cliffs on either side, snow falling around us.

Near Sarajevo, we slept beside a plank bridge. As the temperature dropped during the night, we pulled our coats and beach towels over us and curled together like two spoons. In the morning, I pulled aside the curtains. Fat snowflakes melted slowly on the windows. The roof of a nearby house, the bridge, everything in sight, was blanketed in a soft, white cushion of snow. We drove through a landscape transformed by billows of white—cabbages buried under snow, wet haystacks resembling fat men in black with white top hats, and frosted farm buildings. On the other side of the mountains, the snow turned to slushy rain.

Near a rushing stream, several roadside vendors had set up stalls to serve hungry truck drivers. In front of each makeshift café, a whole lamb revolved over hot coals, the huge spit turned by water. The smell of roasting lamb was impossible to resist. We sat on wobbly stools at a rough wooden table and ate hunks of juicy lamb whacked from the crisp carcass, accompanied by a soup of lamb broth and noodles, fresh bread, and a glass of wine.

The snow had been a warning—winter was coming. South of Dubrovnik, the road looped inland to bypass Albania, a closed country where western tourists were unwelcome. Beyond the new city of Tito-grad, we followed a river gorge with frighteningly precipitous sides, a river hundreds of feet below, and single-lane tunnels blasted directly through solid rock. We saw no other cars and only one truck. I remember thinking as I looked down into the chasm, "At least if we crash over the cliff, we will die instantly." The prospect of surviving a crash in such a deserted place was scarier than death itself.

Once past Albania, travel through the southern half of Yugoslavia loomed ahead. We started at 6:00 a.m. after defrosting the sheet of ice coating our windshield, wound through endless mountains, around sharp curves, up and down steep grades, through solid rock tunnels, past mud slides, ice patches, and fallen boulders on the roadway. We approached the Greek border after dark, both of us exhausted from the arduous drive.

With another 350 miles to Athens, we braced ourselves. On such days, I often read to Tom from our guidebooks and prepared lunch on the move. In the afternoon, the constant motion and humming of the tires on the road left me groggy. The memory of Tom's impatience with Karen when she dozed caused me to struggle against sleep, but invariably I would nod off. That day, I was jarred awake as the van pulled off the pavement.

"Wake up, sleepy, or you'll miss Mount Olympus," Tom said. The majestic mountain stood directly ahead, its snow-capped peak regal above the low, surrounding plains.

Tom, already outside, looked at the mountain through his binoculars. I stood with my back against his warm chest and gazed at the mountain. "I understand now why the ancient Greeks believed Mount Olympus was the home of the gods."

Tom put his arm over my shoulder and his whisper tickled my ear. "Maybe they were right."

Earlier in the day, as we had traveled through towns and villages festooned with blue-and-white national flags, I teased Tom about the good looks of Greek men. I had always been drawn to dark-haired men, the "tall, dark, and handsome" type presented in the movies, and I was pleased with the almost unlimited supply of them in Athens when we arrived. In the falling afternoon light, as we walked along the city street, a man stepped out of a shadowed doorway. His mustache drooped down and his greased hair was swept back in a pompadour. I smelled strong cologne barely masking the scent of perspiration as he brushed past me. He spoke in a low, sexy, sotto voce. "Hello, Blondie."

I grabbed Tom's hand. "Did you hear what he said?"

He grinned at me. "Very suave, indeed. And extremely sophisticated." We both laughed. I would need to reevaluate my opinion of Greek men.

Later, we chose an overnight stop in a parking area across from the ancient Acropolis. As the moon rose, we stood on a low wall and watched the dancing spotlights of a sound-and-light show at the Acropolis. Local lovers came and went late into the night, but they did not disturb our sleep. In the morning, we awoke to the noise of idling bus engines and the voices of tourists.

Athens was crowded with celebrants preparing for a holiday weekend. The Greek Public Health Office made short work of my cholera booster, and we set off for the central market. Inspired by the luscious produce, I wanted to cook like the locals and filled our bags with the makings of a Greek meal. At the meat shop, the butcher told us that in autumn the only local meat he carried was mutton, so I settled for a previously frozen leg of New Zealand lamb. "Return in spring if you want Greek lamb," he said.

At a campground on the coast, we spent our Saturday on chores. Tom cut a new wooden potty seat to replace the worn original, shellacked the storage box, and changed the water filter. I prepared food from my treasures—chunks of lamb and chicken marinated in garlic, olive oil, and lemon juice, waiting to be cooked on sticks I cut from a bush. Tom pulled out our small barbeque and the bag of charcoal from deep storage. I chopped vegetables to make a rough ratatouille and boiled tiny orzo pasta. That night, we ate under a canopy of stars.

On Sunday, our relaxation plans deteriorated. The newly installed filter, an integral part of the van's water system, refused to activate. Our water still tasted of chlorine. Tom tried to force pressurized water through the filter with our hose attached to the camp spigot. Suddenly his voice came from behind the van. "Damn! Fuck!" Then, "Katie, don't use the faucet. I'm shutting down the water."

A few minutes later he came around to the side door holding a two-foot section of broken pipe. What a depressing sight! I was getting tired of the endless repairs, so much hard work for Tom, and the continual stalls to our journey. Things kept wearing out, especially in a home that, day after day, bounced on rough roads. After more than a year of travel, parts of the van were reaching the end of their life expectancy.

It was a two-person job to dismantle the wooden cabinet surrounding the water tank, remove the entire water system, and return the cabinet to lean precariously in its original location. Exhausted, depressed, and grumpy, we needed a hot shower but the water heater in the bathhouse was turned off for the season. The owner lived onsite and Tom tried to cajole him into relighting it for one night. Rather than go to such effort, the man invited us into his home to use his family's shower.

On Monday, we filled our extra plastic jugs with water and returned to Athens, in spite of heavy rain flooding the roads. On the high ground of the Acropolis Hill, above a district of welder's workshops, we listened to the drum of rain on our roof and waited. When the dark clouds moved away, taking the rain with them, Tom tied a rope around the aluminum water tank, made two shoulder straps from the loose ends, hefted the tank to his back, and trudged off down the hill.

I was surprised when he returned in less than an hour, the tank repaired, and the broken pipe reattached. Before putting everything back together, we moved to a better site near a store with a water spigot. We moved the cupboard pieces outside, Tom reinstalled the water tank, and together we refabricated the cupboard around it. Tom tested the system and the filter activated. We had water!

Finally, our Turtle was shipshape again. The sun had reemerged and in the late afternoon glow, we hiked down a narrow dirt path to one of the open-front cafés specializing in souvlaki. This seasoned meat mixture cooked on a vertical spit was new to us, as it had not yet arrived in the fast food centers of California. The cook sliced off slabs of meat from the crispy exterior, wrapped them in soft pita bread and added parsley, onion, and yogurt sauce, while we munched on an appetizer of feta cheese and filo. Perfect!

Next stop—Turkey. Near the border we camped in a vacant lot surrounded by dozens of oceanfront condos under construction. Turkey was gearing up to become a tourist mecca for travelers from northern Europe.

The next morning, while Tom continued to snore on his side of the bed, I reached over to start the fire under the water kettle, then peeked outside. Three uniformed soldiers stood near the window and three more stood a few paces behind them. I dropped the curtain as if it had burned my fingers and shook Tom's shoulder. He looked up, bleary eyed with sleep.

"We're surrounded by soldiers," I whispered.

Tom was instantly on alert. He put his eye to a crack between the curtains. "Quiet. Don't move." He slipped on his jeans, always draped nearby, ready for emergencies.

"Hello. Hello!" Voices from outside were followed by a knock on the windshield.

Tom motioned to me. "Stay in bed and cover up. I'll take care of it." Barefooted and shirtless, he stepped out the driver's door.

I heard the murmur of male voices—no angry shouts, a good sign. After a few minutes, Tom got back in the car. "They think I'm stuck in the mud and want to help," he said. "I'll pull forward so they see it's OK. Stay down. They don't need to know I've got a woman in here."

I did as I was told and kept my head down. As Tom pulled forward, one of the soldiers grinned broadly and waved his arms to direct the car. Tom waved back and we were on our way.

In the center of the old city of Istanbul, a guarded parking area was dominated by vans with European and English license plates. Travelers who stayed there told us they used the nearby public toilets and a Turkish Bath, or *hammam*, only a block away. However, Tom and I had already booked into a campground on the way into the city. It offered showers as well as overland travelers whom Tom could network with.

It was Sunday, the last weekend of Ramadan, and all city museums were half price. At the Blue Mosque, its six minarets reaching for the sky, we removed our shoes and padded about in stocking feet. Countless Oriental carpets covered the floor, reed mats underneath to protect them from the hard stone. When the muezzin called, one of the five calls a day, men flocked into the central part of the mosque to pray.

We crossed a park to the Hagia Sophia, first built in 535 AD as a Christian basilica. In 1453, when the Byzantine empire fell to the Ottoman Turks, the church was rededicated as a mosque. Then, in 1935 it was secularized and became a museum. In the garden behind, a tomb displayed a row of green felt caskets of all sizes, the burial place of a sultan, his female relatives, and thirty-nine princes and princesses. In keeping with the male-dominant culture of Turkey, the caskets of the sultan and boy princes were all topped by turbans.

The Topkapi Palace served for most of the fifteenth century as the main residence of the Ottoman sultans. Befitting its role as a museum dedicated to Ottoman history, the displays were sumptuous—a collection of state robes, gold, jewels, several ornate thrones designed for the recumbent sultan, gardens, and pavilions.

A guide led us around the harem complex, a walled city within a city, through narrow, twisting streets, the sultan's mother's suite, the rooms where sons under sixteen lived, and a dormitory for the special African eunuchs who guarded the harem. We even saw lavatory rooms with keyhole openings in the marble floor, flowing water below, and clean water piped to the sinks. It was amazing to realize bathrooms this sanitary were in use in Turkey in the fifteenth century. In Europe at the same time, even in the fanciest of palaces, the best available toilet was a wooden chair with a chamber pot beneath, not unlike our toilet bucket in the microbus. There was never a morning when I wouldn't have preferred a marble toilet automatically cleansed with running water.

The next day, we walked to the Old Spice Market, a noisy, crowded, jostling hubbub of narrow alleys, the stalls hawking goods from fruit to belts, from meat to plastic dishpans, from carpets to potting soil. Occasionally a truck or taxi came down the alleyway, plowing through the crowds, which pushed, shoved, and yelled as they tried to get out of the way. Porters called *hamals* trotted along the narrow passages, heavy loads strapped to their backs with a leather harness. They moved barrels, crates of live chickens, towering stacks of boxes, bulging canvas sacks, and even furniture through the market. As they picked their way among the crowds, the hamals called out to warn the shoppers who moved aside to clear a way.

The Grand Bazaar, the oldest and largest covered market in the world, was nearby. Though it was tame after the Spice Market, we wandered the covered streets and looked at carpets, clothing, costume jewelry, baskets, gold puzzle rings like Tom's, copperware, and blankets. When Ramadan ended the next day, Turkish Muslims would celebrate and feast with their families. A young man at the bazaar described the celebrations as "Sugar Holiday" and long lines of shoppers waited in front of the candy and pastry shops.

The nights continued to be cold and would be even colder as we traveled east and north over mountain passes. Even when we piled all our coats on top of our bed, we were never warm enough. Tom filled an empty beer bottle with hot water and lodged it against his feet at night. I wore two pairs of socks. In the bazaar, we found a woolen blanket with long, black goat hair interwoven with the yarns. It would be warm! Tom bargained while I pretended disinterest and rummaged through stacks of conventional bed covers. Soon we were the proud owners of a shaggy black blanket!

Back at the campground, Tom roamed the grounds, checked out the facilities, and talked to other travelers. On this part of our journey, up-to-date news could save our lives. The night before, Tom had already gleaned important information for the trip ahead from people returning from India. "Eastern Turkey is inhospitable," he had told me as we nibbled pistachio halva and baklava pastries. "One guy said the shepherd boys throw stones at American cars. Several warned that the high pass between Turkey and Iran is often closed by snow this time of year. And in Afghanistan, the water is so bad we need to purify it with iodine. Bleach won't be strong enough." All of this sounded daunting.

"What about the roads?" I asked.

"The roads are good," he said. "Built by the Americans and British. But there's danger from bandits in the outlying areas. Lots of people prefer to caravan in Afghanistan. They believe they're safer in a group. But a group is only as strong as its weakest member."

"What do you think we should do?"

"I'd rather go on our own . . . If you're OK with that. Together we're levelheaded. I know I can count on you. But we need to be extra cautious. No stopping along the road and no free-camping for a while. Definitely not in Afghanistan, probably not in India, either. They say it's easy to find enclosed compounds in the main cities and almost everywhere in India, even in small towns."

With so much good information, we felt confident. But on our last night in Istanbul, when Tom returned from his rounds, he had a far more worrisome story to share.

"Everyone's talking about two brothers who were ambushed by bandits in the Kabul River Gorge," he said.

"What happened?"

"I'm getting to that," Tom said. I knew he hated to be interrupted when he was telling a story, so I clamped my lips and settled in to listen. "They were trying to walk around the world. Started about a year ago in Minnesota. They made it to New York and flew to Portugal where interested fans gave them a mule, then walked across Europe and the Middle East and from there to Afghanistan. After they left Kabul, they were attacked by local bandits in the gorge. One of them was killed instantly. The rumor is the other brother only survived because he pretended to be dead, remaining motionless on the road next to the body of his brother. One guy said he heard the surviving brother was shot through the lung, but he was rescued and taken to the hospital in Kabul." Tom shook his head. "That hospital was probably almost as bad as lying on the road. Later he was flown back to the United States. Some say he's at the Mayo Clinic."

"How awful!" I said when I was sure the story was complete. "Will we go through the Kabul River Gorge?"

"We pretty much have to. It's the only good road to the Kyber Pass and on to India."

In spite of this news, Tom and I were determined to stay on course. The first bridge across the Bosporus Strait that separated Europe from Asia was under construction, not expected to be complete for several years. We would cross by ferry.

When we arrived at the landing on this first day of the Sugar Holiday, we found several rows of vehicle lines ahead of us with an estimated wait time of several hours. Tom hated lines. He turned up a hill and around a five-star hotel, then down again to approach the ferry from a different angle. Directly in front of us, a funeral procession led by an open hearse with an ornate coffin and mounds of flowers was followed by five taxis with their headlights on, each filled to capacity with mourners. The procession pulled up to the landing and we followed right behind. Tom switched on his headlights and our van became part of the funeral as the guards waved the procession ahead of the lines. We followed closely onto the half-filled boat.

Safely aboard we switched off the headlights. We would have lunch in Asia.

Iran to India, November 1972 to March 1973

Tehran

Mashad

Herat

AFGHANISTAN

IRAN

PAKISTAN

Travelers-Afghanistan

Clothing-Afghanistan

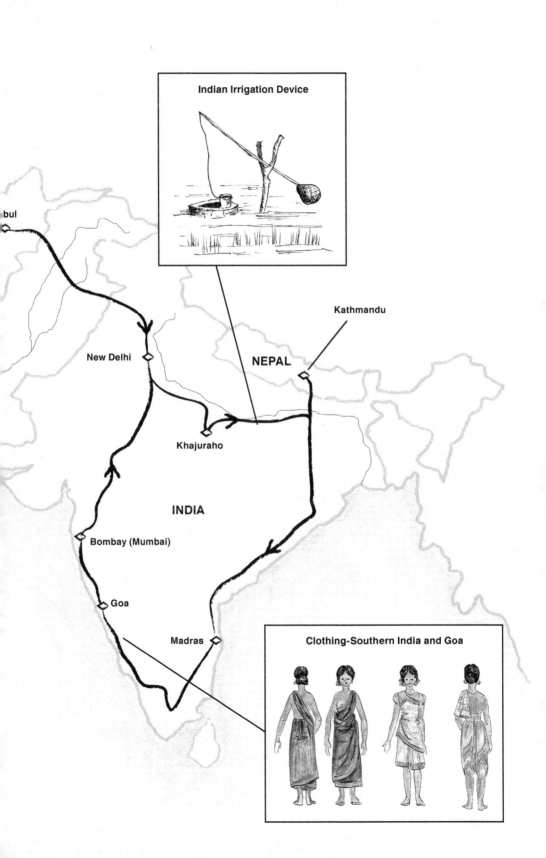

Indian Irrigation Device

Kathmandu

NEPAL

New Delhi

Khajuraho

INDIA

Bombay (Mumbai)

Goa

Madras

Clothing-Southern India and Goa

bul

Chapter 17

Where Others Seldom Venture

On the road to Ankara, we passed villages of houses built in half-timber style, similar to ancient Tudor cottages, mud-colored and squat. Frequently, we saw two-story homes constructed of wood, the second level overhanging the street, the unpainted, weathered exteriors aged to a silver-gray patina. The land was brown, dry, and almost without trees.

"Where'd they get the timber to build all these wooden homes?" I wondered idly.

"There used to be trees here," Tom said. "Turkey had lots of wood-burning trains during the late Ottoman Empire. They cut down all the trees for fuel."

"Are you Zouaving me?"

Tom grinned. "Maybe a little. But I did read about the trains in the museum in Istanbul."

We only stopped in Ankara long enough to go to the American Embassy where, because our passports burst with visa stamps, they pasted new multipage, expandable, accordion sections into each of our travel documents. And yes, of course, we shopped. Groceries, a copy of *Time* magazine (European edition), a small book in English about Oriental carpets, and snow chains. Tom used his last scrap of leftover plywood to make a wide license plate frame to cover up the word "California." We hoped we were ready for all eventualities.

The Anatolian Plateau, east of Ankara, stretched out ahead, a high desert resembling a huge carpet strewn with stones. The stark beauty of the land was revealed at twilight when the sun dipped behind the distant hills and cool, dark shadows slid over the warm ochre of sharp, rock outcroppings and into the clefts of riverbeds. Gradually the scene was enveloped in violet-blackness and the chilly night air descended. Stars like diamond chips shone in the velvet sky, guarded by a crescent moon.

In these desolate expanses, boys and young men watched flocks of black or brown sheep with distinctive, large, bustle-shaped tails. Often the young boys waved as we drove past, or they shouted at us as they stood on a boulder at the verge of the road, a scruffy herding dog at their side. Once, two boys threw rocks at the van, but it felt more a spontaneous exercise than antagonism, similar to when a loose dog barks and chases a passing car.

The days were warm and sunny, but the frigid night air made us grateful for our new, black, shaggy goat blanket. Away from the bazaar atmosphere suffused with spice, sweat, dust, and heat, the odor of randy goat emanated noticeably from the long hairs of our bed cover. In spite of the smell, we were reluctant to crawl out from under its warmth in the morning to scrape the ice off the inside of the windshield glass.

After three and a half days traveling steadily eastward, we entered a broad valley surrounded by snowcapped mountains, Mount Ararat towering in the distance. Close to the Iranian and Syrian borders, the Turkish military had several camps nearby and we shared the road with tanks and jeeps. It began to snow as soon as we entered the mountains.

We crossed over the pass through a misty curtain of snowflakes and descended into a valley where the snow turned to sleet, then drenching rain.

The next day, the sun reflected off puddles where geese and ducks splashed. The Iranian border was only a few miles ahead. We straightened up the inside of the van, put on clean clothes, and Tom trimmed his beard. Being profiled as hippies or druggies might significantly delay the process at the Iranian border. Quickly through the outpost, we waved goodbye to two scruffy, bearded Frenchmen who remained at the border station even though they had arrived several hours before us.

The poorly maintained Turkish road became an Iranian highway, smooth asphalt as far as we could see. In the neat, dun-colored villages, orchards full of laden apple trees were surrounded by low mud walls. Two young boys, watching over a herd of grazing camels, smiled and waved. Groups of nomad women dressed in brightly colored skirts, loose blouses, and gaudy scarves wound in layers around their heads stood at the roadside to watch our green van glide past. The blacks and browns of the Iranian landscape were broken by the shimmer of water—muddy rivers, rushing streams, and irrigation ditches that crisscrossed the fields of cotton or rice stubble. Wherever water flowed, trees grew and cooled the landscape with their foliage and shade, while snowy mountain peaks loomed, a distant backdrop.

In 1972, Americans were well-liked in Persia. The Iranian government was firmly in the hands of Shah Mohammad Reza Pahlavi, a secular Muslim who loved all things Western. The Shah was the latest ruler in a monarchy that had lasted 2,500 years, a continuous line since the founding of the Achaemenid Empire of Cyrus the Great. Shah Reza Pahlavi's policies brought him into conflict with the Shi'a clergy. Working-class citizens favored communism because they disliked the corruption of the ruling elite and the suppression of political dissents by the intelligence service. But the revolution and Ruhollah Khomeini lay seven years in the future.

After a night near the road, we headed for the Tabriz Airport, hoping for a spigot to fill our water tank. Near the terminal, two men washed their cars. When he finished splashing his car with clear water from a hose, one of the men, an Air Force officer trained in the United States, offered to lead us to the city campground. As we followed him, he pulled over at a shop and bought a pint bottle of milk. We assumed his wife had asked him to bring milk home, but he brought the bottle to the van. "This is beautiful milk," he said. "In Persia we share milk with new friends." We all sat together at our little dinette, sipped the cool, creamy milk, and talked about what we each missed from the states. Back on the road, he stopped near his house, pointed us in the direction of the camp, and handed Tom his phone number. "In case you need my help again," he said, "please call me."

In Tabriz, as always, our first chore was to restock our food supplies. While we bought pistachios, a young schoolboy came up. "Americans?" he asked. "I learn English in school. Can I practice with you?" So far, our experience with the Iranian people had been positive and this young lad reminded us of the guides who joined us our first day in North Africa. The boy showed us the way to the local bazaar which had been elusive, hidden amid the labyrinth of twisting alleys. The covered market, illuminated by glass skylights, was filled with busy shoppers.

While in Iran, we had a special goal—to buy a Persian carpet. After studying our new little book, we both favored carpets woven with geometric, tribal designs. In Tabriz, spacious carpet sales rooms were stacked high with carpets and rugs of all sizes. Though the local style was too floral for our tastes, their carpets served as a starting point for understanding quality and prices. The salesmen, not at all pushy, were pleased to educate us with the translation help of our young guide.

Two long days later, we entered Tehran and plunged into chaotic, rush-hour traffic, through streets clogged with trucks, to the ugly city campground hidden in an industrial section. Our first day in the capital was spent gathering up maps and brochures at the tourist information center and exploring the displays at the archeological museum. When we left, the guards locking up behind us, we realized we would again be sucked into Tehran's rush-hour traffic. Cars and trucks swirled around us; no one slowed or yielded. It was a ceaseless free-for-all of honking, bumper-to-bumper turmoil.

I watched silently as Tom's jaw clenched and his hands gripped the wheel till his knuckles were white. "Fuck. Fuck. Watch out asshole." His words were muttered but I could hear them. I had learned to stay quiet when Tom was frustrated by traffic. "It's not worth trying to find the campground," he said. "Navigate me out of town!" We made it to the expressway without a dent or a scratch, and Tom pulled into a deserted lot on a hill. "That's enough," he said. He twisted his head left and right to ease the kinks from his neck and I massaged his shoulders. "Thanks, sweetheart. That was the worst traffic—like shooting the rapids in a rubber raft. A real bumper cruncher's paradise."

Below, the city lights blinked on. From our vantage point, all appeared peaceful. One could almost forget the chaos of the streets below. Across the expressway, an immense white marble arch, the Gate of Cyrus, rose into the sky, illuminated by floodlights. Dedicated only a few weeks before, the arch was a stunning sight, starkly white against the black, star-studded night sky. Renamed the Azadi (Freedom) Tower after the revolution, it would become a symbol of Tehran.

In the morning, we steeled ourselves to reenter traffic hell to try our hand at carpet shopping. Most of the Persian rug merchants were located in one area, near Ferdosé Street. We entered one shop after another, pretending confidence. The profusion of carpets was like an avalanche of color and texture. We repeatedly returned to the deep reds of Baluchi, Bokhara, and Turkoman carpets with their rows of angular, oval shaped *guls*, surrounded by borders of geometric patterns. We looked mainly at three-foot by five-foot rugs, which would fit in our roof box. Depending on quality, they ran about $200 to $500, a price range we could manage.

Mashhad was our gateway to Afghanistan. Our first morning in the border city, we went to the shopping area and filled our grocery bags. Tom and I made an effort to say numbers in Farsi, an essential market skill. At one shop, we struggled to understand the owner when he rattled off the price of several kilos of onions he had bagged. A young man of about twenty, also in the store, offered to help us. His English was excellent. When our bag of onions was paid for, we asked if he knew a good butcher shop.

"I will show you the place my mother goes," he said. "It is only a short distance and the meat is very clean."

Tom and I both preferred lamb to beef, and since Greece, I had begun to buy hunks of lamb or mutton in the native markets. I did not worry about the flies that flitted around the meat in open-air markets or the lack of good refrigeration at the local butcher shops as long as the meat smelled fresh. A leg of mutton, usually around 1,700 grams, cost about three dollars US and could be stretched for several meals. First, I put the meat, bone and all, into the pressure cooker and added onions, garlic, carrots, and, of course, water. I took the tender and flavorful meat off the bone and for several days created meals around this bounty—lamb curry, shepherd's pie with a mashed potato crust, spicy pilaf with morsels of lamb, a hearty stew, or broth soup with barley and tomatoes. We had sandwiches stuffed with the last bits of meat and lamb hash for breakfast with eggs. So far, we hadn't grown weary of lamb.

In Mashhad, we followed our guide through the twists and turns of the market to the butcher's.

"I am happy to help you in any way. I welcome the opportunity to practice English," he said. This disclosure was the inevitable explanation of most youth who offered help. We found it difficult to gauge if these "pilots," always men or boys, sincerely wanted to practice English or if they, under cover of being students, were actually shills who would steer us to a relative's shop. We had decided it didn't matter, as long as they were pleasant company. Tom asked if he knew where beer, always difficult to find in a Muslim country, was sold. "Yes, I know. I will show you." Our guide led us to a shop tucked in the corner of the market. "If you are hungry," he said, "I can take you to a place of good food. The very best camel meat. On a stick of wood. Cooked over hot coals. Very good. Is there a name for this in English?"

"Shish-kebob," Tom said. "Chunks of meat on a stick are called shish-kebob."

He tested the word in his mouth. "Shish-kebob. You want to eat camel shish-kebob?"

Tom turned to me. "What do you think?" I had become the deciding voice in all meal plans.

"I'd love to try them," I said, "but maybe another day. We have all this food to get back to the van and I have broth left from the last batch. We should eat that." Our guide looked crestfallen.

"Is there plenty?" Tom asked and by his slight nod in the direction of our guide, I understood what he meant.

"Yes! Plenty."

Back at the green van with our new friend, I put the pot of lamb broth on the stove. While it came to a boil, I made short work of dicing up a few vegetables and a last bit of meat to add with a handful of soup pasta. I dressed up our meal with the inevitable fried bread with a layer of cheese.

At this point we exchanged names. "I must introduce myself," he said. "I am Beban. In Persia, if we introduce ourselves to new friends, we give a gift. I will have a gift for you when we meet again."

I set the bowls of soup on our tiny table and we ate, shoulder to shoulder, while Tom and I answered questions about America and our impressions of Iran. Tom was the one who first uttered the word "carpets" as he described our afternoon on Ferdosé Street in Tehran.

"Yes, yes," Beban said. "The shops in Ferdosé Street are expensive. They have wealthy people in Tehran. And for tourists, they charge even more." After a polite pause he added, "I can help you look at carpets in Mashhad. My father has a carpet business." So now it was out. Perhaps he was a shill after all. But it had happened so naturally, we wondered if our skepticism was ill placed. Beban continued, "My father sells to merchants in Tehran. Many of those on Ferdosé Street are his customers. He also sells to merchants from foreign countries. If you want to see it, I will take you tomorrow. Today I must soon go home. My mother is waiting."

We arranged to meet the next morning and dropped Beban near his home on our way to the city campground. It was only mid-afternoon, so Tom wandered about the grounds talking to the other travelers while I washed vegetables in chlorine water and put the leg of lamb in the pressure cooker. As I cooked dinner, we realized it was Thanksgiving. We celebrated with patties made from lamb we had watched the butcher grind and a salad of cucumbers and tomatoes garnished with fresh cress sprouts grown from my Danish seeds. Dessert was a large slice of the honey-sweet Persian melon and pistachio baklava. We didn't miss the turkey and pumpkin pie at all.

Beban did not disappoint us. He waited at the appointed time at the same place we had left him the night before. As soon as he got in the van, he presented us with a gift, a small teardrop shaped turquoise and an oval, gray agate. "An introduction present," he said. "Our Persian custom." He navigated Tom down the main street of Mashhad. "See, straight ahead. The golden dome. It is the mosque. Mashhad is a holy city. A place of pilgrimage."

"It's beautiful!" I said. "Is it open to visitors?"

"Sorry. No foreigners who only want to look. There are Muslim pilgrims who come to pray. Especially today. Friday is the holy day. I am so sorry."

We inched our way through the crowded streets. When the pedestrians were so thick we could drive no farther, Beban led us on foot down several narrow streets, clogged with shoppers and pilgrims, to the caravansary. "This was built hundreds of years ago by carpet traders from Russia," he told us. "There were stalls for the camels and donkeys on the ground floor. A kind of stable. The shops for trading are upstairs." Beban was turning out to be an excellent tour guide. He took us to peer into a room next to the entrance. "Here the men fix damage to the carpets." In the dim room, a father taught his young son the respected craft of mending carpets. Fringes were repaired and new yarns of matched colors were tied in spots where tufts had been worn down. As we watched, a man of about thirty-five arrived and greeted Beban with a hug.

"My brother," Beban said. "He does not speak English." The older man nodded his head in greeting and led us up a narrow staircase all the way to the roof. "There is a good view of the mosque's golden dome," Beban said. "Perhaps you want to take a picture?"

Tom, who always carried his SLR Pentax camera and two lenses, began to focus and shoot. On another part of the caravansary roof, several old men beat on rugs to clean them. Dust filled the air and created a golden cloud in the sunshine. Tom switched to his telescopic lens to get a close-up photo without disturbing the workers.

The shop of Beban's family, similar to others, was stacked with towers of carpets. Beban explained to us that only the larger ones were called carpets; smaller examples were referred to as rugs. Tom told him we could probably only buy a rug and that we would not purchase today but would wait until we returned in the spring. Beban nodded and translated for his brother.

Beban's brother continued to smile and motioned toward two low stools. A helper brought hot mint tea in glass cups. Beban showed us how to hold a sugar cube in our mouths and sip the tea through the sugar. He translated for us and for his brother. After about ten minutes, Beban told us his brother would show us carpets. "Only to look," he said. "He understands you won't buy today."

Already the brother had pulled rugs out of the piles and displayed them in front of us. He spread a rug out, smoothed it down, and invited us to touch it. He rattled off information in Farsi and Beban translated—where it was made, how to count the knots on the back side, the colors and dyes (natural or chemical), the age of the rug, and the meanings of the designs. Another rug was set on top of the first, always slightly askew so we could see the edge of the previous one and remember it. Each rug was more beautiful than the last. Gradually he sensed which styles we liked best and only showed us that type.

Once or twice, when we saw one we especially fancied, Tom asked the price "so we can have an idea of the value to set aside enough money to buy when we return."

Beban explained they could not tell us a price from memory. His brother indicated the stiff paper tag wired to the corner of each rug. "Each number is recorded in a ledger," Beban said. "They must look up the price." We were quite impressed by this system. In Tehran, the carpet merchants had always rattled off a price, in spite of an inventory of hundreds of carpets. We figured their quoted prices were so far above the bottom line they didn't need to worry about accuracy. The idea that this merchant looked up prices in a book made him, to our minds, trustworthy. "My brother will look up the ones you find suit your taste," Beban told us.

Carefully, we went back through the entire stack of rugs in front of us, setting aside about a dozen of our favorites. Beban's brother produced a black ledger book, checked the number on the tag, and looked each one up. He explained the quality of each rug as he quoted the prices which ranged from $35 for a small rug he called "third quality" to almost $400 for an antique, "finest quality" Russian Bukhara. It was obvious both Tom and I had fallen in love with the expensive Bukhara, the best of the lot. "My brother is willing to sell to you if you want to buy," our guide told us. This was the softest sell we had encountered either here or in North Africa. We would never know how much Beban was a "pilot" and how much he was truly a new friend. Regretfully we left the fine Russian Bukhara with his brother who continued to smile as he shook Tom's hand. We knew we would return. Perhaps, he did, too.

At our request Beban took us to a turquoise shop near the Mosque. Eastern Iran was one of the only places in the world, besides the American Southwest, where true turquoise could be found. At an upstairs workshop, a man polished the blue-green stones, and though we didn't buy, both the merchant and our guide continued to smile. We again invited Beban to lunch with us and drove back to the quiet shaded street where we had eaten the day before. After our meal, he wanted to show us more of the city. With difficulty, we convinced him we needed to do chores at the campground as we planned to leave the next day. Reluctantly, we parted company, thanked him profusely, and promised to return in spring. We would go to the caravansary, we said, and find his brother.

When we left town the following day, we had to drive through the district where our young friend lived. Surprisingly, Beban appeared in the lane next to us astride his Honda 90. We pulled over to talk through the open window. "I tried to come visit at the campground last night," he said. "I wanted to give you this to remember me by." He handed us a scrap of woven carpet from a bag that hung on the back of his cycle. "The guards wouldn't let me in to see you. They said, 'No natives!' It is lucky to find each other on the road." After more farewells and our promise to return, we parted. Beban would always be the highlight of our fond memories of Iran.

From Mashhad it was only a short drive to the Afghani border. Aware that for the next few weeks, only iodine would be strong enough to kill the prevalent, water-borne Afghani bacteria, we topped off our water tanks and filled up all our extra water jugs with Iranian water. Because service stations would be few and far between and the quality of gasoline poor, Tom filled our gasoline tank and the two red auxiliary gas cans with good petrol. We hoped we would be ready for Afghanistan.

Chapter 18

Like Falling Backward in Time

We arrived at the border in the late afternoon, but it was dark before we cleared the formalities and paperwork. Once across this invisible international boundary, we felt as if we had traveled back in time a hundred years. Though the road, built by the combined interests of the United States and Russia, had a good surface, the countryside was black, no street lights, and no twinkle of electricity as we approached Herat. We hardly knew when we reached the city except suddenly the forms of buildings appeared. Tom drove slowly, both of us searching for any indication of the hotel we had been told to look for. Even the Afghani border guards had warned us to only sleep within a compound. The hotel, labeled by an unlit sign, was surrounded by a high wall edged with broken glass. We rang a bell and a guard came to open the wooden gates and let us into the secure space.

In the morning, we retraced our route, back along the highway to the border. We wanted to re-experience the road we had traveled in darkness—a daylight version of entering Afghanistan. Five minarets of a ruined mosque stood in the distance beyond the border station. The thoroughfare was long and straight, lined with trees, and clogged with traffic. Brightly painted trucks were piled high with dozens of people seated atop their bundles and baskets. We drove past men astride donkeys, herds of sheep, and long strings of camels carrying loads. The vehicles and animals kicked up a golden haze of dust that glowed in the morning sunshine. In town, the dirt streets were lined with open-fronted shops. We saw our first women in burkas, the long, dark, all-concealing garment with only a window of thick lace behind which their eyes were invisible. Men wore baggy trousers, a long tunic-type shirt, and sometimes a vest or long jacket. All the men and boys wore turbans, lengths of colored fabric wound around a skull cap, a loose end hanging down. One toddler, too young to wear pants, scampered across the dusty street dressed in only a shirt and a turban.

We started early and drove long hours to get to the next city before dark. We ate while on the move and stopped only to transfer gasoline or when Tom had to pee. From Herat to Kandahar was over 350 miles. Even today, driving time between the two cities is estimated as eight and a half hours.

The main street of Herat, Afghanistan.

The road looped southward to skirt the southern end of the Hindu Kush mountain range, across miles and miles of dry, flat, barren desert covered with rocks and dusty yellow clumps of vegetation. To the north, jagged hills stood in rows like sharp, brown demon's teeth. The flat landscape was fissured by dry washes where stunted melon vines produced yellowish fruit the size of tennis balls. Occasionally, signs of human habitation broke the monotony, or herds of camels grazed in the distance. Clusters of dome-roofed, dry mud villages squatted among the rocks. A camel caravan, the beasts joined tail to nose, plodded forward, one after the other, at the side of the highway.

We passed an isolated building, a kind of transport center. Men, their woolen sacks of goods at their feet, waited for the gaily painted trucks, which served as public buses. A shop was piled with sweet melons and offered tea from a tall, steaming, brass samovar.

When our fuel gauge showed almost empty, Tom stopped at the side of the road in a spot where we could see for miles in all directions. "I need you to stand outside and be my lookout while I transfer gas," he said. I stood in the middle of the road, scanned the distant rocks and down the dry wash, searching for dark, moving shapes that might be camel-riding bandits. Tom, at the rear of the van, concentrated on transferring the gasoline from our red cans into the gas tank without spilling a drop.

In the afternoon, several hours out of Kandahar, we noticed the land to the right sloped away, no mountains in sight. Almost at the horizon, a dark splotch suggested a grove of trees and a river. Beyond that, in the haze of distance, the earth rippled, a dun-colored sea of sand that extended to infinity. We checked our roadmap. South of us the map showed hundreds of square miles of dunes. The name printed on the paper read: "Desert of Death."

For the last hour, a water course ran parallel to the highway, the life-giving water allowing agriculture to develop. Kandahar was a market town where people from the area came to sell goods, barter, and exchange information. For us it was simply a safe place to sleep in a hotel compound before another grueling day on the road.

Three hundred and twenty miles stood between us and Kabul. Again, the land was unbelievably dry, sunk in drought, rocky and hilly, with brown and treeless expanses of nothing but sand and dust. After four hours of travel through this wasteland, we began to ascend a broad valley shadowed by mountains rising on both sides. Villages squatted in this lowland, their fields fallow, waiting for spring. We passed several ancient walled enclosures with round corner towers melted into ruins. We had learned to identify specks of movement in the distance. Tall, black, loping—a man on camelback. Slow, brown and plodding—a man on a donkey. A slow-moving red spot—a tribal woman dressed in shades of red and purple, crossing the fields on foot, a jug of water on her head.

Kabul lay before us, blanketed by a smoky pall and encircled by snow-covered mountains. The city had the feel of a village grown out of bounds. The streets were clogged and busy. Open shops lined the dusty roads. Meat hung outside at the butcher shop; vegetables and fruits stood piled on the roadside. Small boys sat in front of shops and chopped wood into kindling for braziers used to heat water in the ever-present samovars. Men in turbans herded flocks of sheep across the main thoroughfare, while the brightly painted trucks waited and honked, their passengers clinging to the sides or squatting atop the load. A few cars moved slowly through the congestion of trucks, people, carts, and animals. The main difference between this city and the country villages was the numerous, bareheaded men in western attire, though most women remained buried under their burkas. Even in the center of the city, we saw no tall structures and certainly no modern ones. Street signs were in an unreadable Farsi without Roman letter translations.

We followed another European car to find a hotel compound near the Indian Embassy. The next morning, we went there to fill out a double-paged application, submit the requested photos, pay our 187

Afghanis, and show proof of a minimum of $200 in cash. After taking our passports, the clerk told us to come back in four or five days. We could not get our Pakistani visas until the Indian Embassy completed its process and returned our documents.

Tom had developed a cold over the last few days and the first night in Kabul, I began to cough, too. For the entire trip, though lucky to never be seriously ill, we suffered periodically from the common cold. After over a year on the road, we were rundown, and because we lived so close together, 24/7, it was inevitable that when Tom caught a cold, I would begin blowing my nose within days, and vice versa. The best remedy was rest, and in Kabul regaining our health became our top priority.

The Paris Hotel was a single-story, stucco inn about the size of a California tract home with an enclosed area for van travelers. Best of all, for the cost of 13 cents, we could arrange for a bath. Half an hour after we ordered this luxury, we were led to the bathing room. An old-fashioned, claw-footed tub was filled with hot water and the wood-burning water heater made the entire room toasty warm. The steam and heat helped relieve our stuffy heads, making the entire experience heavenly.

Clean and wrapped in blankets, we sat in the Turtle and read, napped, and sipped hot soup. In Kandahar, we had finally filled our water tank with Afghani water and spiked it with the recommended iodine drops. We soon realized our charcoal filter system was unable to remove the nasty flavor of iodine from the water, leaving us gagging from the unpleasant taste of our morning coffee and tea.

In England, I had learned an effective cold cure and, in Kabul, I dosed us with aspirin tablets dissolved in hot lemonade. Sweetened with honey and fortified with rum, the drink was strong enough to camouflage our water's substandard taste. This uplifting beverage relieved our sore throats enough that we set off to explore the neighborhood. Nearby antique shops sold guns and other paraphernalia; carpet shops displayed stacks of rugs and kilims; gem shops were lined with glass cabinets filled with tourmaline, garnets, emeralds, and lapis lazuli; and a general store sold magazines, canned goods, and sodas. I bought more lamb at the butcher's market to make into soup and vegetables, which I washed in iodine water. At a nearby street called Chicken Street, we were directed to a café. Near the door, several large kettles filled with milk continually simmered over wood fires. For ten *afghanis* (about 13 cents), the owner ladled a liter of hot milk into a plastic bag or a bottle supplied by the customer. We returned to the van with a bulging plastic bag of warm milk and immediately made ourselves hot cocoa. The rich chocolatey drink made us feel pampered.

After five days in Kabul, both Tom and I still coughed through the night and our energy level plunged. Other travelers at The Paris suffered from coughs and chest congestion, too, and we nicknamed the syndrome the "Kabul Cough." In this city, where wood was used almost exclusively for heating and cooking, we took smoke into our lungs with each breath. Still, Tom and I wondered if an illness more serious than the common cold was being spread around. Tom suggested we go to the US Embassy for a medical reference. They sent us to the local C.A.R.E. hospital where a doctor listened to our chests, reassured us we didn't have pneumonia, and prescribed a pill to help us sleep.

At 1:30 p.m. on our seventh day in Kabul, the clerk at the Pakistani Embassy handed us our passports with the needed visa stamp. We sprinted for the van. The India–Pakistani border was only open at one location, one day a week—Thursday. It was already midafternoon on Tuesday and we had over five hundred miles to travel. If we missed the open day, we would be stuck in Pakistan for a full week.

As we left the capital, we passed an open market where meat hung in the stalls nearest the road. We were out of lamb and broth. "Can we stop and buy meat?" I asked. "I can cook it in the pressure cooker tonight or even while we drive."

Tom pulled over and we grabbed our shopping bag. At the nearest stall, meat hung suspended from hooks inside a screened box. A few flies buzzed around the dark, red chunks of roughly textured muscle, coarser than any meat we had seen before. "It's probably camel," I whispered to Tom.

The vendor must have heard me and understood a few words of English. "No, No. Memsahib, beef. Not camel!" He grinned to reveal a mouth of brown teeth. "Good beef, Memsahib. Good beef."

Tom and I looked around. Of all the stalls, this one was perhaps the cleanest, though admittedly not by much. "Remember in Mashhad, Beban told us the camel skewers were good," I said. "Shall we try it?"

"It's up to you. It might be beef. Water buffalo, maybe. Or camel."

"Whatever it is, after an hour in the pressure cooker, it's simply cooked meat. I can add lots of spices and make a stew."

The butcher wrapped a chunk of the mystery meat in newspaper, and we carried it back to the van where I transferred it to a clean container and put it in our refrigerator. In less than ten minutes, we were on our way again. About a mile down the road, we passed a line of three wooden carts pulled by tired camels. They rolled toward the market, each loaded with brown, hide-covered haunches cut from a large animal, unmistakably camel by their color and the soft padded shape of the projecting hoofs. We turned to each other and grinned. "Pretty sure we bought camel," Tom said.

"I knew he was lying. It'll be fine if I cook it long enough."

For the next few weeks, we traveled the historic Grand Trunk Road, originally built by the Persian conquerors of India, extended by the Mughal Emperors, then improved by the colonial British. At its height, the route extended from Kabul, over the Khyber Pass, through Lahore to Delhi, and on to Calcutta (now called Kolkata). Not long after leaving the butcher's market, the road ascended a gradual incline and entered a tunnel. At the end of the darkness, we emerged into sunshine again and found ourselves at the top of the narrow and dramatic Kabul River Gorge, the river at its bottom so far away it was invisible. This was the unlucky place where the two American brothers were ambushed only a few months before.

Tom gripped the steering wheel and turned to me. "Keep your eyes open for movement along the road or any strange shapes or shadows," he said. "I don't intend to stop for anything."

The two-lane road wound, rope-like, down the side of the gorge in tight hairpin turns, one stacked on top of another. Both Tom and I were vigilant, scanning ahead as we rounded each curve. Tom drove as fast as he could in safety, and we made it to the bottom of the gorge, directly below where we had begun. We were through the worst of it . . . alive. The road continued next to the river until it entered a valley of farmland and orchards. We didn't stop until we had reached the Afghan border station after dark. Our papers were quickly stamped and we waited out the night in the buffer mile between Afghanistan and Pakistan.

Up at dawn, we joined a line of waiting trucks and inched toward the Pakistani border kiosk. After a two-hour ordeal, the legendary Khyber Pass lay ahead. Well-fortified by rows of concrete, tank-stopping teeth, the road surface improved and truck traffic increased. Signs directed caravans with camels to use a dirt track parallel to the highway. At the top of the pass, we entered a flat plateau with scattered dry-mud forts, each with a single high tower. In the villages, turbaned men with rifles strode the streets. We kept moving. Gradually, the land changed to forbidding, black rocks and sharp crags. By afternoon, the mountains came to an abrupt halt and the Punjab Plain, smothered under a thick soup of dust, stretched out as far as the eye could see. We were safely out of the notorious Northwest Frontier Province.

In the lowlands, trees, villages, people, and towns multiplied. The road was clogged with bullock carts, pedestrians, and horse-drawn taxis transporting veiled women passengers. We crossed the Indus River, both banks formed of dark rock blanketed by cushiony layers of white sand. The farther we progressed, the more tropical the land became. We saw our first banana tree since Panama and the first man dressed in a dhoti, a typical white sarong-like garment.

When night descended, the unlit road remained congested with bicycles and bullock carts, most without lights, though occasionally a cart had a lit kerosene lantern tied to its rear axle. We peered into the blackness searching for dangers. In Lahore, we asked directions to the nearest border station at Ferozepur. When we arrived in "no-man's-land," we were stopped by a sentry. "No crossing here," he said. "Go to Wagah. You must cross there in the morning."

Back in Lahore, we asked directions to Wagah. A group of men in turbans pointed toward a sign to Amritsar. At about 11:00 p.m., we were halted at a bridge by soldiers who waved us to a nearby dirt lot filled with dozens of vans, semi-trucks, and buses. "Seven a.m.," one soldier said as he pointed to his watch. "You cross at seven a.m." Tom parked our van between two huge trucks and within minutes, we collapsed into bed. We were confident the sound of the trucks revving their engines would serve as an alarm clock.

But it was a soft tap on our window that woke us. Tom pulled aside the curtains and we looked out at a deserted expanse of dust. A teenage boy stood by the window and pointed toward the bridge. All the trucks and buses that had filled the field the night before formed a queue at the barrier gate. Before we were fully dressed, the line of vehicles inched forward. Last in line, we followed a jumble of cars and trucks around a dusty brown Pakistani border control building, where their drivers stood in lines waiting to get their paperwork stamped. Tom joined them, while I made breakfast and carried it to him, then washed the dishes. I put the "camel" in the pressure cooker, along with onions, carrots, garlic, curry, and water, and set it on the stove. The jiggle of the pot's pressure gauge was a constant reminder of dinner cooking. A few minutes before 1:00 p.m., our paperwork was completed.

The actual border demarcation was in the middle of a bridge across the Ravi River. On one side of the bridge, a truck had stopped and Pakistani laborers in green shirts unloaded bags and bales, which they carried to a line painted across the road between two archways. The workers, stopped by armed soldiers, stacked the entire contents of the truck at the demarcation line. A group of men in blue shirts came from the Indian side and picked up the cargo left by the Pakistani laborers. The Indian men lifted the burdens on their heads, turned, and returned to the other end of the bridge. The goods had arrived in India without a single worker setting foot across the border.

The customs process to enter India was more efficient than our morning experience. The station was shaded by palm trees, and flower beds added color. Friendly soldiers in immaculate turbans and khaki uniforms patrolled the area and went in and out of the pink stucco offices. Hundreds of travelers relaxed in the shade and waited their turn to get their documents stamped at several tables set up on the green lawns. Our customs inspection was accomplished in the late afternoon by a sari-clad, woman officer who told us we were free to go.

We had made it to India!

Chapter 19

Another World Entirely

This was not Tom's first time in India. Arriving by ship with his work, he had visited the port of Bombay, the Pakistani port of Karachi, and other seaports in the Far East. But for me, each mile we now traveled was a journey in a storied, exotic land.

Violet-blue twilight enveloped this land as we drove from the border station to Amritsar. Along the way, we passed men on bicycles, their brightly colored turbans bobbing and weaving along the side of the road. At a gated compound where van travelers were allowed to stay the night, I opened the pressure cooker and ladled out the stew. It smelled great, but, even after hours of cooking, the mystery meat remained tough and gamey. Undoubtedly, it had been an extremely old camel. In the end, we threw the meat away and settled for a dinner of rice and broth. Nearby, tied to a post, two Brahman cows with curved horns, prominent shoulder humps, and hanging dewlaps munched on clumps of dry grass.

In Amritsar, we found a street of shops that sold fabric and clothing. While in India, I wanted to occasionally wear a sari like the local women. As a teen, I had learned how to wrap the long swath of cloth and create the stack of folds in front from an aunt who had lived in India. In one of the shops, I bought an inexpensive sari, a simple length of sheer cotton printed in a bold pattern of yellow and white flowers with brown swirls. Since it had no border or end trim, it cost less than a dollar. To wear it properly, I needed the appropriate undergarments—a cropped and fitted bodice and an underskirt with a drawstring waist. The sari merchant, who spoke English, accompanied me down the street to a stall that sold the underclothing and helped me get a yellow, ready-to-wear, stretch-knit top and a tan cotton slip. I would wear my new outfit in Delhi.

In Amritsar, at the Golden Temple, the holiest shrine of the Sikh religion, a guard instructed us to remove our shoes and socks and wash our feet, a religious ritual all must follow to enter. On a marble island in the middle of a huge square pool of water, the gold-topped shrine dominated the compound. A white stone causeway stretched across the pond to the temple. First, we padded around the surrounding covered colonnade, the marble floor cool under our bare feet. We passed a bathhouse, several additional gates, a smaller shrine, and two sacred trees. Completing the circuit, we joined the throngs on the causeway. Inside the shrine, pilgrims chanted, sang, and prayed. A young man carrying a banana-leaf bundle led us up to the second story, where a group of old men sat around a clock and recited from religious books. Our guide opened his bundle of shiny, dark-green leaves to reveal a lump he described as holy food. He offered us a taste and pinched a bit off with his fingers. It was smooth and sticky and tasted of wheat, sugar, and *ghee* (super-clarified butter).

Perhaps because of this, our first India experience, Tom and I both became enamored of Sikhs and their culture. The area around Amritsar, the Punjab, was the home of the Sikhs, a relatively recent religion founded in the fifteenth century. We were told that Sikhism combined elements of Hinduism and Islam. Though they believed in reincarnation and karma, they also believed salvation was attained through God's grace. Among the colonial British, Sikhs were valued for their fierceness as soldiers, and among modern-day travelers in India, they had become known for their finesse as truck and taxi drivers. We found them to stand out among their countrymen for their height, strength, good looks, and intelligence (perhaps because of their protein-rich, non-vegetarian diet). The men never cut their hair or beards. Well-dressed businessmen rolled their facial hair into a chignon under their chin and held it in place with a hairnet. Sikh men wrapped their long, uncut hair into a neatly arranged, immaculate turban. Small boys, too young for turbans, wore their hair in a topknot, covered with a square of cloth. Tom and I quickly discovered if we needed directions or information, we had better luck finding an English speaker if we talked to a Sikh. We said to each other, "When you need help, seek a Sikh."

After our morning at the Golden Temple, hungry for Indian food, we spotted a café where the cook squatted on a raised platform and prepared chapattis. He patted balls of dough into flat disks between his hands, much as Mexican women form tortillas, then slapped the rounds of dough onto the sides of the earthen tandoor oven inside the platform. There the dough clung to the hot clay sides until the bread was done. He lifted the finished bread out with tongs and handed it to us with a portion of hard-boiled egg curry ladled from a bubbling pot. We figured if the food, spicy and satisfying, was made fresh in front of us, it was safe to eat.

The next day, we headed for New Delhi under gray and rainy skies. Vendors and buses gathered at the crossroads; ducks and children splashed in mud puddles; carts pulled by camels lumbered next to large, Indian-built, *Tata* trucks. That night we slept in the compound of a fancy hotel in the planned, modern state capital of Chandigarh, the dream city of Jawaharlal Nehru, the first prime minister of India.

Morning dawned bright, a clear sky overhead. As we approached Delhi, a kaleidoscope of scenes slid by. Bullock carts filled with straw or cane trundled down dirt roads. Groups of white Brahma bulls and cows huddled in the shade of a tree. Women strode alongside the road, dressed in colorful skirts, thick silver bangles around their ankles, earthenware or brass jugs balanced on their heads. Thin men, dressed only in a wrap of fabric called a lungi, guided bullocks pulling plows through the rich, dark soil. The fields were neatly divided into squares and rectangles, often graced with a tree in the center to offer shade at midday. Water wheels, clay jugs lashed to each rung, turned by cow power. At each turn of the wheel, the sparkle of clear water poured from the jugs down into irrigation channels that fed the land. In the villages, at communal ponds, women washed clothes while boys splashed water on the backs of black water buffalo. Naked, brown toddlers played in the dust by their doorsteps or in the fields at their mother's feet. Women and young girls, clay jugs balanced on their hips, waited their turn to lower a bucket into the village well. After traveling through Afghanistan where women were seldom allowed in public, it was a pleasure to see wives and daughters, dressed in bright colors, out and about, doing their domestic chores.

We passed groups of schoolchildren seated in the dirt under the shade of a banyan tree. While the students concentrated on their lessons, their teacher squatted nearby, waving the buzzing flies away with a paper fan. In the heat of midday, men lounged in front of their dry-mud cottages on charpoys, bed frames laced with hide strips. More than once, we passed an enclosure surrounded by a tumbled down wall, the space inside filled with a heap of animal bones and carcasses. Scores of vultures hovered nearby or tore at the shreds of decomposing meat that clung to the bones. Mangy dogs slunk around the perimeter, waiting for more animal remains to be added to the pile.

Delhi boasted the only tourist campground in India, a fenced-in lot at the convergence of two main roads near the center of New Delhi, not far from the gate to the old walled city. Tom and I explored and did the inevitable chores only possible in a big city. I wore my new sari, convinced my efforts to blend into the culture would be appreciated. I don't know exactly how the locals reacted to me, an obviously western lady, dressed in a cheap sari. Whatever they thought, I never felt the sting of criticism or angry looks.

First, mail and an American meal in the U.S. Embassy cafeteria. At their bookstore, I purchased *Fodor's Guide to India* and a copy of *Indian Cookery* by Dharamjit Singh. Published in Britain, this cookbook became my introduction to authentic Indian cooking. At the Red Fort, we hired a guide for five *rupees* (50 cents) to explain the history and important details of this luxurious palace from the Mogul Empire. One afternoon, we walked through the exhibits of the Asia '72 Expo, where crowds of city folk swarmed past exposed iron rebar protruding from the concrete floor, a hazard that would fail any safety inspection in California.

The streets of India's capital were a constant jam of pedestrians, pedicabs, and bullock carts. Shops with living quarters above lined the streets. Saris dried in the breeze on balcony railings and charpoys hung from pegs on the outer walls to clear the limited floor space during the daytime. Enclosed wooden stalls on the sidewalk offered pedestrians a cool drink of water dispensed from a spouted brass container.

One afternoon, we walked by a building under construction, a surprisingly modern design. Workmen swept the bare concrete floor with brooms and shoveled up concrete debris. Others unloaded panes of glass from a nearby truck and carried them into the site. Tom introduced himself as an American engineer to the man in charge and asked about the project. "It will be a fine arts theater and music center," the man explained. "It will seat eight hundred people and have practice studios on the upper floors." He was the glass contractor and he waved his arms proudly to encompass the glass-walled lobby, where his workers installed sheets of plate glass. "We must work fast," he said. "A Ravi

Shankar concert is scheduled for the grand opening in two weeks."

Tom became cranky when he was hungry, and after only a few hours without nourishment, he needed a snack, so our tourist days were punctuated by local treats. At a stand near the Red Fort, we bought deep-fried samosas, small turnovers filled with cumin and potatoes or spicy lentils. At a stand-up counter in the old city, we sampled tandoori lamb kebabs with freshly made naan bread.

My search for a better sari led us to an elegant shop that catered to a wealthy clientele. Well-lit and air-conditioned, the interior was lined with shelves, each filled with stack after stack of silk saris in every color imaginable, the borders woven of gold thread. A low platform covered with spotless, white, cotton fabric ran the length of the room in front of the shelves of folded silk. Several salesmen sat cross-legged on the platform and spread selected saris for their lady customers, who sat on a low bench in front of the platform. The women fingered the goods to test the fabric's quality and haggled over prices. Tom asked the cost of one particularly rich sari, a length of gold and pink silk. "Six hundred and fifty rupees," the salesman told us. Tom made a quick calculation in his notebook and pointed to his answer. Seventy-five dollars US! On our budget, that was a fortune. We asked if they had cotton saris and were directed upstairs to stacks of brightly colored cotton garments and the heavily taxed saris of polyester blends. I found a soft cotton sari, the lightness of a batiste baby smock, printed with a dark green pattern and spots of orange, edged with a printed border. For a total of 36 rupees ($4.00 US) it was mine!

From Delhi, we headed to Agra, the home of the Taj Mahal, where we stayed at our first PWD (Public Works Department) Rest House, or Dak bungalow. These enclosed compounds were originally built in the late nineteenth century by the British colonial administration to offer a safe and clean overnight sanctuary for traveling government officials. Still maintained by the Indian government, they usually included a pleasant, shady garden, a bungalow with rooms for travelers, a hose bib, and a cold-water bathing room. A watchman let us into the compound and collected the fee, as much as twenty cents, though often free. It was possible to free-camp in India without danger but we preferred the PWD compounds. No matter how deserted the countryside seemed in the evening, we inevitably woke up surrounded by a ring of curious children, village dogs, and free-roaming cattle. When Tom went out to dump the green bucket, curious boys trailed behind him, only to jump back in disgust.

Though we visited several other Mogul sites in and near Agra, our main destination was the Taj Mahal, a monument to love built by Shah Jahan as a tomb for his beloved. When we walked under the arched, red stone entrance, the domed, white marble tomb stood before us, glowing in the sun. We strolled hand in hand between the reflecting pools, circled the exterior of the mausoleum and admired the lacy walls inlaid with semi-precious stones. The visual experience was breathtaking, the beauty of the monument unmatched. Young Indian tourists ignored signs that forbade making noise and called for respectful silence. Their loud yells created echoes that bounced around the stone walls inside. Tom and I lingered behind the monument to soak up the view of the Jumna River, a wide expanse of sand and blue water with a village in the distance. Later, we sat close together on a stone bench near the entrance gate as the long shadows cast by the two towers moved across the marble platform in the setting sun. As the evening descended, a full moon rose into the star-studded sky above the Taj Mahal. The grounds were finally silent and empty. We walked in the bright moonlight and kissed in the shadow of one of the white stone towers.

The next morning, on the way out of town, we saw four, bearded holy men, dressed in saffron robes, traveling with their elephant. The huge beast was adorned with bells that jangled as he lumbered along. One of the monks walked while stroking the elephant's flapping ear, another strode behind with the tail in his hand. I was reminded of the parable of the blind men and the elephant in which six sightless wise men describe the beast based on what part of the animal they touched. It seemed the perfect story to explain the varied impressions of people who travel across the Indian subcontinent. Some see only the poverty. Others are enchanted by the colors and culture. The spiritual may see only the sweep of Buddhism or Hindu rituals. A lucky few are able to actually touch the heart of the people. I wondered what I would remember most.

In order to visit a UNESCO World Heritage site, we turned off the main highway, down a road so narrow we had to pull over onto the dirt shoulder to pass each bullock cart. Khajuraho, built in the tenth century AD, consisted of scattered groupings of Hindu and Jain temples famous for their erotic sculptures. The central group of temples sat on grounds with green lawns, trees and bushes of magenta bougainvillea against which goats, unfazed by the thorns, stood on their hind legs and nibbled the tender parts of the vivid blossoms. The stepped temples, topped by soaring layered roofs, were covered inside and out with sculptures carved into the gray stone. The reliefs, so fully in the round the figures seemed free of the stone, depicted gods and goddesses, voluptuous maidens at all manner of daily tasks, and couples in fond, passionate, and intimate embrace. The frankly depicted erotic poses were athletic and Tom and I studied them at length to puzzle out if they might be possible for mere mortals such as us. Often the full-breasted woman was helped by a maidservant to maintain her position on the member of her partner. The profusion of figures, depicted in various sizes around the temples, lent an almost Baroque feel to the sculptures, though these were definitely not cupids, angels, or ladies resting on clouds.

Returning to the Ganges river valley, yellow fields of mustard gradually evolved into a dry rocky landscape, where old stone forts stood atop jagged escarpments, then turned into a lush land of palm trees and rice paddies. As we neared Benares (also called Varanasi), we passed four men who trotted along the roadside, each balancing on one shoulder the handle of a pallet that supported a body wrapped in a white sheet. Mourners followed behind, some on foot, others in pedicabs.

Varanasi, regarded as the Hindu spiritual capital of India, was listed in our guidebook as the home of almost two thousand temples. The narrow streets of the city were clogged with pilgrims, residents, and cows. Only a block from the Ganges river, we found a safe spot to park our van. For three miles along the riverbank, broad steps called *ghats* led down to the water's edge.

At the stairs, men in loincloths bathed, brushed their teeth, or performed religious ablutions. Children frolicked and swam about, though never far from the edge, and modest women poured water over their heads while fully clothed in saris. The best way to view the activity of Varanasi was from the river. We were immediately approached by a boatman, a muscular, pot-bellied man who pulled the oars of his boat with strength and spoke rudimentary English. He pointed, smiled, and shared basic information in simple language as we glided along the water in the warm December sun.

We passed two sections set aside for laundry. Men and women beat clothes on smooth rocks, and long ropes draped with vividly colored pants and saris crisscrossed the area. Laundry that found no space on the lines was spread on the stone banks. At another spot, water buffalo wallowed, only their heads and shoulders showing, while their owners scrubbed their backs. We floated by a bevy of anchored boats, sturdy and colorfully painted fishermen's quarters. Our boatman pointed to one and claimed it was the home of "hippies."

The bathing ghats were crowded with people. They lathered up with soap, scrubbed their bodies and their hair, rubbed their heels on the rough stone steps as if they were pumice, and rinsed in the river water with great splashes and gurgles. The larger ghats were used by everyone while others were set aside for a specific group or organization. Several of the bathing ghats had semi-enclosed structures the size of a shower stall where modest, upper caste women could bathe. A ghat reserved only for women was alive with hundreds of gossiping bathers in colorful saris, more boatloads of women continually arriving.

Varanasi had two burning ghats reserved as spots for the cremation of bodies. At the main location, several fires burned brightly. On one of the pyres, amid the smoke and yellow flames, a foot had come free of the shroud and stuck out, gradually blackening as it burned. Another pyre was laid nearby. Cords of wood were stacked in an orderly manner while two bodies wrapped in cloth awaited their turn. Our guide told us women were shrouded in red, men wrapped in white. The open cremations were strangely peaceful and free of any odor other than the smoky aroma of burning wood.

After the excursion, we climbed the stairs where women squatted to sell red powders used to paint the soles of hands and feet or imprint the red forehead dot of auspiciousness. Walking back to the van, we passed shops where vendors sat on platforms next to the street, encircled by displays of bangles, incense, lacquered toys, or flowers. A line of beggars, bowls held in both hands, asked for alms, while cows ambled past. A holy man, one of the millions of wandering ascetics in India, strode by us completely nude, clean from his bath in the Ganges and pushing a bicycle. His image was quite different from others we had seen along the highway—thin, dusty men dressed in loincloths, their hair matted, a begging bowl hung from a string at their waist and a trident walking stick in hand.

In spite of rough road conditions, I managed to read parts of our *Fodor's Guide of India* and shared the information with Tom as he clutched the wheel, his eyes always looking ahead for problems. "This state, Bihar, is one of the most populated areas in all of India," I told him. "There's an average of eight hundred people per square mile!"

"I believe that!" Tom responded as he tried to avoid the dozens of bicycles and the carts pulled by camels.

For a time, we drove parallel to a narrow-gauge railroad line and overtook two trains, each a couple of wooden carriages pulled by a small, coal-burning locomotive that spewed smoke and embers into the air. I leaned out the window and waved to the Indians who filled the cars and clung precariously to the doors and exterior to catch the air.

The road was lined with palms. High in the palm fronds, clay jars were wired to the trunks below a gash that dripped sap, and I found a reference in our guidebook to an alcoholic drink made from palm sap. Farmers harvested golden stalks of ripe rice, and their women threshed the grain and spread it on mats to dry. At the edge of many fields, we saw a type of man-powered irrigation device constructed of a long, limber bamboo pole balanced over a forked, slingshot-shaped section of an old tree limb. One end of the bamboo pole was weighted with a huge lump of dried clay and, from the other slender end of the pole, a bucket tied to a rope hung down. A farmer would pull down the high end of the pole and dip the bucket into a nearby well. With the help of the heavy mud counterweight, he would then lift the dripping container, swing it over, and pour the water into a nearby irrigation canal.

On Christmas day, at a PWD Dak bungalow shaded by a gigantic tree, we settled in for a day of rest. Breakfast featured nut pancakes and fresh papaya. For our evening meal, I pulled out our only can of "Banquet" chicken. The bird, not much bigger than a large Cornish game hen, slid whole from the quart-sized can. I made gravy from the juices and a can of English mushrooms, reconstituted a German package of dried green beans, and cooked a pseudo stuffing of rice and herbs. We ended the meal with our last two shots of Drambuie and a dessert of homemade candied walnuts. It was a nostalgic meal, and thoughts of the goose and red cabbage my family would be sharing at home made me a little homesick.

Though we missed our families, especially Mike and Michelle at this holiday time, Tom and I agreed India was all we had hoped—the color, the sun, exotic sights, magnificent temples, and forts. We had watched monkeys and bears dance for coins under the watchful eye of a trainer. We had marveled at a snake charmer seated in the dust on the sidewalk as he blew a thin tune on a gourd flute while his cobra swayed languidly out of a woven basket.

There had also been sights that depressed or saddened us. The scrawny cows, the crowds and congestion in the cities, the carcasses and vultures, but most of all, the children with dirty hands, ragged clothes, and thick mucus draining from their noses. There had been beggars— women lining the streets in Varanasi, men with atrophied legs who scooted around on padded hands and knees, and children with mental deficiencies led by a parent who begged for coins. In those days, almost fifty years ago and well before the technological revolution, India was, in almost every way, a Third World Country with primitive infrastructure and an enormous population, most in poverty.

Yet, in spite of all this, we loved India. It was different from anywhere else we had traveled, more exotic than North Africa, poorer and more densely populated than Central America, and in many ways, more beautiful and filled with history than Europe. With each day, we gained new insight into the way the people of India lived and loved, thought and died. Our journey would influence our view of the world and humankind for the rest of our lives.

Chapter 20

Mountains and Danish Friends

The morning after Christmas, we awoke in the warm, flat lowlands of India. By evening, we were in Nepal in the foothills of the Himalayas, lush with bamboo, large-leafed forest trees, and bananas, on our way to Kathmandu.

The one hundred miles of torturous, two-lane roads to the capital of Nepal would take us seven hours to drive. We traveled upward, curling around innumerable hairpin turns cut into the mountain slopes. No bridges or tunnels shortened the distance or straightened out the curves. The road was a long ribbon laid along the contours of the hills. Almost every slope was cut and layered into terraced fields, like gigantic stairways designed by a drunken architect. Each crest in the road revealed another terraced valley and layer after layer of mountains. In the hazy blue distance, the snow-capped, high Himalayas stretched across the horizon, an entire row of famous mountains, Mount Everest, so far away it was indiscernible from the others.

In India, we had gotten used to seeing men and women carrying burdens on their heads, a method well-suited for flat country. But in the mountainous terrain of Nepal, the native people carried their burdens either Chinese fashion from the two ends of a shoulder pole or in a conical basket on their back with a woven strap that transferred the weight to their forehead. The village women no longer wore saris but wore a wrapped skirt, topped by a long-sleeved blouse. They often added a wide strip of fabric wound in layers around their waist into which they tucked small items and even chubby, chapped-cheeked babies. All this allowed for hands-free hiking along the narrow, mountain pathways.

We crossed one summit after another, past isolated villages and tumbling streams. At one point, only slightly off the road, we were surprised to encounter a parked, white caravan (trailer) with Danish license plates. This was an odd sight—a lone trailer, no car, no evidence of passengers. We drove on, wondering what disaster had caused it to be abandoned in such a lonely spot. From the crest of a final mountain pass, we saw the city of Kathmandu spread out below across a mist-shrouded valley. Before nightfall, we found our hotel, the enclosure already populated by several vans.

Later, when we were in bed, we heard a commotion at the gate as a tardy guest arrived. We peeked out of our window to see a Land Rover towing the white trailer we had seen stranded along the road. They parked not far from us and all was quiet again. The next day, we learned the latecomers were a Danish family, a man, his wife and their children, three boys ages sixteen, fourteen, and ten, and a girl fifteen years old. We wondered at their bravery to journey so far with their family. We had found we were not always the most adventurous travelers.

Tom and I were eager to explore Kathmandu. The old, central area was a maze of mud-brick buildings with carved, wooden window frames and veranda posts, the streets mainly hard-packed dirt. All around were piles of crumbling stones and pagodas. It was the king's birthday and crowds of people filled the center of the city as there was to be a parade. In the main square, Tom positioned himself at the corner of a building on a high step, and I stood on the doorjamb of the van, an equally fine vantage point. One group after another moved through the square at widely spaced intervals—villagers in traditional costumes, bands with cymbals, flutes, and long curved horns, floats transported on truck beds, men twirling flags on long poles, and a grand finale of an animated cloth dragon. Among it all, a huge, muscular bull hobbled around the square on a gimpy leg and ate remnants of food garbage left by the crowds.

The next day, the old square was less crowded. Still, at every turn, we were bombarded by exotic sights perfect for Tom's telescopic camera lens and the stuff of my dreams. Small shops lined the street-level selling beans, rice, strange barks, colorful powders, soap, or canned goods. We looked into a dark cubbyhole where a tailor bent over a hand-powered machine, stitching a jacket. Women squatted near fountains and washed clothes in round metal tubs, bathed wrapped to the waist in wet fabric, or sat in the sun nearby to comb their black, glistening hair. On a raised stone platform surrounded by pagoda roofed temples, grain was spread to dry in the sun. In one alleyway, women laid down dry grass so passing cars could do their threshing. We saw countless hairy pigs, some so pregnant their bellies scraped the ground. Near the river, temples of all sizes stood next to shops that sold curios and hashish.

The weather in Kathmandu was sunny—warm in the daytime and crisply cold at night. On the last day of December, I stayed in the Turtle while Tom rented a bicycle and explored on his own. I wrote letters,

Two Women of Nepal: (left) typical village dress and (right) traditional costume of a Tibetan refugee.

washed my hair, and prepared a pilaf of rice and yellow lentils, a recipe from my new Indian cookbook.

We had become friendly with the Danish family. The parents and the two oldest children, Mas and Linnea, spoke proficient English. The youngest boy, Bjorn, was a pistol, always laughing and eager to make mischief. Tom referred to him as "Little Fart," an affectionate nickname we were confident no one actually understood. Like his mother, the middle boy, Karl, was quiet and studious, too shy to practice English, which he had only studied for a year. Anders, the father, told us New Year's Eve was a special time in Denmark and invited us to join their family celebration. Tom and I brought popcorn and they served tea and cakes. Before midnight, we were back in our own van to celebrate a more intimate New Year's Eve with a flurry of kisses.

Tom and I greeted 1973 by dipping our toes into a five-star lifestyle. Nepal was slowly being discovered as an adventure destination. Not far from our compound, the Soaltee, a luxury hotel, stood amid land-scaped grounds. With a view across the valley to the distant Himalayas, it offered wealthy travelers spacious rooms, a world-class restaurant, a pool, and gracious hospitality.

Our intention was to ask permission to fill our water tank at one of the hotel's garden spigots. Tom entered the lobby with our large, white, plastic water jug and was directed to the kitchen in the basement where he could fill the container at the room service area from a filtered water tap. He returned to the van and poured the clear water into our tank. "They said to come back for more. As much as we need," he told me. "You've got to come with me this time. It's fabulous."

We walked through the lobby with its marble floors, polished wood, and gilt-framed mirrors to the service elevator. In the basement, I glimpsed the kitchen with special stations for different types of food—salads in one place, seafood and poultry in another, and separate areas for Indian, Nepalese, and Chinese preparations. Dozens of cooks washed and chopped vegetables, tossed salad, cleaned fish, and cut up meat.

After our water tank was topped off, we wandered through the arcade of shops filled with jewels, silks, carpets, and embroidered bags. I scanned the restaurant menu, lusting after the gourmet dishes priced well above our budget. A drink would be an affordable New Year's treat. We sat on high stools at the bar and Tom ordered a beer. I was tempted by fresh lemonade with ice. Wow! The gregarious English bartender set dishes of toasted yellow lentils and salted peanuts on the counter for us and chatted while we sipped.

That evening, we tried the Utsee, a restaurant our bartender friend had recommended for its Tibetan specialties. We could not understand the menu, so we pointed to several items. Soon the waiter brought us a table full of dumplings similar to wonton, each cooked a different way. Dumplings in soup, steamed dumplings, and dumplings sautéed in butter—all a mixture of savory pork encased in tender noodle dough. We continued with two stir-fried meat and vegetable dishes and ended with a Tibetan dessert of sweet rice with a sauce of fruits, and a pot of green tea. We managed to finish this surfeit of food and waddled out after paying the bill for $2.10!

We hoped to travel the hundred plus miles across Nepal to Pokhara, but our plans were dashed the next day. At the Office of the Road Builders, we learned they could issue only two permits per day. Travel was restricted to an assigned day and the first available date was more than a week in the future. Disappointed, we tried to lift our spirits with consumerism. Delighted by the low prices, our stash of souvenirs grew—a soft, cream-colored woolen shawl for me, several polished stones (agates, moonstones, and opals), old coins (for Tom), and two burgundy and purple, cotton Nepalese saris. Charmed by the way the young girls wound red yarn into their braids, I bought several similar hair adornments for myself.

Nepal was known at the time as the main escape valve for Tibetan refugees who fled the Chinese regime in their home country. In 1950, the People's Liberation Army marched into Tibet and took over the government. The first peace agreement allowed an autonomous administration headed by the Dalai Lama. However, in 1955, that agreement was rewritten to exclude the Dalai Lama's government and create a fully communist system. Several years of unrest and uprisings followed. Under a threat to his life by Chinese forces, the Dalai Lama fled to India in 1959. Between 1959 and 1961, of the more than 80,000 refugees who followed their spiritual leader, over 20,000 Tibetans traveled no farther than Nepal where they settled in refugee camps hoping to eventually return home. By the time of our visit to Kathmandu, the refugee camp in Patan, a short drive from the capital, was well established, run on a communal basis, and a favorite excursion for western visitors.

At the refugee center, we were greeted by a swarm of ragged children dressed in long, woolen Tibetan robes. They clustered around us to sell bangles and other trinkets, but within minutes we were deserted in favor of tourists in a black sedan with a tour guide. I had worn my Nepalese sari skirt and twisted red yarn and tassels into my blond braid in hopes of not looking like a rich tourist and I had succeeded. Tom and I headed for the carpet-weaving workshop. One entire room was devoted to spinning and twisting the yarns needed to make carpets. Another was filled with looms that held colorful works in progress depicting designs of Chinese characters or dragons.

The bigger carpets were worked by teams of two to five men and women, a finished carpet with the same design draped over the top of the looms. As the first rows were woven, the artisans sat on the floor, a basket of colorful yarns beside them. We watched the weavers' fingers fly as they twisted the yarns around the warp, and with a long, knitting needle-sized rod, held the yarn out in a series of loops. When a section was done, the weavers pounded the yarns down firmly, cut the threads from the rod, pounded again, and trimmed the nap with large shears. Slowly these pounded lines of yarn tufts rose upward on the loom. When the work got too high to reach, the weavers added one cushion after the other to sit on, their pile growing taller so they were always level with the work. By the end, the weavers sat cross-legged on a tower of pillows.

Next door, the communal shop sold carpets, jackets, sweaters, tea bowls of wood and silver, prayer wheels, prayer flags, and small statues of Buddha. Across the road, two-story brick buildings formed a circle around an open ground, where puppies frolicked in the dry grass. Carpets hung from the second story balconies. Women and children approached us with items to sell, everything from belts to old coins, from rugs no bigger than a doormat to yarn hair ties. One man pointed to a carpet suspended from a balcony and indicated we should follow him upstairs. In a corner room, he displayed two matched carpets, each with a creamy background and a pair of dragons in three shades of blue. They were beautiful, though totally different from Iranian carpets, and the price the man quoted was low. Tom and I whispered together. Perhaps these rugs might be a valuable investment. However, we would have to become vendors ourselves to get the needed cash.

As we left, we noticed the grassy central area, once the domain of puppies and children, was filling with adults who streamed from the weavers' workshop and the surrounding buildings. They crowded into the gathering space where a man in a suit stood on a wooden platform. An important meeting was about to begin.

The next morning, we drove to the central market in Kathmandu to sell "trade goods." Mas, the oldest Danish boy, came along, intrigued by the idea of selling stuff. The old shock absorbers Tom had hoarded proved unsalable. However, his camera tripod, used only twice in the last year, brought eighteen dollars. Then we got twenty-eight dollars for Tom's binoculars. Richer than the previous day, we returned to the Tibetan Refugee Center. It was immediately apparent that the area was strangely quiet. No children hawked trinkets. No carpets were displayed from balconies. When we knocked on our carpet man's door, no one answered. Near a closed curio shop, we saw a girl who had showed us a coin the day before and we asked if she still had it.

"No. No coin." She kept glancing sideways as she spoke, as if she were afraid of being seen with to us. "Yesterday. Big meet-up," she said in a low voice. "No more sell. Only at shop." She pointed across the square to the approved communal store. "Big fine we sell. Big fine."

We were stuck with a relative fortune in Nepalese currency unusable in India. Tom, Mas, and I returned to the streets of Kathmandu to spend our Nepalese rupees, an almost impossible task. We added two more Nepalese saris, a couple of ancient coins, a matched set of polished opals, three tiny moonstones, and spices to our stash. Still we had money left. We would eat out for the rest of our time in Nepal.

On January 7, we reluctantly left Kathmandu. Twelve days was not enough, but we had two-thirds of India left to see and our Indian visa had a four-month time limit. We caravanned with the Danish family as we had become fond of their children, and as a result, felt protective of them. Tom was concerned about the condition of their trailer's hitch, which kept breaking, the reason it had been temporarily abandoned on the mountain road. Anders repeatedly had the hitch repaired but Tom foresaw continuing difficulties.

Traveling behind the Land Rover/trailer, our progress was slow, but by nightfall, we made it to the PWD where Tom and I had spent Christmas. Tom was well into a cold and coughed most of that night. We blamed our frequent colds on a combination of being rundown and germs. Kids with runny noses, endemic in India and Nepal, touched everything, including our hands and clothing. The colds often put a damper on our energy.

Tom insisted he was OK to drive the next morning. The day was an agony of slow progress along the Ganges river, up across the edge of the central plateau, past red rock outcroppings and hundreds of green parrots perched on telephone wires, and through the maze of streets in the town of Gaya. All along the way, we stayed in sight of the swaying Danish caravan. Finally, we arrived at Bodh Gaya, the place of Buddha's enlightenment and a site of pilgrimage. A cluster of stalls surrounded an impressive Buddhist temple complex. Across the street, a PWD Dak bungalow offered a garden and a safe place for all of us to relax. As soon as he turned off the engine, Tom crawled in back and collapsed on the bed.

While Tom rested, I joined Anders and his four children to explore. I bought bananas, oranges, and a papaya, as well as tomatoes, eggs, and chilies. We nibbled on cauliflower *pokora* and spicy potato *samosas*. In front of the shrine a man beat a drum and chanted. The air was filled with the sounds of bird calls, beggars' cries, and the murmur of pilgrims' prayers.

When I returned to the van, Tom looked miserable. I felt his forehead and fever radiated through my fingers. I made him undress and get under the sheet, dosed him with aspirin, and set a glass of water nearby. No better in the morning, Tom gratefully remained in bed, sleeping and drinking fluids. I filled the day with the usual downtime activities, including washing my hair under an outdoor faucet in the garden. By evening, Tom's temperature had broken. He ate scrambled eggs and a banana and suggested a game of Scrabble.

We remained in Bodh Gaya another day to allow Tom to recuperate. In the evening, he and I walked to the temple where hundreds of oil candles were lit, a wonderland of flickering lights. Spotlights shone on the carved stone tower, a reverse silhouette against the dark, starry sky. Hundreds of monks gathered near the altar and in stately pairs, joined together for rituals of prayer and chanting.

Traveling with the Danish family changed our style. Each morning the two families would agree on a final destination and the route we would take. We no longer stayed in sight of each other, but Tom and I always knew they were ahead of us and if they encountered trouble with their trailer hitch, we would find them. On the second day out of Bodh Gaya, our agreed route went around a large industrial town, the home of the famous maker of Tata trucks. Fearing difficulties due to congestion and road construction, we planned to stay close together as we navigated the city. When we reached the place where we expected to find a new bypass, construction workers flagged us over and conveyed the message that the road ahead was closed. They pointed toward a detour directly through the center of town.

Once we entered the narrow streets of the city, our van and the Danish rig were engulfed by crowds celebrating a local holiday. Groups of men, beating drums and drunk on the hypnotic sound (or maybe on palm wine), danced and chanted. Each group had its own votive shrine filled with painted gods and goddesses and bedecked with flowers. The crowds swamped us and we lost sight of the Danish caravan for a few minutes. On the other side of the city, the narrow detour continued, crossing riverbeds via low, concrete wash bridges designed to allow the heavy rains of the monsoon season to flow over them. On one of these, the Danish trailer hit a bump and what Tom had feared happened—the trailer hitch fractured in two places. Ahead a fence surrounded a group of buildings. Anders carefully maneuvered his rig to the gate of what turned out to be a government town for the workers of an atomic energy plant. Most of the next day we waited at the facility's guest house while Anders got the hitch rewelded yet again.

Our group moved south, headed toward the low-lying coastal areas of East Bengal and the state of Orissa. Coconut palms lined the roads and waterways, rice paddies, pools, canals, rivers, and the expanse of the Bay of Bengal.

At the town of Cuttack, we camped in the yard of a tax office. That evening, Tom and Anders inspected the new welds on the trailer's hitch and discovered they were already starting to crack and separate. Tom took charge. He had been muttering for days that the root cause of the problem was the different suspension of the two Danish vehicles. The Land Rover, designed for rough roads had high, stiff suspension so it took the roads like a pogo stick, bouncing up and down on its shocks. The trailer, on the other hand, had a single axle and soft suspension. It traveled the road like a wheeled teeter-totter. The two vehicles constantly fought each other and the stress was carried to the trailer's hitch. Tom convinced Anders to let him redesign the connection and have it fabricated and installed. He had the tongue of the hitch widened and added flexible bolts that would allow for more movement between the vehicles. If the bolts broke, they could easily be replaced by a cache Anders would need to have on hand. Tom was sure the new repair would solve the problem.

We missed our freedom but agreed to stay with Anders and his family a while longer. Puri, a pilgrimage center and beach resort, was close by and another rest stop would be welcome. Our tourist bungalow enclosure was next to the beach, the sand at our doorstep. Within minutes Tom was in the surf, swimming and skimboarding in the nude. I was not far behind him. Though I didn't remove the bottom of my bikini, I swam out into the warm water, the small waves lapping against the sensitive skin of my bare breasts. This idyllic lifestyle of swimming, sunbathing, skimboarding, napping, nibbling fruit at noon, and eating fresh fish at the tourist restaurant kept us happy for two days.

On the third day, after our swim, we took Linnea, the Danish daughter, and headed for Puri's famous temple. It had been a long time since I had enjoyed the company of another female who shared my interest in saris and bangles.

The main street up to the temple was lined with beggars. Rows of lepers sat in the dust along the street, their bandaged limbs outstretched. Their calls for alms filled the air. I have to admit, after experiencing India for more than a month, I was inured to misery on display. It may have been hard-hearted, but I could pass beggars without agonizing over their plight or longing to drop coins into their outstretched hands. I knew by this time a few coins would make no dent in the causes of poverty in India.

Near the temple, shops sold fabric, saris, glass bangles, bronzeware, toys, and other temptations to get pilgrims to part with their rupees. Linnea and I looked at stacks of fine cotton and silk saris, and I showed her how to wrap the lengths of cloth around her slim hips. From the rainbow

Linnea and I shop for saris in Puri, India.

piles of saris, I selected one of fine, pure-white batiste trimmed with an embroidered blue border and blue fringe on one end. It would add elegance to my wardrobe.

The next day, again with Linnea for company, we drove to Konarak to see an ancient temple, now only a ruin. A huge stone structure, it stood atop a sandy hill surrounded by coconut palms. Most impressive were the animal sculptures, including two gigantic elephants, each carved from a single boulder.

Most of our planned route to Madras went through the state of Andhra Pradesh where news told of civil disturbances. We expected several intense days of driving with no stops, except to sleep in a protected Dak enclosure. Only a few miles into the state, we encountered two other Volkswagen vans and stopped to discuss the situation. A young German couple drove a Westfalia camper, and a single man in another van traveled with them. It was decided that, considering the riots and upheaval, we would all stick together. Tom and I led the group—three Volkswagen vans and one Range Rover pulling a trailer.

Our second morning together, we entered the labyrinth of narrow streets in a town. I peered into the rearview mirror every few minutes in an effort to keep the other vans and the Land Rover in sight amidst the heavy crowds of people, pedicabs, trucks, and bullock carts.

"Wait. Pull over a minute. I can't see them anymore," I told Tom.

"There's no place to stop." But he stopped in the middle of the street and waited. People and carts flowed around us. "I can't stay here," he said. "Do you see them yet?"

"No. Nothing."

An elephant with a man in a dhoti astride the beast's broad shoulders lumbered past. Pedestrians slowed and stared at us. One exuberant youth even slapped his palm on the side of the van.

"Fuck it. I have to keep moving." Tom pressed carefully on the accelerator and returned to the flow of traffic. I continually looked down side streets and behind us for a glimpse of our friends. There was nothing we could do beyond hope they were together and we would find them later. Once free of the city's congestion, we continued to drive slowly, constantly turning to look behind us. Finally, we sighted the Danes and the Germans stopped for lunch by the side of the road. "Damn," Tom swore under his breath, "all that worry and they were safe all along."

"Maybe it's time for us to go on our own," I suggested. "You've fixed the hitch and they have the Germans to travel with now. It would be nice not to worry about them every day."

"I agree, just you and me. I've had it with caravanning."

"Me too! You told me months ago—a group is only as strong as its weakest member. Now I know what you meant."

We hugged the Danish children, shook hands with their parents and the Germans, and told them we would see them in Madras. We had enjoyed Mas and Linnea and "Little Fart," the same way we had liked traveling with Mike and Michelle. But we needed to be on our own again, independent and free to consider only each other.

The long drive through the rest of Andhra Pradesh was ahead. In the middle of the afternoon, we approached the city of Rajamundry on the banks of the Godavari River. Surrounded by sugar cane fields, banana plantations, and velvety, green paddies planted with new rice, the town was a cultural center. In other times we would have stopped. However, demonstrators were out in force. Groups of young men carried flags and banners and had set up traffic barricades. With energetic waving and shouting, they forced cars and trucks to drive on the wrong side of the road. In India, as a result of long years of English colonial rule, the right side was (and still is) the wrong side. Changing sides slowed traffic, caused confusion, and created a potential for accidents. At first, Tom and I found the situation mildly amusing. After all, we were used to driving on the right-hand side and our vehicle was designed for it. However, passage became increasingly difficult. Indian trucks, cars, oxcarts, bicycles, and pedestrians kept switching back and forth from right to left. It was total bedlam.

Even beyond the city, Tom remained on constant alert through the unpredictable and chaotic traffic. The narrow highway was often blocked by chanting crowds. After several tense hours, we arrived at a PWD bungalow protected by a high wall and washed the stress of the afternoon off with buckets of cold water in the enclosed bathing room. The Danish family and the German contingent arrived an hour later, followed almost immediately by a platoon of soldiers who set up camp and turned the compound into army operations headquarters. Tom and I couldn't wait to get on the road the next morning. We woke at dawn and drove out of the area as fast as possible, relieved to cross into the politically calm state of Tamil Nadu. Not far ahead, the city of Madras (now known as Chennai), offered a YWCA. The German and Danish travelers straggled in after 10:00 p.m.

We had all survived the grueling trip.

Chapter 21

Through Better and Worse, We Are a Couple

Madras was the entryway to a month in paradise and naturally, it was also a mail stop. The morning after we arrived, we went directly to the U.S. consulate, only to find it closed to commemorate the funeral of President Lyndon Johnson held that day in Washington, DC. The duty officer assigned to deal with emergency issues searched for our mail and returned to the lobby with a fat packet of letters. The officer, who introduced himself as Kevin, was about our age and on impulse, he invited us to join him for lunch. His home was beautifully furnished with overhead fans that whirred quietly. The meal was served on the open veranda by the houseman—onion soup, shrimp and egg salad, and chocolate brownies. Kevin had been the Dean of Men at the University of the Americas in Mexico City the same year I attended. What a small world!

Kevin drew us a map to the Madras branch of the British retailer, Marks and Spencer, a modern supermarket full of imported foods, as well as Indian cooking ingredients. After my shopping spree there, I prepared sandwiches of crisp English bacon, thick slices of Indian vine-ripened tomatoes, and Danish sprouts, a meal that, in spite of its international components, made us nostalgic for home.

Madras harbor was a perfect place to while away a leisurely Sunday afternoon. A tree-lined boulevard ran the length of the beach park where middle-class couples strolled. Families clustered around blankets spread on the grass and nibbled from metal dishes filled with curry, dahl, pickles, and mounds of rice. There was a marine aquarium, a children's carousel with brightly painted horses, and vendors hawking snacks and candies. Tom and I strolled among the happy families, past fishing boats and piles of driftwood strewn on the sand.

On our last day in Madras, we checked for mail and said goodbye to Kevin. After talking for an hour in his office, we insisted we needed to get on the road, but Kevin implored us, "Stay another night and join me for dinner!"

Tom and I looked at each other, an unspoken question passing between us.

"Please stay," Kevin urged. "I can get my cook to prepare a traditional Indian meal. He's a great chef."

Of course, Tom knew it would be impossible to decline with the promise of local cuisine. The rest of the afternoon, visions of curry danced through my mind. We took a cold, bucket shower at the YWCA bungalow and dressed—Tom in his embroidered shirt and me in my new white and blue sari. I was pleased with the swish of the front folds of fabric as we walked up the porch steps to the cool veranda.

The meal matched my expectations. First an exceptional prawn curry, creamy with coconut milk and the perfect heat from chilies and spices. A tomato, onion, and green chili salad, rice, and yellow dahl scented with asafetida were presented in small metal and wooden dishes from which we could ladle our own portions. There were also two kinds of chutney—a chunky, sweet mango chutney and an unbelievably hot chili paste.

A side dish of bananas and coconut offered a sweet contrast. In the center of the dining table, the cook set a platter heaped with fried *pappadams*, a thin, crisp Indian cracker bread made from gram (chickpea) flour.

When we had eaten as much as we could manage, we moved to the living room and settled into comfortable chairs. Kevin poured us each a glass of amber-colored port. When the houseman brought a plate of sliced apples and a chunk of cheese, we knew we had come full circle and were again in Western mode.

I took a sip of my wine and the warmth of the sweet liquor relaxed me. Curious about signs we'd seen, I turned to Kevin. "We've noticed banners across the boulevards that encourage birth control and vasectomy," I said. "Is the advertising having any impact on overpopulation here?"

Kevin frowned. "There is some effect. The better educated understand the importance of lowering the birth rate. But in poor families, the campaign is gaining little traction, though many women would prefer smaller families. Repeated childbirth takes a toll on their health. But in this society, women are afraid to practice birth control without their husbands' permission."

"Why are the men against it?" I asked.

"Ah, Indian men," Kevin said. He shrugged as if it were a hopeless case. "Farmers want sons to help with the work. Even city dwellers believe a man without a son is only half a man. And they're afraid vasectomy will affect their prowess. It'll take a mammoth amount of education to change their minds."

Tom leaned forward. "What about health care for pregnant women and for babies?" he asked. "We see swarms of young children on the streets. Always with runny noses. And more than a few with disabilities like club foot and cleft palate that would be corrected at home."

"The Indian government is trying," Kevin said. "But the problems are overwhelming. It'll probably take a few generations to build up the health care system."

"Before we came to India, Katie and I intended to one day adopt a child from Asia. Now we're not so sure. So many children seem to have disabilities and mental deficiencies."

"I know it sounds callous," I added, "but it takes a special kind of person to raise a child with extra needs and I don't think I have what it takes. I can't help but wonder if the children with physical and mental challenges are the result of a lack of prenatal care and poor childhood nutrition."

"These things are certainly a factor," Kevin admitted. "The international community. . . you know, UNICEF and other organizations . . . They help in these areas. But as I said, everything takes time."

Though we ended on a somber note discussing health, education, and population issues, I was pleased to have a conversation with an adult other than Tom, especially a man who knew India and its problems.

South of Madras, we drove along a coastal road, the sea nearby, and followed a sandy track along the seashore where we bought freshly caught fish from a local fisherman. We stopped for the night near the ancient temples of Mahabalipuram. As soon as Tom parked the van at our shaded PWD bungalow compound, I got out my Indian cookbook to prepare fish curry for lunch. With the help of this book, better than a textbook, my repertoire expanded and I learned about Indian cooking. After lunch, we visited one of the temples, a wind-worn creation of stone set on the water's edge.

The tropical heat of a new day woke us early, and we set off on foot along a lagoon under the scattered shade of palm trees. The temples of Mahabalipuram, no longer used for worship, did not attract pilgrims, though they were a popular place for sightseeing. We shared the grounds with a local family, a couple of other westerners, and a busload of schoolgirls. These temples were created from a natural group of pink granite boulders that rose inexplicably from their sandy surroundings. I was in awe of the sculptures of figures—magnificent elephants, mythical beasts, and columns carved in deep relief directly into the sides of

People of Southern India: (left to right) a schoolgirl, a matron of Madras, a businessman, and a fisherman.

the mammoth stones. Later, we drove to another group of five temples individually carved from colossal stones. Near them towered three gargantuan animals—an elephant, a sacred cow, and a lion—each also created from one boulder.

With the sun directly overhead, we sat in a shady area, sipped cold Cokes purchased from a vendor, and watched as two monument keepers and the schoolgirls ate a meal of rice, vegetable curry, and condiments, priced at 1.50 rupees or the equivalent of 15 cents, and served on individual banana leaves. The girls, in matching *salwar kameez* (long tunic shirts and baggy trousers with narrow ankles), ate their lunch using two fingers to scoop it into their mouths.

Tom often repeated the old adage, "Only mad dogs and Englishmen go out in the midday sun" and we tried to keep this saying in mind as we traveled. In the tropical south we rose early, saw whatever there was to see in the morning, drove in the afternoon (or all day), swam when we were near the sea, and finally, bedded down at dusk in a PWD bungalow.

In the Cardamom Hills, acre after acre was planted with coffee bushes shaded by trees to protect the delicate coffee from the strong sun. Other hills were blanketed by closely clipped, green mounds of tea bushes, the slopes twined with narrow footpaths for pickers, all women and girls, who plucked the tender new leaves with their quick fingers.

Amidst the terraces of tea bushes, we happened onto a tea processing plant. When we stopped, an Indian gentleman came out of the two-story structure to greet his unexpected guests. His dark face wreathed in a smile, he offered his hand. "Mr. Patel. I am master tea maker here. I would be pleased to offer you a tour of our facilities."

Tom and I eagerly accepted his offer. "We begin to harvest tea in the cool of the night," he explained. "We finished several hours ago. Now we have started the curing process." Built into the slope of a hill, the upper level of the plant was filled with machines to remove moisture from the freshly picked leaves. Machines downstairs were used for further drying, curing, and mixing. In an adjacent room, we watched as the last of the previous night's harvest was sent through a machine that magnetically pulled out small stems. In the sorting room, we carefully trod past tall hills of tea leaves. Several machines busily shook the tea through screens of various gauges sorting the dry leaves by size. Another machine blew away the last bits of chaff. The area hummed with machine noise and slanted shafts of sunshine danced with tea dust. In the packaging room, foil-lined boxes stood in rows ready to be filled.

Mr. Patel led us to his office and displayed samples of the five grades of tea from the day's production. He was especially proud of his unbroken leaves, the best grade. "These will be exported," he said proudly. "We also export broken leaves. They're good for mixtures and blends. Also, for tea bags which you Americans use." He gestured toward the last three samples on his table. "These are the lesser grades," he explained. "Crumbled or finely broken remnants. We call all three 'dust tea.' We sell most of this type of product in India. The dust brews into a rich, full-bodied tea that can stand up to the addition of milk and sugar. This is how Indians drink tea. We even mix in spices."

"Do you harvest year-round?" Tom asked.

The tea master nodded. "Here, in the Kerala Hills, we have the advantage of year-round growth. But the tea produced here does not reach the premium flavor of mountain teas grown in a cooler climate, as in Darjeeling. There the harvest is seasonal."

I was thrilled to learn so much about tea, my beverage of choice.

"We also grow cardamom on this plantation," the tea master said. "Would you like to see the cardamom shed?"

In the cool building, the air had the fragrance of Christmas cake. A single layer of pale green pods was arranged on drying tables. He picked up one of the pods and cracked the thin, brittle husk between his fingernails to reveal the sticky black, aromatic seeds within. He handed the broken pod to me, and I raised it reverently to my nose, inhaling the sweet aroma. "The pods grow on tendrils, which trail on the surface of the ground," he said. "Picking them is difficult work but not as delicate as tea harvesting."

"At home, in the US, cardamom is in a soft white pod, kind of puffy looking. And it's expensive," I told the tea master.

"I'm not familiar with this," he said.

"I have a few I brought all the way from California."

"I'll get some to show you," Tom said and returned to the van. He came back with several of our white pods in the palm of his hand and offered them to Patel. "A gift for you. To thank you for showing us around."

The tea master inspected the white pods and broke one open with his fingers. I knew the black seeds inside were dryer and less aromatic than his, but he simply sniffed the broken pod and nodded politely. He scooped up a handful of the green cardamom and offered them to me. "A gift to you," he said. "It has been a pleasure to show my work. A pleasure to share it with a lady who enjoys my product."

That week, we traveled almost to the tip of the Indian subcontinent, then turned north along the Malabar Coast of the Indian Ocean. The low wetlands of Kerala surrounded us. The land glistened emerald green and blue, edged by white sand beaches fringed with swaying coconut palms. Grass-green rice paddies were etched with the crisscrossing lines of blue canals, while fishing canoes bobbed on the surface of backwater bays. Workmen in knee-length lungi (sarongs) pushed heavy carts filled with rope and doormats made of coir (coconut fiber) or loaded white, powdery bales of rubber sheets onto boats. As usual, I studied the ways the women of the south wore their saris and how the men folded their wrapped garments to shorten them so the sea breeze would cool their legs. Each night, before I forgot the details of the folds and drapes, I sketched the local way of dress and my pages of colored pencil, "costume" studies multiplied.

When we arrived in Cochin (Kochi), Tom was excited to share a town he had visited several times by ship. The city had been a port since 1341 when a flood carved out a harbor and Arab, Chinese, and European merchants took advantage of the new anchorage. Cochin was broken up into areas separated by waterways, many festooned with giant, wing-like, Chinese-style fishing nets. The old sections of Cochin maintained remnants of an ancient Jewish colony founded in the sixth century B.C. and a Portuguese colony founded a thousand years later. In the Jewish section, we were surprised to see street signs that read "Jew Town." This area was also the district of wholesale spice merchants. On the quay across from the warehouses, great heaps of black peppercorns, ginger root, turmeric root, and cinnamon bark were loaded onto tenders, small boats which took the goods out to anchored ships. I couldn't resist buying spices from one of the merchants and came away with two kilos of peppercorns for a cost of $1.20 US, enough to last for years.

Cochin was unbearably hot in the middle of the day, so we retreated to the Malabar Hotel, where a few rupees got us into their swimming pool. We spent the afternoon in the water and at sunset reclined on lawn chairs, a cool lime drink in hand. The longer we traveled, the more we longed for occasional respites from the discomforts of van life. We anticipated a beach holiday farther north in Goa. A Portuguese colony until 1961, this tiny, new state boasted miles of sandy beaches fringed by palm groves. Goa was known as a haven for van travelers.

Two ferries took us across inland waterways to reach our goal. The first was nothing more than a flat raft pulled by a motor launch, and the second had ramps so steep our overladen van scraped bottom going up the incline. It was dusk when we arrived in Calangute, the only real town in Goa, and almost immediately, we spotted the van of a couple we had met in Afghanistan. We flagged them down and followed them to a spot that would be our home in paradise.

Shaded by several spindly trees and a couple of palms, the site was near the beach, close to a well, a fifteen-minute trek to a market, and not far from several small restaurants. Two van neighbors camped within shouting distance.

Calangute Beach, as yet undiscovered by the tourist mass market, was a Mecca for hippies and druggies of all ages, travelers from France, Germany, America, and Canada, as well as a few Indian tourists on the slum. The Westerners mainly lived in their vans or in rented palm-roofed bungalows for ten to fifty dollars a month. One young Canadian woman had recently given birth to her first child in one of these cottages with only her husband in attendance.

We shared the wells with locals whose shacks were scattered along the sandy hills behind the shore. Our fellow van travelers dressed in sarongs, loincloths, shorts, or nothing at all, sunbathed and swam in the nude, ate in the local restaurants, took drugs, and generally relished the laid-back atmosphere. Tom and I were determined to live the hippie lifestyle, minus the drugs, during our vacation in Goa.

Most of our time was spent on the beach, in the speckled shade near our site, or visiting with our neighbors. On the first day, we drove to a fishermen's market and bought a whole fish that still glistened with seawater. In the falling light of evening, Tom squatted outside the van, our camp lantern in the sand beside him, and cleaned the fish with the help of a small Indian boy who appeared out of the darkness. He was our neighbor as his family lived in a nearby two-room cottage with a palm frond roof. Not quite old enough for school, this child was their youngest. He often scampered over to sit for a moment of pleasure on our folding, canvas camp stool, exactly the right size for him. He was happy and energetic but his persistent cough concerned us. There wasn't much we could do to help as neither of his parents spoke English and they were shy around us. We gave him oranges and hoped he would get better with the addition of expensive citrus to his diet. Another neighbor was an Australian couple who had lived in their bungalow for two years. Their ten-year-old daughter spoke excellent Hindi and played happily with the local children.

The days were sticky and hot, the humidity high. Each night the residual heat filled the van and clung to our skin. Our tray of Danish sprouts shriveled and died in the tropical heat. To catch the ocean breeze at night, we slept with all the windows open, the cloth screens snapped into place to stop bugs. Not long after sunrise, a vendor arrived, a basket of fresh bread on her head, her call waking us. Later, women with eggs, fruit, or sweets came to our spot, hoping to get their share of our money.

We used the well, along with all our neighbors and, as usual, purified the water with chlorine. We did not use the primitive outhouse, which was a walled, concrete block cubicle with a tattered cloth door and an opening in the back where the village pig entered to scavenge. However, with few other options, this was where Tom carried our bucket each morning to empty it. Trash disposal was a classic case of primitive recycling. There was a midden near the outhouse where everyone took their refuse. As soon as a bag or bucket was emptied at the site, the recycling began. Within seconds, dozens of crows swooped down and grabbed any choice scraps. Then, the neighborhood dog bounded over to drag off whatever seemed tasty, followed by chickens that pecked among the debris. Finally, the village pig ambled over to root through whatever remained. This left only papers, bits of cardboard and an occasional jar or can contributed by us Westerners. Cans and unbroken jars were collected for various uses by the local people, and occasionally the papers and other remains were burned. In spite of several families living in this spot, the trash pile never grew.

Mornings and afternoons, we lounged on the wide, sandy beach. Tom, completely nude, skimboarded along the shoreline, while I sat on a towel in my bikini bottom, slathered sunscreen on my bare breasts, read or wrote letters, and ran into the surf to cool off. Fully clothed, Indian tourists walked along the shore with parasols to protect them from the sun. We were told upper-caste Indians did not swim because it was an activity associated with lowly fishermen.

One evening, after a long and restful day, we decided to eat at a popular beachfront café called Tito's. We were served on the palm-roofed

Our Paradise Campsite in Goa.
Look for the van among the trees and the small figure of me dumping trash.

veranda while the sky darkened and the stars sparkled against the velvet expanse. By the time we finished our meal of fried shark, prawns, and potatoes, a full moon had risen. The beach was flooded with moonglow and the low dunes shone white. The night air brushed our skin on our walk back to the van and the sandy ground looked as beautiful as silk sheets. Low spots nestled between the hilly dunes whispered of romance.

We had only a few garments to strip off. I pulled my loose dress over my head and flung it into the night. Tom removed his shorts, folded them carefully under his head, and lay down on the sand, his arms stretched up in invitation. I lowered myself, one knee on each side of his hips and looked down at the bearded face of my lover. As his love filled me, I tipped my head back and absorbed the galaxy of stars above. The sweep of my loose hair tickled my bare back. I closed my eyes, imagined a scene like in *From Here to Eternity* without the waves, and lost myself in the passion of the moment.

Later, exhausted and satiated, I snuggled next to Tom and we stared up at the spangled sky. I had lived my most romantic daydream—sex on a tropical beach under a full moon. This moment would last me a lifetime. Tom reached behind his head for his shorts. Suddenly on his knees, he groped about in the sand.

"I can't find my shorts," he said. "They're not here."

I rolled over, romantic thoughts broken into a thousand shards. "I know you put them under your head. They must be here." Now, I sifted through the sand, too.

Tom stood up. "Come on! We've got to go back to the van. The car keys were in my pocket!"

I grabbed my dress and panties from the beautiful pile where I had flung them, and we ran naked through the hillocky sand to our camp spot. If the Turtle was gone, all we owned in the world would be gone with it. What a relief to see our beloved green home in the clearing!

"My wallet was in the pocket, too," Tom said. "I'll get the spare key from the bumper and let you in. I'm going back to look again." But twenty minutes later, when he returned, he had found nothing. "In the dark, I wasn't even sure I could tell where we were."

"How much money was in your wallet?" I asked. "It couldn't have been much."

"It's not the money. There was only about twenty rupees. But my Coast Guard ID was in the wallet, too."

I knew this was important—we had used it several times to gain access to military bases in Europe. But we probably wouldn't need it again until we returned to the United States, so I didn't fully understand his concern. "Is that a big deal?" I asked. "We have your passport." We always kept our passports and our California driver's licenses hidden in the van.

"The Coast Guard ID is my career," he said. "It's our livelihood when we get home. If someone tries to use it and gets a job pretending to be me, it could be a disaster. At the least, it would cause a problem that might take months to untangle."

"I doubt that will happen." I hoped to calm Tom down. "The thief only cares about the money. Most likely, your shorts are already discarded in a trash heap behind some cottage."

"You know people go through the trash here. The card's worth money. It could be sold. It could mean a job for anyone smart enough to use it!" By this time, I knew Tom well enough to realize he could always envision the worst-case scenario, while I always expected the best. I also knew I would get nowhere arguing with him. I could only hope, as the days passed, he would worry less. One thing we both agreed on— the idea of the thief with a set of keys to our home terrified us.

"One of us has to stay nearby from now on," I said. "We can't risk the thief figuring out which Volkswagen those keys belong to while we're at the beach."

"We won't leave it unguarded for a minute," Tom declared.

The next day, depressed and unsettled, we drove into town to change some of our stashed US dollars. With rupees in his pocket, Tom was more relaxed and we drove to another beach where we could swim close enough to the van to keep an eye on it. Later we ordered dinner at the café near our clearing. One huge lobster with enough sweet white meat to satisfy us both lifted our spirits.

In preparation for our departure, Tom began a complete check of the car—front end, brakes, oil . . . whatever. While he worked, I walked across the backyards of the nearby bungalows and headed toward our infamous spot, compelled to search one last time. I took a stick and prodded and poked the sandy gulley where we had made love. I searched up and down the undulating hills. Behind a tuft of grass and a stunted shrub, I found Tom's shorts, half buried by sand. Triumphant, I shook them off. I groped into the pocket and felt the weight of the car keys. Safe in the other pocket, I found the spiral notebook where Tom recorded all our expenses. But no wallet. I carefully searched the area again, hoping against hope the thief had simply grabbed the cash and tossed the wallet, the precious Coast Guard ID still inside. But no luck.

Making the most of my limited good fortune, I returned waving the shorts and the car keys gaily in the sunshine. "Look what I found," I called. "Even your notebook."

I didn't mind his blackened, greasy hands as he hugged me. A sigh of relief passed between us. "You are amazing," he said.

"I'm sorry. I looked, but I couldn't find the wallet."

"Well, it's a long shot any of these hippies will realize the value of the ID," he said. "The thief must have been a gringo. An Indian would have kept the shorts." I knew he was right about that. "Can you imagine the story our hippie told his friends . . . how he lifted the wallet right from under my head while we were screwing? What an eyeful he got."

This vision was too much. I remembered how I had straddled Tom's hips and moved in abandon. "Oh, my God! If only I had kept my eyes open, none of this would have happened."

"It wasn't your fault," Tom whispered in my ear. "It was lovely. I was completely oblivious, too. I didn't even feel him pull the shorts from under my head!"

"We may have rolled around a bit. We'll laugh at this when we're sixty."

"I guess we ought to move on in a few days," Tom said. "I want to get to Bombay to report the theft of my ID. When it's on record at the American Consulate, I'll feel better."

Tom spent the next day with car maintenance and hauled enough water for me to do laundry. I scrubbed down the stove and the refrigerator, which had been switched off, and washed our sheets, towels, and the clothing we had worn for the last several weeks. Tom helped me string rope between the palm trees and by afternoon the area flapped with lines of wet saris, shorts, T-shirts, and linens. The warm sea breezes dried everything quickly. Before dinner, our bed was remade, our clean towels were stashed away, and our clothing was carefully folded into the cardboard box I used as accessible storage for the items we wore most often. We kept the box of clothes in the back on the bed during the day. At night, we moved it to the front passenger seat.

While we worked, we noticed people coming and going. Amplified Indian music blared across the hillocks of sand and dune grass. We could see vendor stands being erected and a shrine, usually ignored, was decorated with flags and streamers. In the late afternoon, Indian families walked through our clearing headed for the Hindi fiesta. As the sky darkened, lanterns and strings of electric lights flickered on.

Intrigued by the festivities, we joined the crowds. Gaily festooned stalls sold candy, fruit, toys, and incense. An aisle of banners and awnings led to the shrine which stood under the expansive branches of a tree, its trunk now painted with white spots. The villagers bought candy and incense which they left at the shrine. Everyone was in a festive mood, and after they offered their gifts to the goddess, they bought snacks and socialized. Tom and I sipped barely chilled Coke from one of the stands. Tired after our day of work, we left while the fiesta was still in full swing. Tom moved our van to a quieter spot behind one of the bungalows and we fell asleep to the hum of distant voices and the rhythms of Indian music drifting in our open windows.

I woke early, needing to pee. As I sat on the commode, I glanced over to the window for a view of our tropical paradise. What I saw was a long slash of torn screen and an empty cardboard box. All the freshly laundered and folded clothes . . . gone! Tom was jarred awake by my scream, "We've been ripped off again!"

We didn't try to go back to sleep. Tom had lost two pairs of khaki shorts (including the pair I had just found), two tank tops, two shirts bought in Mexico, and a swimsuit, while my losses included two loose dresses, two pairs of shorts, one sleeveless blouse, an embroidered shirt from Morocco, two sari tops, a sari underskirt, and my two favorite saris, including the white one with the blue border, worn only once. This time we guessed the thief was probably an Indian who had been at the fiesta, though with such a treasure it could have been a hippie who would sell the clothes downtown to get drug money. For the rest of the day, Tom and I sat glumly at camp in our underwear, all we had left suitable for the tropic heat. It was time to leave Goa.

Bombay was a two-day drive through arid, drought-stricken countryside. We had heard that beyond the city, famine had crept across the land. The farther north we headed, the drier the landscape became, more desolate with each mile, the air so hot it sapped our energy.

In Bombay (now called Mumbai), at the Gateway of India, an immense triumphal archway that faced the boat-filled harbor, we parked in the middle of the stone-paved plaza active with hucksters, balloon vendors, and tourists in line for the boats to the Elephant Cave. Across a busy road, the Taj Mahal hotel reigned, its uniformed doormen standing sentinel. Next door to the Taj, a park displayed a bronze sculpture and beyond that, an odiferous public latrine. At one side of the park there was an Indian army recruitment center where young men sat in their underwear and waited to be called for their physicals.

We had been told vanners "camped" in the plaza behind the Gateway, but the spot was without shade or water. Others drove forty-five minutes to Juhu Beach where there was a campground of sorts. The nearby downtown YMCA allowed campers to park overnight on their grounds, but it was a narrow space with only enough room for three vans. Travelers often parked on the street for several days before they could get in. Good timing and good luck for us! Only two vans were parked inside the gates and there was room for us with no wait. The hot, confined space gave us access to running water and a primitive bathroom where we could have a cold shower. Best of all, it was across the street from a general store and only a few blocks from an area of food vendors.

Bombay, a center of commerce, boasted the colorful Crawford Market, several government-run emporiums, a business center with modern buildings, and vast slums of poverty and squalor. Clusters of famine refugees lived on the sidewalks behind the Taj Hotel, and dead rats lay on the street at dawn. Other neighborhoods were beautiful with parks and old Victorian homes built by the British.

The YMCA was unbearable during the day when the sun beat down into the enclosure and radiated off the walls. Tom and I, travel-weary, often ate lunch at the Taj coffee shop, one day even going upstairs to the hotel's elegant buffet. In the sweltering afternoons, we lounged about the public spaces and ogled the expensive items in the boutiques. We would soon leave India, so we shopped in earnest, traveling from the bazaar to the Handloom House to the new Cottage Industries Emporium by taxi leaving our van to maintain its spot at the Y. The markets and shops offered a cornucopia of treasures—silver shirt studs, a tablecloth with napkins, a batik bedspread, spices, ten kilos of Darjeeling tea and enough fresh food to get us to Delhi. Because of the low cost of almost everything in India (10 cents for a cauliflower the size of a human head, 40 cents for a half-dozen eggs, and $5.00 for a batik tablecloth), these purchases hardly dented our budget.

Tom knew Bombay well from the past and wanted to show me the city beyond the markets. At his direction, the taxi driver cruised Marine Drive and up to the Hanging Gardens for the magnificent view, then turned deeper into the city to the crowded, bawdy, red-light district known as The Cages. The streets were filled with jostling men and horse carriages. Prostitutes waited for customers in narrow lighted doorways and beckoned from the windows of three-story buildings so close together they shared a common wall.

I looked at Tom, my question obvious though unspoken.

My husband laughed. "Yes, I've been here before with a group of guys from the ship. But honestly, I never went upstairs with any of the girls."

"Truly?" I asked.

"Truly," he repeated. "It's a bit unsanitary here for my taste. One of the other guys did. He didn't come down with the clap, but he did pick up a nasty dose of crabs."

After five days in the city, our roof box filled with purchased goodies, it was time to leave. One last lunch at the Taj and we headed north into the area of drought and famine. Even before we left the city, I knew I was coming down with a cold, my first in several weeks. My throat was sore and my head ached. Outside, the land became ever drier, dust swirling up from the roads and into the car windows, open to keep us from suffocating in the heat. The dust made my sore throat worse. Tom suggested I put a wet handkerchief over my nose and mouth, but I refused. . . why I don't know. I only remember I was sick and grouchy and my throat was on fire. When he found a place to park in the falling dark, I made him cook his own dinner while I lay miserably on the bed.

That night I couldn't sleep. My throat was raw and I burned with fever, sweating and shaking with chills, tossing and turning. A few times I dozed off, only to jerk awake, barely able to swallow. Each time, I reached for the aspirin bottle, the only medicine we had, and took a few more. For several hours before dawn, I lay awake, consumed by the pain. In the morning, I refused to get out of the bed. Tom drove on while I moaned in back, the bed sheets soaked with perspiration. I swallowed a few more aspirin to no effect. Then I began to hear faint music.

"Tom," I called weakly. "I hear a band. A marching band. Is there a parade?"

"Nothing. We're in the middle of nowhere."

"But I hear John Philip Souza. A Souza march. Maybe there's a parade in the village."

"Katie, there's no parade. There's a famine here. Nobody is marching. You've probably overdosed on aspirin."

I had barely enough sense left to realize he was right. Midmorning Tom located a small guest house with a water spigot and stopped to nurse me. He plied me with water, brewed hot lemon juice for me to drink, wiped my forehead with a damp cloth, and rinsed the sweat-soaked sheets in the laundry bucket. The hot wind dried the sheets in less than an hour. My throat was an inferno, I still burned with fever, and I was no longer allowed aspirin.

"We need to head straight for Delhi," Tom said. "I want to get you to a doctor." I simply groaned. I didn't want to miss Rajasthan, our next planned stop, but I was miserable and scared. "I'm going to start driving again," he said. "If you get worse, at least I want to be closer to Delhi and out of this godforsaken drought area." I could only nod agreement. Back on the road, I lay spread-eagle on the bed with (finally) a wet handkerchief over my face. More comfortable with clean sheets, I fell asleep in spite of the bouncing of the van on the bad roads. While I slept, Tom passed the turnoff for Rajasthan and continued on the road to Delhi.

Gradually, the pain in my throat eased and my fever broke. After long hours of driving, Tom made us scrambled eggs for dinner, slept, then started again at daybreak. He was determined to get me to Delhi that afternoon. By midday, I felt much better, but I stayed in the back of the car in bed. Tom drove like a demon in order to get me to medical help and I wanted him to feel his efforts were needed. It was already midafternoon when we approached a wide river and a detour. A soldier waved us onto a two-lane dirt road. Off to our left, the asphalt ended at the remains of a wide, concrete bridge split in the middle as if it were a

California freeway overpass after a 7.0 earthquake. One half of the bridge had dropped down six feet lower than the roadway and lay in the water and sand of the river. Pedestrians, Indian women with jars on their heads and men with bundles on their shoulders, proceeded carefully across the bridge, helping each other as they clambered down the drop between the sections and waded through the water that flowed over the concrete.

I moved to the front of the van as Tom followed a line of trucks and a few cars descending a steep incline to a sandy riverbank. Ahead stretched the daunting prospect of a pontoon bridge. A wooden road surface followed the ups and downs between huge, floating steel drums that supported the makeshift bridge. One at a time, the transport trucks slowly crossed the undulations, their long wheelbases carrying them from one steel cylinder to another.

When it was our turn, Tom inched the van forward. Because of our shorter length, we dipped down into each valley between the pontoons, our front and rear bumpers scraping the wood planks. At the top of each rise, our undercarriage threatened to catch and hang us up. Below, the swift river water splashed and swirled. When we reached the far side and climbed the bank, the dirt road continued on, no connection to the asphalt highway anywhere in sight.

Tom pulled to the side of the road and tried to communicate with a soldier posted there. "Road to Delhi?" he shouted and waved his arm in the direction of the main highway.

The soldier trotted over and motioned for us to move on. "No, no. You must go. Pakistani army is near. Maybe they bomb the bridge." The soldier waved his rifle in the direction of the traffic moving down the dirt road. "You go!" he ordered.

For hours we crossed fields and passed villages. Gradually the traffic turned off into towns along the way and we were almost the only motorized vehicle crawling through the backcountry. Ahead an oxcart churned up dust. Down the road, a shack crouched in the shade of a scrawny tree.

"Look. What's that?" I asked.

Tom peered into the setting sun and swirls of road dust. "It's a guard shack of some kind. There's a barrier gate like at a railroad crossing." We pulled over to watch as the oxcart approached the shack. When the cart stopped at the lowered gate, a skinny attendant in khaki shorts came out of the shade and talked to the farmer. He returned to the lean-to, raised the barrier, and allowed the cart to pass.

"It's a toll gate," Tom said. "I'm not paying a toll for this shitty road!" He put the van into gear. "Give me a couple of rupee bills in case I need them." He drove steadily toward the lowered toll barrier, honking the horn. Tom extended his arm out the window, the rupee bills clearly dangling from his hand.

The Indian toll taker stood on the side of the road and waved his arms and shouted what must have been the Hindi words for "Stop!" His voice was drowned by the noise of our engine. Tom kept waving the rupee bills, a tempting flag, but he did not slow down.

"What're you doing?"

"Watch this," Tom said. "He'll raise the gate again."

The toll man stood still like a deer caught in headlights. Then he ran toward us to grab the money, releasing his hold on the control bar. The gate flew up, Tom pulled his arm with the rupees back into the van, and we sailed through in a cloud of dust. As we passed, the toll guard pumped his fist in anger. In answer, Tom leaned on the horn, a loud blast of noise that obliterated the man's shouts. When we caught up with the oxcart, Tom cranked the steering wheel and we slid by the lumbering cart, bumping over the rutted shoulder of the dirt road.

I was shaking. "You're crazy! What if you'd hit him?"

"Well, I didn't!"

We reached Delhi well after dark. By then, my throat was only mildly uncomfortable and my fever gone. At the central campground, we collapsed into bed, exhausted. We would go to the embassy and get a recommendation for a doctor first thing in the morning.

India to Yugoslavia, March to May 1973

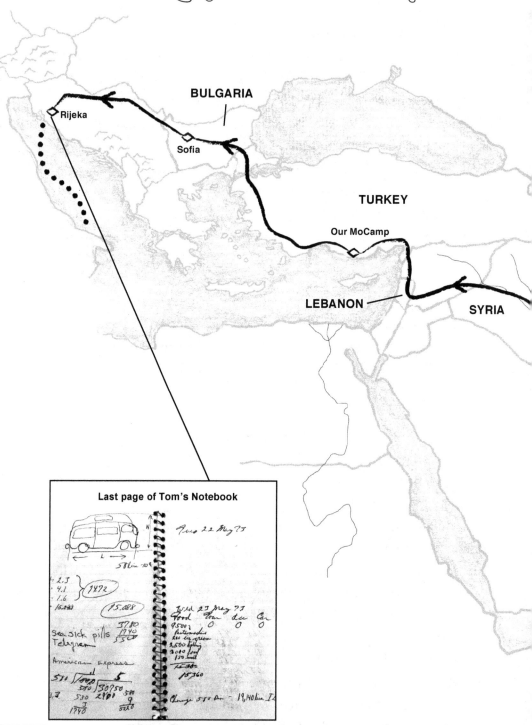

BULGARIA

◇ Rijeka

◇ Sofia

TURKEY

Our MoCamp ◇

LEBANON

SYRIA

Last page of Tom's Notebook

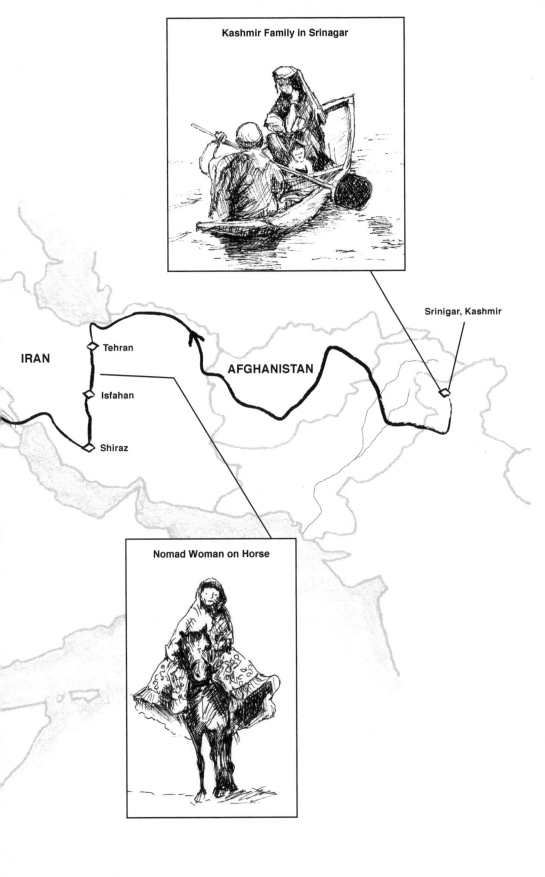

Kashmir Family in Srinagar

Srinigar, Kashmir

IRAN

Tehran

Isfahan

Shiraz

AFGHANISTAN

Nomad Woman on Horse

Chapter 22

Middle East Express

The Harvard-educated doctor recommended by the American Embassy declared I did not have strep throat but prescribed penicillin tablets for me anyway. Perhaps we would yet have time to drive to Kashmir before our Indian visa expired on March 21. But, as we knew by now, travel could be a series of changed plans.

During the long bumpy ride to Delhi, our refrigerator broke a Freon tube. The touchy appliance was now totally dead and needed to be repaired, a much more complicated project than expected. After days of effort side by side with a Sikh refrigeration expert who found electrical problems in addition to the Freon leak, Tom gave up. We would have to continue without refrigeration.

We pored over our maps to plan our return trip across the Middle East. Neither of us wanted to go the same way we had come. We talked to travelers who had crossed Iraq and Syria on their way to India. It seemed an exciting option and we could get the needed visas in Delhi.

At the Iraqi Embassy, the clerks were pleasant but warned us the process could be drawn out. We filled out the paperwork, presented our photos, and moved on. The Syrian visa officer told us he could have the paperwork approved within twenty-four hours. Great news! The Iranian visa was a simple process and we settled in to wait for the Iraqi approval. Each day we went to the embassy to hear, "No. Not yet. Maybe tomorrow." We would not make it to the India/Pakistan border for the weekly crossing day before our Indian visa expired.

Getting the visa extended required an interview with a high official. If he didn't believe our reasons were important or if he simply didn't approve of our looks, the interviewer had the power to deny an extension. We dressed carefully, clean and well-groomed. I wore my best sari and hoped the Indian officials appreciated this nod to their culture. The interview and the masses of paperwork, each page done in quadruplicate with carbon paper between the layers, took a full day. But finally we got the extension.

After two weeks in the capital, our Iraqi visas were approved. Determined to get a glimpse of Kashmir, we set out with only five days to make the journey and get to the border crossing. From the flat, wheat plains of the Punjab, we entered the foothills on a road that ran close to the Pakistani border and was maintained by the military. The highway was lined with countless military bases and installations and served as the convoy route to the contested territories of Kashmir.

The farther we traveled, the steeper the terrain and the more deteriorated the road. Frequently, one edge of the road was only inches from a deep chasm, a narrow river strewn with boulders below. The two narrow lanes were often covered by landslides of dirt and rubble which had tumbled down, totally burying the pavement. In other sections, half the pavement had dropped down the precipice. We stopped at a place where both lanes had fallen into the gorge below. The army had laid two steel H-beams across the void to serve as a bridge.

Most of the traffic consisted of military trucks with much wider wheelbases than our Volkswagen, and the makeshift bridge had been laid accordingly. The beams were wide and Tom thought he could cross safely on their inner edges. He inched the van forward while I closed my eyes. Only trust would get me through. If we crashed into the abyss, we would die together—a fitting romantic finale. When the van again bounced on the rubble of the road, I opened my eyes. We had made it!

Later, we arrived at a stretch of road totally covered under several feet of loose earth. Tom followed tire grooves already etched into the soft rubble of the landslide. At a blind curve, moving slowly across the mounds of dirt and rock, we met an Indian military jeep head-on. Our van was jolted by the impact as the shorter, heavier vehicle bounced off our front-mounted spare tire. An army officer in the jeep jumped out, quite irritated. He shook his finger at us. "No passing in the turning," he shouted. "Wrong side! No passing!" But there were only two tire ruts in the dirt and in the end, his Jeep had to back up to let us pass.

We camped at a Dak bungalow halfway up the mountains and at dawn began the final stretch. After hours of torturous driving through a valley and up hairpin turns to the snow level, we entered a narrow, one-way tunnel carved through solid rock and plunged into darkness. For more than a mile, we held our breath and hoped the tunnel had been engineered better than the road. At the far end, the broad Kashmir Valley lay below, blanketed in haze.

The flat, dusty valley ringed by snowcapped peaks was softened by lines of poplar trees, fields of canary yellow mustard, and orchards of fruit trees cloaked in pink and white blossoms. We had only twenty-four hours to soak up the romance of this idyllic spot, and we intended to make the most of it. With *Fodor's India* on my lap, I directed Tom around Dal Lake to gardens built by the Mogul emperors when Kashmir was their summer retreat. Hints of past luxury remained in the gardens—pavilions, fountains, now dry water channels, and petunia-filled flower beds.

Hundreds of houseboats—elaborate, Victorian, floating mobile homes—were moored along the shores of the lake and the floating artificial islands. At the tourist center, Tom struck up a conversation with a young American couple who invited us to come for cocktails at their rented houseboat. After dinner, we took a *shikara*, one of the light flat-bottomed boats used as water taxis. As the boatman paddled across the silvery water, Tom and I reclined against flowered cushions, while curtains from the canopy fluttered in the breeze. The lights of houseboats moored all around flickered on as we approached our destination. Neil and Susan welcomed us into an elegant room with walls of reddish-blond cedar wood that contributed a subtle, spicy aroma to the interior. There were three bedrooms, a parlor, a dining room, and a pantry. At the rear of the boat, a gangway led to a kitchen and servants' quarters on the lakeshore. For us it seemed unbelievably decadent, but we vowed we would rent a houseboat if we ever returned.

We slept near one of the Mogul gardens, and after breakfast, we regretfully headed down the mountains toward the Pakistani border. We arrived at Amritsar by noon of the second day, eighteen hours before the border gate would open.

The next afternoon we were in Pakistan, heading for the Khyber Pass. Thirty-six hours later, with one overnight stop, we reached the Afghan border. Less than a mile into Afghanistan, we saw an odd group traveling toward Pakistan. First an Afghan military jeep with four fully armed soldiers in back, rifles at the ready. Behind them, a black mule hitched to a loaded wagon and two tall, blond, young men wearing Western clothing. A second military jeep with armed soldiers brought up the rear.

A Kashmiri Couple.

"They look like they could almost be those American brothers we kept hearing about," Tom said.

"I thought one of them was murdered by bandits. How can it be them?"

Tom swerved to the side of the road and stopped. "Let's find out." He jumped out of the car and crossed the highway with me close behind. The walkers slowed their pace to greet us. The military jeeps put on their brakes and waited patiently. Tom and I soon had the entire story from the brothers' lips.

One of the men was indeed Dave Kunst, the brother who had been shot in the lung during the bandit massacre in the Kabul Gorge. Dave explained that after he had been shot the previous October, he was rescued and flown back to the United States, where he had spent several months at the Mayo Clinic. During his recuperation, he managed to convince his third brother, Pete, they should continue the trek as a way to honor their murdered sibling. Dave and Pete had flown back to Afghanistan where the government insisted, this time, on an armed guard from Kabul, past the site of the shooting, to the Pakistani border. The American Embassy helped the brothers get a new mule and wagon and facilitated transportation to the exact spot of the ambush where the brothers would restart their walk. They were now only a few days into the new journey and intended to complete a circuit of the world before they stopped.

Tom and I drove through the infamous Kabul River Gorge at dusk with the story of the Kunst brothers fresh in our minds. We were happy to arrive in the Afghan capital. For three days we shopped, cleaned the van, and drank hot cocoa while hail pelted the roof. Our route across the deserts of Afghanistan, all the way to Tehran, would be the same as in November. Now, in the first week of April, much of the land was softened by the bright colors of spring wild flowers and nomad caravans on the move.

We arrived at Mashhad, Iran, eager to bargain for our Persian carpets. If we selected carefully, we had room in our roof box and money enough

We traveled back across Afghanistan in the spring.

for three rugs. We returned to Beban's brother's shop and sat down with the carpet merchant to begin our selection. Again, we were surrounded by dozens of carpets. The quoted prices were lower than before, so perhaps, after all, Beban, who was never mentioned by the merchant, had been an agent who would have gotten a "finder's fee." We chose three Baluchi carpets with medallion shaped *guls* and geometric border designs, each a slightly different size and range of colors. One was only a few years old, the wool tufts bright red, black, and deep blue with beautiful borders all around. We were told the other two were older, about thirty years, and therefore more valuable. One was woven in red, brown, and orange, the other with a stepped pattern in reds and blacks. After two hours of negotiation and two cups of sweetened, mint tea each, Tom and I left the caravansary with three carpets bundled under our arms.

From Tehran, we headed south, across desert country to Isfahan, a pretty city of gardens, an Armenian cathedral, and the Jameh Mosque. To one side of the mosque, a long, covered-brick arcade was lined with expensive shops selling jewelry, precious stones, tiles, intricate brass-ware, and carpets. Outside the entrance of the bazaar, we explored a street of metal workers, the air filled with the tapping of hammers on brass, copper, and silver as artisans created patterns on trays, urns, and samovars. At the first stall we ran into our American friends, Susan and Neil, whom we had met in Kashmir and later in Kabul. On a trip such as ours, crossing paths with travelers more than once made us old friends and we spent the rest of the day with them. Susan was impressed with my ability to bargain, developed over the last two years, as she watched me purchase a wood-block printed tablecloth and a fine nugget of tur-quoise, thus emptying Tom's pocket of loose Iranian *rial*. They took us to a carpet gallery to see a display of three fabulous carpets made espe-cially for the Shah by the students of the Fine Arts University. These carpets were so tightly knotted and of such fine, soft wool, our Mash-had purchases paled in comparison. Over dinner in our van, we showed them our three carpet treasures. We all agreed, though not Shah qual-ity, ours were perfect for a young couple starting out.

We drove across fertile valleys, soft with young wheat, to Persepolis, built 2,500 years before, through Shiraz and into another valley alive with the pageantry of nomads. Dozens of family groups were strung out along the highway on their yearly move to higher altitudes for the summer. Lines of donkeys and camels, laden with folded tents, poles, pots, and colorful Kilim saddlebags, were followed by turbaned men herding flocks of sheep and goats. The wealthier men and women rode fine horses, the ladies handsome in flowered scarves and voluminous, multicolored skirts spread out across their mount's rump. Women who walked with the flocks swished their skirts, smiled, and waved. Young animals romped beside their mothers, and one young camel rode atop a stack of bundles and blankets on the back of an adult beast, reminiscent of similar sights in Morocco.

As we approached the Persian Gulf, the land gradually changed from rocky desert in bloom to green valleys, then to sand dunes, salt flats, and reeds. With nothing to entice us into Abadan, we camped in the parking lot of the local airport and set off in the morning for the nearby Iraq border. Due to diplomatic and political problems between Iran and Iraq, the border was only open to international travelers—local people could not cross either way. On a narrow dirt road, we finally located the outpost, a wooden shack in the middle of a deserted expanse of sand and shrub. There were no officials in sight. Tom hollered "Hello" into the slightly open door and a single guard shambled out in a wrinkled uniform, rubbing his eyes as if he had just woken up. He looked at our passports and waved us on, then went back to finish his nap. On the other side of the border, the narrow road cut through a dusty grove of date palms before it deposited us on the highway to Baghdad.

Iraq seemed endlessly flat, dusty, and almost treeless, not at all as I imagined the "Fertile Crescent." Patches of irrigated fields planted with wheat were isolated spots of green surrounded by dull brown. We bypassed Baghdad, spent our only night in Iraq in a date palm oasis, then drove on till the road turned west into a forsaken landscape, rocky and endlessly bleak all the way to the Syrian border. The customs and immigration checkpoints for the two countries lay miles apart, a desolate no man's land in between and nothing to mark the actual border except two guardhouses.

In Syria, we found ourselves sharing the road with convoys of military vehicles loaded with soldiers. Happily, they were headed toward the desert, not in our direction. The border station stood on the crest of the mountains between the Syrian desert and the rich, agricultural fields of Lebanon's inland valley. A lower range of mountains separated this agricultural area from the Mediterranean coast, the domain of fishermen, tourists, and the financial center of Beirut, a cosmopolitan city not yet destroyed by war and bombs.

We arrived in Beirut on a Tuesday, exactly one week after raids by the Israel Defense Forces, which targeted PLO members in retaliation for the massacre of the Israeli athletes in Munich the previous summer.

The city was on edge. Though the Lebanese government had not been attacked, all official sites were on high alert. At a heavily guarded U.S. Embassy, I willingly walked past armed soldiers, jeeps, military trucks, and a half-track with a manned machine gun to retrieve our mail with the help of a U.S. Marine guard. Mail in hand, we went to the waterfront to read family news, including the word that Mike and Michelle would again join us for the summer. To celebrate, we splurged on two cheeseburgers at a local "Wimpy's." Yes, fast food had come to the Middle East.

The unrest, raids, and military movement, both in Lebanon and earlier in Syria, made us uneasy. We would move on to Turkey as fast as we could. We crossed into (and out of) Syria's coastal window to the sea, and with relief, entered Turkey several hours after dark the same night.

Chapter 23

Turkish Spring

I n coastal Turkey, famous for beaches and Roman ruins, we had heard there was a Mocamp (short for motorcamp) located on the bay of Antalya near the town of Silifke. The camp, owned and run by British Petroleum, was said to be modern, with all the conveniences, and after our long drive from India, Tom and I planned a stress-free, beach vacation. The Mocamp provided plenty of hot water, shade from pine trees, a delightful view out to an island crag topped by the remains of a castle, and the Mediterranean Sea a few steps from our door. We set up our beach chairs on a rocky shelf skirted by azure water and soaked up the sun. Most evenings, we relished the Turkish cuisine served at the camp café—stuffed grape leaves known as dolma, green beans vinaigrette, flaky cheese filled pastries called *sigara böreği*, shish-kebob, and grilled trout. Each meal was accompanied by a thick, savory yogurt sauce with garlic, olive oil, and chopped parsley. We felt our muscles gradually relax as our thoughts drifted over our experiences, past and yet to come.

After a three-day holiday, we felt rested, healthy and ready to sightsee. We followed a yellow sign with the English words, "Historical Ruins," and stumbled onto an old pirate city, a jumble of barrel-vaulted stone remains spread along a sandy beach. Our appetite whetted, we visited a Byzantine church and roamed castle ruins atop a rocky spur near a popular beach resort. Antique, white marble columns, the remains of a Roman town, lay scattered among vacation bungalows and fishermen's cottages. We strolled around the town, peeked into gardens of flowers and fig trees, examined the carvings on the fallen pediments, and climbed up to a well-preserved amphitheater. At noon, we parked near a sunny cove and bought sigara böreği to go from an open-air café. These flaky cheese nibbles (the Turkish name translated as "cigar pastry" to indicate their shape and size), had become a favorite. I mixed up an herb and lettuce salad to accompany the crunchy, hot, melted cheese-filled pastries. After our meal, we donned our bathing suits and splashed in the sea.

We had heard about a local restaurant described as the best in Turkey. The family-style, fixed menu, cooked by the owner's wife and mother, was served one dish after another—bread, a plate of tomato, cucumber and pepper salad, stewed green beans, and the entrée, a fish soup, the exquisite flavor fatally marred by tiny fish bones and scales afloat in the creamy broth. Luckily the wine was good. We strolled back to our home in the mild night, grousing the entire way about the small portions, the restaurant price, and the bones in the soup. Complaining together about our mutual irritations with the outside world was strangely unifying. Soon we laughed over the ridiculous soup and hurried to make love by the sea.

Further on, Pamukkale, a mineral hot-springs resort, perched atop white travertine cliffs. Layer after layer of snow-white mineral and calcium terraces like petrified waterfalls descended to the green fields below. Formations near the top formed lily-pad shaped thermal pools in irregular, overlapping rows. Misty steam rose from the pools and the water channels, which crisscrossed the plateau amid modern hotels, Byzantine ruins, and tourists soaking in the warm, healing water.

Another day, we explored the ancient Greek city of Aphrodisias—a fine residence, a white marble theater missing only its roof, a stadium, and the Temple of Aphrodite. We walked the streets paved with their original white and gray stones and listened to the sound of water flowing through the ancient water system.

With no refrigeration since India, it was a daily necessity to shop for fresh food. In a town on the Aegean Coast, we hit the jackpot. I sighted a butcher shop as we bumped along a village street. Not unexpectedly, none of the burly butchers spoke English. A few lamb chops and sausages were displayed in their glass case, but I was after a whole leg of spring lamb. I would ask using "sign language." Tom stood back and watched, a grin on his face, as I slapped my thigh, rubbed my butt, and bleated, "Baa, baaaa." At first the Turkish butcher looked incredulous. What was this American woman doing? But after a second performance, he grinned, went into the back room and brought out a beautiful, pink leg of lamb. Success!

Several blocks further on, both sides of the road were lined with stalls of staples, produce, pots, and pans. Farm women squatted beside baskets of lettuce, beets, green onions, spinach, asparagus, radishes, and chard. A young woman, her rounded abdomen promising the arrival of a baby, sold bound bundles of parsley, dill, small baskets of black olives, and chunks of chalky white cheese. Another woman, her old face wrinkled with smiles, sat behind a large basket covered with a damp, spotlessly white, linen dishtowel. One corner of the cloth was turned back to reveal mounds of snowy yogurt, thick as double-whipped cream.

"That's what they used to make the garlic yogurt at the Mocamp," I said. "We've got to get some."

Further on, a man with a drooping mustache trundled his pushcart down the street, calling out, "*Yultka. Yultka.*" In the cart he had stacks of the flat, paper-thin, wheat pastry, each about the size of a dinner plate, used to make the crisp, "cigar" cheese rolls. Tom reached in his pocket for coins while I held open one of the shopping bags. Laden with parcels of yogurt and yultka, fresh herbs and vegetables poking through the holes of our string bags, we returned to the van. I couldn't wait to prepare dinner.

I smeared chunks from the tender end of the lamb leg with thick yogurt mixed with chopped garlic, chives, and parsley. As the meat marinated, I carefully wrapped the thin, pliable, yultka sheets around mounds of seasoned, fresh cheese. With more than a dozen "cigars" laid out, I was pleased with my efforts. Tom, returned from his nightly tour of our campground, started the barbeque, threaded the lamb on wooden skewers, and grilled the shish-kebob. A salad of chopped cucumbers, spring onions, olives, and sprigs of Danish cress (once again growing well) was the perfect foil for the pastries fried in hot olive oil. The meal was as good as any we had eaten at the Mocamp café.

I had gone overboard at the market and needed to keep my hoard fresh without a refrigerator. I had developed several strategies to keep food from turning bad on warm days. I kept fresh vegetables and cooked meat in a plastic dishpan covered with a wet dishcloth, always set in the shade or a well-ventilated spot. Any breeze blowing across the damp towel, frequently refreshed with more water, served as a primitive air conditioner, similar to the cooling of drinking water in a canvas bag hung from the car bumper on my childhood trips across the desert. The growth of mold on cheese could be forestalled by wrapping it in a cloth soaked in diluted vinegar. Occasionally, in Turkey, we found ice, but not often. When we did, we added the frozen chunks to the dishpan and used the defunct refrigerator as if it were an ice chest.

In the middle of a five-day holiday at another seaside camp, we drove to the ancient Greco-Roman city of Ephesus. Jubilant crowds of Turks had come by bus for the celebration of a spring festival and to watch a national dance competition. From the top row of stone seats in the perfectly preserved Roman amphitheater, we watched colorful groups of athletic dancers from all over the country swirl and stomp to bring honor to their home towns. We walked the remains of the ancient city, down the paved thoroughfare that stretched from the amphitheater to the *agora* (market area), past the ruins of once beautiful fountains, around magnificent temple facades, the Roman Baths, a brothel, and down a paved side street, to an ancient public toilet. Marble squatter holes, poised over a water channel, lined the walls of a square courtyard with a hand-washing fountain in the center. Again, I envied the ancients.

We had arranged with Tom's parents to send money to Athens, but it was beginning to look like a miscalculation. We had lingered too long in Turkey, and Tom, aware shipping dates were fluid, was anxious to know exactly when our Jugolinija ship would sail for New York. "I'd prefer to drive straight to Rijeka," he said one evening. "I want to find out the current schedule and complete the final paperwork for our passage."

"Can we cancel the money wire if your mom hasn't sent it yet?' I asked.

"I'm not sure. I hope, once our booking is secure, we can return to Greece."

"Whatever you think. You're the one who has to do all the extra driving. I'm simply along for the ride." This was an attitude developed over the last two years. Wherever the road led, there was always a wonderful experience waiting around the bend.

He unfolded our road map and studied the notated mileages. "What about going by way of Bulgaria?" he asked. "I've heard visas are available at the border."

"Bulgaria's part of the Soviet Bloc. As Americans, can we do it without problems?"

"According to a guy I talked to yesterday who came south through Bulgaria, they offer a twenty-four-hour visa. He said the main problem was speed traps. With only one day to get through the country and good roads, I guess it's tempting to drive too fast. He said Bulgarian towns take advantage. They set up places to stop tourists and collect hefty cash speeding fines. But, even going slow, we should be able to cut our travel time in half."

We crossed the Dardanelles by ferry a short distance from the Bulgarian border, excited to try our first experience behind the Iron Curtain. The early morning traffic was light, and it continued that way most of the day with only a few other foreign travelers, trucks, and an occasional cart using the road. At one point, in spite of Tom's cautious speed, four men jumped from behind a copse of bushes into the lane in front of us and held up their hands to indicate we should stop. They were not in uniform, but each had an official-looking badge pinned to his chest. One man spoke a little English and he kept repeating, "Too fast. You go too fast." He rubbed his fingers together and named his price while his companions stood by ready to cause trouble if we didn't pay. Tom paid the fine and the posse allowed us to continue.

During the eight-hour, nonstop journey, we were struck by the austerity of the drab towns, little more than a series of old apartment buildings, deserted streets, and stores stocked with limited goods. In residential areas, an occasional parked car covered by a tarp waited for an event worthy of the expense of gasoline. The entire atmosphere was one of grayness. In the capital of Sofia, an old European city of darkened stone structures unchanged since World War II, the streets hummed with streetcars and the sidewalks were alive with families, seniors, couples holding hands, and young women pushing baby carriages, all out for an evening promenade.

On our arrival at the Yugoslavian seaport of Rijeka, we went directly to the Jugolinija offices. Tom had been right to take the speedy route. Due to various shipping contingencies (an Italian strike, dry-dock time, maritime problems), the schedule was in disarray, the type of delays he had anticipated. Three ships would sail in the next week, one in two days, another four days later. In a week, the *Klek* would sail, the last sailing until midsummer. The *Klek* would be our ship.

We had one problem—the money sent to Athens. We were at a loss. Due to its communist government, there was no American Express office in Yugoslavia. The Italian town of Trieste, only sixty minutes away, had an American Express office, but when we got there, it was manned only by a representative unable to transfer money from the Athens office. Was it worth driving the additional three hours to Venice? Our previous experience with the American Express in Rome clearly in our memory, we gave up. We would deal with our money issues back in the United States.

At the Jugolinija offices, we paid our passage ($300 each). Midway into signing the documents for shipping the van on the same vessel, we were told the cost varied according to the size of the vehicle—$250 for cars up to 15.99 cubic meters and $350 for vehicles 16 cubic meters and over. Our van was definitely over as it stood, but Tom was eager to strip it down to save the $100. He wanted to have it measured that afternoon, but we had to return to the campground to do the work. Tom removed the bumpers, the spare tire, the gasoline cans mounted on the rear, and even our wooden roof box full of treasures. If we passed the measurement test, all this stuff would have to fit inside the microbus for the ocean passage.

Tom was pretty sure we would pass, but it would be close. However, when we returned to the office, the shipping agent was busy. The clerk told us, "We don't care. We'll sell you the lower-priced ticket and they'll measure it on the dock before they load you. If it's too big, you can pay the extra then."

For the next few days, we organized our possessions, made a list of souvenirs for our U.S Customs declaration, read, and played Scrabble on the rocky beach. Most days we drove into town to get the latest news about the *Klek*.

One morning, after we had skipped the trip to town the day before, the Jugolinija agent told us our ship was already at the dock and would sail early the next day, May 19! They wanted to load us before noon and it was already ten. We rushed back to the campground to strip the van down again. While Tom removed bumpers, gas cans, etc., I hurriedly packed our suitcases with clothes for the voyage. I gave neighbor campers our leftover food, except for a bag of cheese and crackers to take along. Tom bolted the divider between the cab and the rear section. Together we emptied the roof box and stashed all our precious items carefully in the overhead compartment where our suitcases had been. Finally, the wooden storage box itself came down. The bumpers, gas cans, water jugs, tools, and spare tire went into the van, the empty roof box wedged on top of it all. Tom made sure the inside was secure, backed out of the rear tailgate, and locked it. A well-oiled team, we finished the job in an hour.

I sat perched on top of both suitcases in the passenger seat, bags of games and books around my feet as Tom sped back to the dock. Two government men and the agent waited for us with their tape measure. Tom and I kept a close watch on the procedure to make sure all the measurements were accurate, but in the end, we came in at 16.2 cubic meters and the officials would not let this slide. After we paid the $100, we were left with only forty-two US dollars for miscellaneous costs on the ship and in ports along the way. We would manage. We had learned to live frugally for the last two years.

Chapter 24

Family Summer

The *Klek* was a bulk cargo vessel that carried a maximum of nine passengers, a practice that allowed for sailing without a doctor on board. Because it was similar to the ships he usually worked on, Tom was familiar with the type of accommodations (simple) and activities (none other than port calls) provided for passengers. Our cabin, three times as large as our Turtle, was furnished with two beds and a sturdy desk. And we had our very own bathroom. Breakfast was served at 7:30 a.m., lunch at noon, and dinner at 6:00 p.m. We ate with the ship's officers and Tom soon made friends with the second mate.

Life aboard the ship settled into a routine. Between meals we played Scrabble in the lounge, read, wrote letters, or chatted with the other passengers, including four young children who taught us how to play Rummy. In pleasant weather, we reclined in deck chairs or leaned on the rail and watched the sea. We explored the ports of call—Genova, Alicante, Lisbon—then settled in for the ocean crossing.

One late afternoon in the middle of the Atlantic, we gazed across the glassy water. We hoped to see a school of dolphins breach the surface. "Look," Tom said and pointed across the vacant ocean toward the horizon. "There's something strange floating out there."

I saw it, too, a dark shape that bobbed like a buoy. As the ship came closer, we recognized it as the bow of a small boat sticking straight up, the rest of the craft waterlogged and sunken like an iceberg below the surface.

"It's a wreck," Tom said. "There's probably a pocket of air in the bow preventing it from sinking." Aware of the importance of the remains of a boat at sea and familiar with proper procedure, he went to the bridge to inform the mate.

Within minutes, the *Klek* doubled back to investigate. Soon the other passengers gathered at the rail to watch the rescue at sea. On the bridge, the captain gave orders. A flare was thrown over the side to mark the spot and four of the crew lowered a lifeboat and rowed over to the wreckage.

"There could be survivors in the bow, breathing the trapped air," Tom said. The other passengers looked to him as the expert and hung on his words. As the sun dipped below the horizon, the lifeboat crew towed the wreck to the side of the *Klek* and, under the illumination of spotlights, attached cables to the bow of the boat. Slowly the wreck was lifted higher and higher out of the water, till we could make out its Florida registration and the name written on the side of the fiber-glass hull, *Billfisher*.

"It's an open-deck, charter-type sport-fishing boat," Tom told his audience. "See the foot lockers for tackle." By now, most of the wreck was clear of the water, but as it swung from the cables, we heard the groan of the structure ripping apart. "It's too waterlogged and damaged," Tom said. "The weight of the hull is too much. They won't be able to lift it on board without it being pulled to pieces."

Already the captain had ordered the boat to be lowered back into the ocean. "Do you think there might have been people in there?" I asked.

"No. The guys in the lifeboat checked that out first, before they ever started to hoist it out of the water. There was no one there."

"What will they do now?" one of the other passengers asked.

"The captain has to report it to the Coast Guard. He'll leave a flare, mark the coordinates on the map, and let them know. The Coast Guard will be out to inspect it and get the registration number. In the end, they'll sink it so it's not a hazard."

Dinner was late and the conversation was all about the wreck and the rescue effort. It was the high point of a decidedly uneventful crossing.

Three days later, the Statue of Liberty greeted us with her raised torch. Manhattan's skyscrapers towered as welcome sentinels. We quickly cleared U.S. Customs, put everything back in its proper place, and drove toward my uncle's home on Long Island. As he had no idea when we would arrive, not even the exact day, we had time to spare until my relatives returned from work and school. First lunch at a McDonald's, then a trip to the bank and to a laundromat! Though a long way from California, we felt as if we were home.

After our visit with my relatives, we headed for Connecticut and Tom's brother's home on a large rural property where we could get the van in order after two years of rugged travel. We parked in their driveway, slept in our van, cleaned cupboards, sorted souvenirs, and shipped several boxes of goodies to California. Tom converted the under-seat storage into an ice chest by lining it with aluminum sheeting and drilling a hole through the bottom of the car as a drain. With this addition, and the availability of ice, we again had basic cold storage.

For me, the excitement of our adventure was over. On June 15, I mailed home the last of my series of detailed journal letters. From then on, I kept only a cursory diary and condensed each day's activities into a sentence or two in a spiral notebook. These notes recorded a typical summer vacation.

To avoid having the kids sleep on the front seat and floor of the van for another summer, I had asked my parents to ship us their Westfalia

Camper tent, which was designed to attach to the side of a Volkswagen microbus. My mother dutifully put the tent on a Greyhound, addressed to Tom's brother in Brookline, Connecticut. But it never arrived. Eager to get started on the American version of Tommy's Tours, we borrowed a large, canvas tent from Tom's brother and set off. Our route for the first six weeks consisted of several loops around the East Coast, doubling back three times to Connecticut in the vain hope of finding a Westfalia tent waiting for us.

Finally, it was the first week of August with less than a month to get the kids home before school started. We circled back to Connecticut one last time, returned the borrowed tent, then headed south. With my parents' tent irretrievably lost in the ether of Greyhound-land, we returned to our cozy sleeping arrangements like four peas curled together in a pod.

In our dash for the west coast, we stopped only once, in Stone Mountain, Georgia, to visit my college friend, Lindsay, and her husband, Matt. They lived in a cabin-style house with a spare room, where Mike and Michelle could sleep inside. Tom and I bunked in our beloved Turtle on their rambling front lawn. Matt kept a skiff tied to a rickety dock and Mike and Michelle rowed around their private pond. One afternoon the kids spotted a water snake, and when Matt came home, Mike couldn't wait to tell him about it.

"It was thick as this," he said, holding up his skinny arm. "Black and long . . . in the middle of the pond. Out there past the willow."

Matt squinted against the sun. The pond reflected the golden sky against inky water. "Was it this big?" He stretched his arms out as far as they would go.

Michelle nodded. "Maybe bigger," she whispered.

"Probably the old black water moccasin," Matt told them. "I see him mostly in the late afternoon."

"Is it poisonous?" Mike asked.

"He's a pit viper. His fangs are full of poison and a good bite would kill you." Matt was serious in his warning. "He's an old guy and he'd rather keep to himself. Don't bother him if you see him again."

Mike and Michelle never swam in the pond again, and when they were in the boat, one of them was always on the lookout for the snake.

We were invited to go along on a planned whitewater rafting trip with Lindsay, Matt, three of their friends, and a nephew of one of them as a companion for Mike and Michelle. On Saturday, we all rose before the sun and set off toward South Carolina, a caravan of three cars—our van, Lindsay and Matt in their pickup truck, and their friends in another car. We arrived at the Chattooga River by midmorning and I cooked a pan of scrambled eggs for the group. Matt and Tom drove Lindsay, the three kids, and me up to the top of a relatively calm stretch of river rated as a Class II float experience. Our rubber boat was roomy, and we had snacks and lemonade, towels and sunscreen. Lindsay and I waved goodbye to our husbands, while the children paddled the boat into the current.

The river flowed green and clear. We drifted through the dappled sunlight cast by tree branches. Sometimes the water moved so slowly we could swim alongside the raft. Other times we thrilled to the excitement of shooting small rapids, then swam in the sandy pools at the bottom. The kids splashed, hollered, and jumped off rocks while Lindsay and I lay back against the warm rubber boat and talked about our lives since college.

"What will you do when you get back to California?" she asked me during one of these lulls.

I stretched out lazily, and watched the kids build a rock dam across a nearby streamlet. "First, we have to get Tom back on the shipping list so he can work again. And I'll need to find a new teaching position. I'm worried about finding anything. My sister wrote the schools were cutting back and jobs in education were difficult to find because the population of school-age children has dropped. At any rate, there's no hurry."

"Where will you live? Laguna or Los Angeles?"

"It doesn't matter where we live once Tom starts work again. He has a friend, another engineer, who lives in Colorado. Other guys live in San Francisco and near Seattle. As long as we're near an airport, he can always fly to any port. Of course, I'd rather live in Laguna or at least near the ocean."

Lindsay frowned. "Won't you miss Tom when he goes off?" She spoke seriously. "I miss Matt when he's on the road. Usually a week at the most. How will you manage months, especially now you've been together all this time?"

"I don't know. It's kind of sad to think about." The thought was a weight in my chest. "I'll have to keep busy, I guess."

At about 6:00 p.m., our group arrived at our breakfast spot. We had been given the task of driving Matt's truck and our van from that parking area to the location where the three men, including Tom, and the two other women would emerge after their adventure. They had taken rafts down Section III, a much rougher stretch with multiple rapids.

The final rapid they would contend with was Bull Sluice, rated as Class IV Plus. Always popular because of a large swimming hole at its base, Bull Sluice was notorious because it had been featured in the recently released film, *Deliverance*, with Burt Reynolds and Jon Voight. We moved the cars to a rock overlook where we had a good view of the sluice. Mike spotted our group in the fading light of the summer evening. Surrounded by whitewater, they roared down a drop of fourteen feet through a narrow jumble of boulders and submerged rocks. We ran to the beachhead to welcome them.

Tom stepped ashore, his feet a bit unsteady on terra-firma, elation in his eyes. "I loved it!" he said as he hugged me. "I can't wait to do that again." The buckles of his life jacket dug into my chest, but I was glad to have him in my arms.

From Georgia, we hurried on to New Orleans, where on August 14, we celebrated our second anniversary. New Orleans marked the beginning and the end of our adventure. The last stretch across Texas, New Mexico, and Arizona was no more than familiar desert we had to cross.

What would our life be like now?

Chapter 25

A Lifestyle Choice

When we were a dating couple, Tom and I had been happy with the lifestyle mandated by his job as a marine engineer. Depending on his ship, its route, and his assignment, separations could be anywhere from one to four months. The separations when he worked gave me space to do my own thing. His long vacations gave us quality time together. It had seemed an ideal life. But after two years of constant togetherness, learning to make our relationship work, and deciding everything together, we weren't sure we wanted to be apart for months at a time.

On our return to California, we settled into the cottage which, except for my father's draftsman who still occupied the large bedroom, had remained vacant, waiting for us. We unloaded the van. No longer the repository of all our worldly goods, it would be the Turtle no more.

As soon as possible, Tom flew to San Francisco to put his name and license number on the union listing of engineers available for work.

Though it was important for him to be on the list in San Francisco, the main West Coast port, he could check his status at the San Pedro (Port of Los Angeles) union hall. He was also required to attend monthly union meetings in order to keep his number active as it progressed up the list. Tom knew it could take a while, maybe four to six months, for his number to get close enough to the top of the list for him to pick up a good seafaring job.

We had plenty to do while we waited. There were friendships to renew, family to visit, and a less adventurous lifestyle to get used to. We unpacked the boxes sent home from Denmark and Germany and rediscovered our treasures as we freed them from the shredded newspaper. Tom built a cupboard to hold our Danish dishes, cutlery, linens and glassware, and I painted it a bright, sunny yellow. I hung my saris in the closet and wondered if I would wear them in California. I pulled out my Singer sewing machine to make a blouse decorated with a section of Afghani embroidery embedded with mirrors. I continued to try Indian recipes with the spices I had purchased in Madras and Bombay. I even found pleasure at the local laundromat where the magical machines tumbled and spun our dirty clothes in half the time it took to wash them by hand in a bucket. In the evenings, we cuddled on the couch, laughed together at Johnny Carson's monologue, and went to bed for intimate caresses.

Slowly, feeling it was what I ought to do, I researched nearby school districts. I wasn't eager to enter a new school midyear, so I looked halfheartedly, didn't find anything, and didn't look further afield. I briefly considered substitute teaching, which I had done before I taught full time and had disliked intensely. I would look again in the spring, when positions for the 1974 school year would be listed. Meanwhile, in an effort to look useful, I located a boutique that sold custom children's clothes and designed and sewed for them. Tom, always supportive, suggested I buy a new sewing machine, a Swedish machine with all the latest features.

Tom had a harder time adjusting to a life of leisure. He puttered around the house, looked for improvement projects, and worked on the van to bring it back to pre-trip condition. Once a week, he drove up to San Pedro to check his status and peruse the listings on the union job board. Occasionally he picked up a twelve-hour night relief job in port.

Once, simply for the fun of an outing with him, I accompanied Tom on his trek to San Pedro. After he checked the job board and found nothing, the dispatcher suggested he return for the late afternoon call. "There might be a short-term job available you could get," he said.

To fill the time, we drove out to the Palos Verdes headlands for a picnic. Not far from the Point Vicente Lighthouse, we stood on the bluff, breathed in the salt air, and watched the waves break against the rocks below. The Pacific Ocean stretched to the horizon, the dim outline of Catalina Island a dark shape between the blue of the sea and the blue of the sky. Behind us lay Los Angeles—homes, skyscrapers, freeways, noise, and congestion from the coast to the mountains. The winds whipped my hair and I snuggled into Tom's shoulder to keep warm.

"I'll miss you when you go back to sea," I whispered into his chest. "I'm so used to having you near."

"You'll be fine." He opened his jacket, wrapped it around us both, and pulled me close to his warm body.

"I know I'll be OK," I said. "I'm not worried, only sad. Sad in anticipation, I guess. I wish we could stay together all the time."

"Well, there are options. There are shoreside jobs in the maritime industry—jobs on the docks, in the union hall, in dry docks, or with a maritime insurance company."

I leaned back against his embrace and looked up, my mood suddenly brighter. "What about other land jobs? With your degree in mechanical engineering, wouldn't you be able to get a job at a hospital or a university? Don't they have their own in-house power plants . . . complex facilities that need a mechanical engineer onsite?"

"Sure. I'll take a look at shore jobs."

The dispatcher grinned when we returned to the union hall. "Hey, Slattery, how'd you like to sail to San Diego?" he asked. "There's an overnight position on a ship tonight. They have a second engineer ready to ship out from San Diego, but they can't wait for him to come to LA. So, if you want it, you're in."

Tom looked at me. "Do you mind driving home and then down to San Diego tomorrow?" he asked. "We can visit your sister and the kids after you pick me up."

The next afternoon, while Tom napped on my sister's sofa, exhausted after a long night on duty, she and I took the kids to the park and prepared a pot of spaghetti for dinner. Later, on the drive home, Tom and I talked about how hard my sister was working as a new teacher and a single mom.

True to form, Tom thought of how he could help by fixing or building. "Her house needs a lot of work," he said. Tom was silent for a while and I could tell he was mulling over an idea before he spoke. "Though I'm probably crazy to offer," he said, "I could remodel her kitchen. It'd only take a couple of months."

"Are you sure you want to?"

"I keep thinking about building our dream house. Wherever we end up, I want to build it myself, or remodel a fixer upper to make it perfect for us."

"I'd want a big gourmet kitchen! I'm tired of cooking in cramped spaces."

Tom laughed. "We're not there yet! But the project for your sister would be good practice."

Tom had proved himself as a builder of small improvements in the van and as the sole builder of his parent's remodel completed during the first six months we had dated. I had studied drafting and had paid for my college tuition as the assistant to an interior decorator. Together we would be a dynamic, dream-house building duo.

The deal was soon arranged. Tom and I packed a few bags, I took my new sewing machine and a few of my favorite spices, and we moved part time to San Diego. Before we knew it, the Christmas holidays were past, it was 1974, and we still lived most of our days amid the confusion of a remodel in someone else's home. During a quick trip to Los Angeles so Tom could go to the union hall, I enrolled in a Chinese cooking class in Laguna. From then on, I drove each week to the class and returned to San Diego excited to try my new skills. Mike and Michelle were a captive and receptive audience. They watched in awe as I chopped and sliced with my Chinese cleaver, mixed up sauces, and deep-fried in a wide, iron wok. I taught them to eat with chopsticks and they helped me form spring rolls and fold wonton.

Meanwhile Tom pushed himself. By early February the remodel was finished and we returned to our cozy Laguna cottage.

Though he wasn't particularly enthusiastic, Tom didn't forget his promise to consider a shoreside job. On a trip to San Pedro in late February, he learned about an opening for a marine engineer with the American Bureau of Shipping, a nonprofit organization responsible for the certification of the safety on merchant ships, naval vessels, and marine structures. The Bureau had posted a job for a marine engineer to oversee compliance to safety regulations during the construction of three tankers in the San Diego shipyard, and Tom decided to apply for the position. Before long, he was called in for an interview, quickly followed by a request for another. When he returned from San Diego after his second meeting with the hiring officer, he told me they wanted to see him again and he was certain he would be offered the job.

"That's good news!"

"We ought to talk this out before I go back for the third interview. We need to agree on what I should say if they offer me the job."

I was surprised at his lack of enthusiasm. "Is there something about the job you don't like?"

"We simply need to be sure this is the life we want. It's a big decision . . . a huge change from what I used to do."

"You're right. Let's list the benefits and disadvantages and compare working for the American Bureau with the lifestyle we would have if you return to shipping out." At the top of a sheet of notebook paper, I wrote "Shore Job with A.B." I drew a line down the center of the page and wrote "Pros" on top of the left column and "Cons" on the right.

At the top of the Pro column I wrote, "Together every night!" and drew a heart. "I'd like to live near Mike and Michelle," I said. "We could have so much fun."

"Might be for only a year or two. After the tankers are finished, I could be assigned to another shipyard . . . like New Orleans."

"Very cool!"

"Or Newark."

"Well, at least it's close to New York."

"There'd be lots of long hours, too," Tom said, "especially if there's a deadline. I might be called in on weekends, too, when there's a safety concern. The pay is lower and chances for advancement will be limited compared to a seagoing job."

"I'm pretty sure I can find a job in San Diego," I said. "It's a huge school district. At any rate, I could substitute."

"In the beginning I'd only get two weeks of vacation a year, and it might not be during your school's summer break," Tom said.

The reality of the shore job was not quite as perfect as I had envisioned. We would live together and sleep in the same bed each night, but our quality time together would be limited. And when he was transferred, I might be looking for a new teaching position every year or so. I had another thought. "If we have children in a few years, with this job you'd be home for our kids, right?"

"Yes," he agreed. "But with shipping out, remember, I'd have paid vacation equal to the time I'm gone. We'd have lots of family time when I'm home. And we could all travel together."

We looked at the lists. There were four notations in the Pro column: Together every night! San Diego, New Orleans (?), and home for kids. Though a little longer, the list below the word Cons was more substantial: transfers to other shipyards, long hours, weekends (?), lower pay, short vacations, teach or substitute.

I sighed. "I keep coming back to how much I'd miss you when you're at sea."

"And I'd miss you. You'd have to be in charge when I'm gone, but I know you're up to it. Besides, we could stay here in Laguna Beach. You'd have both our parents nearby to help out when I'm away."

This was an important consideration. I had come almost full circle, back to what we had imagined our future life would be. I put a horizontal line across the middle of the page and wrote under it, "Shipping out."

In the left Pro column, I wrote "Long vacations = Quality time," "Live in Laguna near family," and "Better pay." In the Con column, "Long separations."

"What about travel?" I asked. "We'd have your long vacations to travel, right?"

"Sure. With more money and four to six months' vacation every year, we'd be able to travel a lot more."

I added "More travel" in the Pro column.

"When I'm teaching, if I find a job . . . I hope you can get your vacations to match mine at least in the summer."

"Do you want to teach again?" Tom asked. "Because, if I'm an officer on a ship, I'll make enough you wouldn't need to work. Of course, if you want to teach, you can. Otherwise you could stay home and paint, sew, or draw. Even travel on your own. Whatever."

Tom definitely knew my soft spot.

"Truly?" I said. "Sounds too good to be true. I know I'd never be bored . . . I could always go back to teaching later, if I want."

I wrote "Stay home/No teaching" in our Pro list.

"Look at the lists, Katie. It's obvious. Our life will be more flexible if I'm shipping out. More interesting, too. Do you want to settle into a staid suburban life? Nine to five. Commuting. Weekends and two weeks in the summer. PTA. Little League. Is that the life you want?"

"No. Definitely not," I conceded. "I don't want to live in a suburban tract and only see you when you're tired after work." I grinned. "And I love the idea of not having to teach. I could do my art. Or take classes. We could live in Laguna. We'd have more time to build our dream house together, too. And we could travel more, right?"

Tom wrapped his arms around me. "I'll call the American Bureau tomorrow and cancel my appointment with regrets."

"Can we go to Japan?" I asked. "Maybe all of Southeast Asia. We didn't get that far in the van."

"You'll do anything for a trip, won't you?"

"Just about," I said. "I'll even be a kept woman."

Tom laughed and nibbled my ear. Then he looked serious again. "I'd like to ask your dad if we can buy this property. We could build our dream house right here."

"Yes, let's!"

A few weeks later, when his name was close to the top of the union list, Tom decided we should drive to San Francisco. Before we left, he called his old company and let them know he'd be in the Bay Area. They told him a third engineer's job would post on the union call-board the next day, and, if he could make it, he should be prepared to leave.

We drove straight through and arrived at the union hall as it opened. There it was—a position for third assistant engineer on the *President Jefferson*. Tom entered his number to bid on the job. "If nobody with a higher number bids, I'll get the job," he explained. "Normally, when there's an opening, like when an engineer goes on vacation, the permanent officers are promoted up the ranks. If they have the correct license, the second then becomes the first, say, and the third would become the second. The Hall can supply a third from open call on a temporary basis. That way, only the lowest position is a newbie."

"So later, you could advance, too, right? Because you have a higher license than third."

"Sure, but it's not my job yet."

Just then, a guy shambled into the hall and inspected the board.

"I know that guy," Tom whispered. "He's a lazy worker and he drinks a lot."

As the man spoke to the dispatcher, Tom moved close enough to hear. I strained to eavesdrop. The dispatcher handed paperwork to the man, looked past him to Tom, and sadly shook his head. I heard the guy say to the dispatcher, "What do I do now?"

"I suggest you go out and get drunk," the dispatcher said and winked at Tom. After the man headed for the door, the dispatcher motioned to Tom. "Come back this afternoon. I wouldn't be surprised if the job opens up again."

"What happened?" I asked.

"That idiot only has a third's license, but his number was one higher than mine. He got the job."

"So that's it? We wait for another opening?"

"Maybe. But if he takes the dispatcher's suggestion . . . naturally said in jest . . . if he shows up drunk or doesn't show up at all . . . the job might be back on the board again this afternoon."

When we entered the union hall for the afternoon call, the dispatcher waved Tom over, a grin on his face. "The third never checked in on the *Jefferson*," he said. "The job's yours if you want it!" He handed Tom the paperwork. "Good luck! Get to the dock as fast as you can. They're set to sail this evening on the tide."

Less than an hour later, Tom and I stood on the dock at the foot of the gangway, our arms wrapped around each other. "I'll miss you," I whispered, the lonely months ahead on my mind.

"I'll write," he said. "If you drive up to San Francisco when the ship comes back in two months, we'll have a couple of days together. Now that we're married, you can stay overnight with me on the ship."

"Of course, I'll come up."

Tom slung his huge, khaki duffel bag over his shoulder. "I have to get going. Take care on the drive home, sweetheart." He started up the gangway, then turned and smiled, his eyes sparkling the way I loved. "Start plans for our trip to Asia," he said. "We can go when I come home for vacation. I want to show you Singapore and Hong Kong. You'll love 'em!"

"Japan, too?"

"Anything we can do in two or three months." Tom strode to the top of the gangway, then turned, waved and disappeared from sight.

I walked slowly back to the green van. It would be a long, lonely drive home. But I was elated. Our new life was falling into place.

My life had been totally changed by the promise of travel, the journey with Tom, and the prospect of more travel in the future. I had entered the adventure as a twenty-eight-year-old, single woman—an art teacher off to explore the world with her lover. Getting married had simply been a romantic gesture for me, a choice I could reverse if it didn't work out. Two years later, I had returned to the United States as part of a committed, married couple. We looked forward to a life together, building a home, continued travel, and having children who would share our love of international travel.

Travel had opened up the world for me. It had relaxed my views and judgments about people from different backgrounds. I had journeyed across four continents and seen that no two countries were exactly the same—different history, different food, different kinds of homes, different styles of dressing, different expectations for their lives, different ways of working. Yet in all these places, people thrived and suffered, worked, went to school, and loved their families. My judgments about people and what they did would forever be colored by my knowledge of the varied way people lived their lives.

My love and respect for Tom had grown exponentially over our two years on the road. My understanding of myself had also expanded. I was totally committed to the unusual lifestyle we chose together. I was grateful for Tom's gift of time and freedom to follow my creative passions. His strength, confidence in my abilities, and the financial stability he offered would be my rock. Though his love for me would never be couched in flowers, sweet words, or romantic gifts, I knew, without a doubt, he loved me, flaws and all.

When I arrived home, our cozy cottage felt plainer and less homey without my husband. I took out the Tartan wool I had bought in Edinburgh and rubbed the scratchy fabric against my cheek. It seemed to emit the smell of Scotland. I laid out the pattern pieces for a man's shirt, pinned them in place, and began to cut. When I was finished, I brewed myself a cup of tea, curled up in the corner of the old, tweed couch, and spread our big atlas across my lap. I opened to the pages of Asian maps and traced my finger along the edges of the continent, around the islands and the peninsulas. Where should we go? Much of Asia was closed or at war. Still, there were plenty of great places to visit. I began a mental list—first, Japan, then Hong Kong, Malaysia, Thailand, Singapore, and Bali.

Yes, definitely Bali.

Epilogue

ess than a year later, Tom and I were in Bali.

It was the final stop at the end of two months of travel through Asia. We had jumped from country to country in a plane, stayed in a Ryokan in Kyoto, taken a tiny train from Bangkok to Chiang Mai, and driven a rental car from northern Malaysia to Singapore, where we ate satay at the outdoor food stalls. In Manila, we bought a container load of mahogany lumber for our dream house and had the wood shipped home on an American President Lines vessel with one of Tom's friends watching over it.

On our return, building our dream house (a complete remodel of the beach cottage we bought from my father) became all-consuming for Tom. I was his enthusiastic helper for the first five years, and then I became a mother. Our daughter, Erin, was born the same month the county issued our building permit. Some of the earliest pictures in her baby book show Erin in the back carrier, peering over her father's shoulder as he sets the survey markers for our second-story living room. Another shows her sitting in her mechanical swing while I make sandwiches in a roofless cottage kitchen.

After five years of work, we finally moved upstairs into the still unfinished remodel. For Erin, the weathered plywood floors, rough wood kitchen counters supported by two-by-fours, and curtains used as bathroom doors

Tom surveys for new construction with Erin in back carrier. 1977

were normal. A photo of Erin from this period shows her leaning over the deck railing, pretending to help her dad nail siding. Meanwhile, I was beginning to long for a finished home.

After years of living in construction mode, my enthusiasm began to waver. Work progressed only during Tom's long vacations. He insisted on doing almost all the labor himself—everything from placing the rebar for the concrete foundations to raising the walls, from installing the plumbing to building all the cabinets, and from milling the rough mahogany boards we bought in the Philippines into siding to creating tiny wooden plugs to conceal screw heads on the exterior. I taught adult cooking classes and volunteered as a Girl Scout leader. These activities were a distraction from the mess at home and a much-needed creative outlet.

After two years living upstairs amid the mess of construction, we decided to add to our family. I was almost forty and felt I couldn't wait much longer if I wanted a second child. My only demand was for the installation of hardwood floors before the baby began to crawl, a request Tom honored the week after our son Ethan was born.

As the years passed, I felt more trapped by the constant disarray of construction and the budget constraints set by Tom's insistence that we pay for everything totally out of pocket and free of any loan obligation. Though I ventured on a few short trips by myself and we drove the old Turtle to San Francisco once a year, it had been ten years since our trip to Asia. The longer my passport languished without new stamps, the more discontent I became.

The stress and decisions of the remodel often put Tom and me on opposite sides. I saw clearly that we were our best as a couple when we were traveling. In 1985, I insisted that, on Tom's next vacation, we set aside building in favor of travel. With Erin and Ethan in tow, we spent a month in New Zealand. Erin and Ethan each had their own passport. Mainly extra baggage, our eighteen-month-old son was the one who now rode high on his dad's shoulders in the back carrier. We traveled and slept in a rented motorhome and, in lieu of a crib, a large appliance carton with one side cut away served as Ethan's bed. Nine-and-a-half-year-old Erin learned to swing Mauri Poi balls, panned for gold, sat at the helm of the *Lake Victoria* steamboat, and watched sheep being sheared, experiences that more than

Our family with our mini-Winni.
Left to right: Tom, myself, and Erin, with Ethan in front.

made up for the weeks away from 4th grade. She was well on her way to becoming a lifelong, world traveler. We had so much fun on this trip that the following year, Tom and I bought a twenty-four-foot motorhome with bunk beds for the kids. For fifteen years we concentrated on traveling around the United States in our mini-Winni, the nickname for a small Winnebago.

Though Tom and I continued to travel together

throughout the thirty-two years of our marriage, the stress of the remodel drove a wedge between us and gradually our sense of intimacy and togetherness disappeared. Still, we loved each other and we struggled to stay together. When Tom was at sea, I tried to relax and do what made me happy. I loved being a mom, found my work with the Girl Scouts rewarding, traveled occasionally while Tom was home on vacation and could stay with the kids, continued to cook for the joy of it, helped our aging parents, and began to write. In many ways it was a satisfying life and certainly a full one, but I felt frustrated and lonely in my struggles to regain the romance of my marriage.

Nothing seemed to be working, but I hung on year after year—through the death of all four of our parents, through Tom's bout with cancer (during which I took out a loan and hired a contractor to finish the house) and into his retirement. I continued to hope our marriage could be salvaged through Erin's years at university and Ethan's deployment to Afghanistan and Iraq with U.S. Marine Corps Reconnaissance. Finally, Tom and I decided to separate and then later to divorce.

He and I remain friends. Though we are both with new partners, he is still my best advisor on all things automotive and home repair. We know each other so well and have loved each other so long, we cannot envision any other way of being.

Tom remains one of my most enthusiastic supporters. When I mentioned I wanted to write a memoir of our adventure in the van, he returned the next day with his multipaged passport and eight small spiral notebooks, those treasures of penciled notes, tiny sketches, and money conversion tables that he carried in his shirt pocket for two years. He read my finished manuscript and gave it his approval. I feel I am the luckiest of women to have shared so much of my life with this man, to have an ongoing relationship with the adults Mike and Michelle have become, to have two wonderful children who value travel, and to have a new partner who has brought happiness and art back into my life.

Memoir Timeline

1971

January	Proposal
July	Tom returns from ship
August 14	Wedding
September 9	We leave Laguna Beach, California
October 16 to November 7	Major car repairs in Guadalajara, Mexico
December 15	Arrive in Panama

1972

January 6	Board SS *Donizetti* and sail for Spain
January 22	Arrive in Spain
March 16	Argument in Malaga
March 17	Take ferry to North Africa
April 13	Take ferry from Tunisia to Sicily
April 21 to May 5	Wait for money in Rome
July 4	Arrive in Dover, England
July 10	Mike and Michelle arrive in London
July 26	Stratford on Avon, Katie's 29th birthday
July 31	Mike's 11th birthday

August 9	Ferry from Harwich, England, to Belgium
August 14	Our first wedding anniversary, Eindhoven, Holland
August 21	Airline snafu when Mike and Michelle fly home from Copenhagen, Denmark
September 5	Tom's 30th birthday in Stockholm, Sweden
September 22	Leave Copenhagen, Denmark, for the second time
October 14	Leave Heidelberg, Germany, for the final time
October 21	Enter Yugoslavia
November 4	Cross into Turkey
November 14	Cross border into Iran
November 23	Thanksgiving in Mashhad, Iran
November 25	Cross border into Afghanistan
December 25	Christmas near Patna, India

1973

January 1	Kathmandu, Nepal
January 25	Arrive in Madras, India
February 15–24	Goa, India
March 23	Leave New Delhi, India
March 28	Cross border into Pakistan
April 3	Leave Kabul
April 6	Buy carpets in Mashhad, Iran

April 17	Beirut, Lebanon
April 18	Enter Turkey
May 7	Drive through Bulgaria
May 9	Rijeka, Yugoslavia
May 16	Sail from Rijeka on the SS *Klek*
June 7	Arrive in New York
June 20	Mike and Michelle arrive in New York
July 26	Katie's Birthday in Williamsburg
July 31	Mike's Birthday in Washington, DC
August 11	Rafting on the river
August 14	Second wedding anniversary in New Orleans
August 20	Return to California
Fall and Winter	Tom and Katie live in Laguna Beach and Tom begins going to San Pedro to the Union Hall

1974

February	Tom interviews for American Bureau of Shipping
Spring	Tom gets job on SS *President Jefferson*

Acknowledgments

I have been blessed with wonderful people who have encouraged and supported me as I wrote this memoir.

Special thanks and appreciation to the following people:

- Tom Slattery, who made the adventure possible
- Ron Whitacre, who encouraged me to write about it and read every draft
- Karen Lang, Mike Pierce, and Michelle Pierce Reed for sharing their memories with me

Wherever the Road Leads could not have been written without the help of a myriad of readers, editors, and advisors. Continuing thanks to the loyal women of my writing group: Donna Feeney, Donna Becker, Denise Yaru, Elene Wilder, and the sadly missed Ruth Baumgartner. Special thanks to my dedicated beta readers, who struggled through a much longer version of the manuscript. These include Erika Vincent, Carol Hanke, Ron Langdon, Diana Smith, Jeannette Pease, Roger Owens, and Chris Catsimanes. Various writers and editors offered help and advice that gave me confidence to move forward. They include Nick White, Georgeanne Brennan, Janet Long, Verna Mitchell, and Jill J. Hall. For help finding the last few errors, whether typos, glitches, or misspelling, I thank Barbara Miller and her eagle eyes.

To my indominable editor, Lorraine Fico-White, for her support, suggestions, and tireless answering of questions, I offer my unmitigated gratitude. We work as a team to make my writing the best it can be.

For their help as I prepared the book for publication, special thanks go to my book-designer, Lorie DeWorken, always responsive and helpful, and to Cole Waidley who used his graphic talents to create the layouts for the section maps and the book cover. I extend a special shout-out to my beta readers, my friend, Ricki Older, and my daughter, Erin Slattery, for helping me select the photos and drawings to illustrate *Wherever the Road Leads*.

Every book is a group endeavor and this memoir is no exception. If I have forgotten anyone, I sincerely apologize—please blame my forgetfulness on a tired brain, not a lack of appreciation.

Discussion Questions for Your Book Group

1. Why are readers drawn to stories about real people and events? What pleasures can be found in a travel memoir? Does *Wherever the Road Leads* fulfill your expectations for a travel memoir?

2. The author starts the story with a short episode that takes place in Paris. Did this vignette help you get immediately involved in the story and the characters? What details did this section reveal about Tom and Katie?

3. Tom wants to get married "so it will be easier to cross borders." Why do you think Katie agrees to marry Tom?

4. The author includes an afternoon at the beginning of the trip when she and Tom discuss the meaning of the word "Zouave." What does this episode show about Katie? About Tom?

5. The author uses conversations to reveal much of the feeling and emotion between the couple. In the preface she says, "I . . . created dialogue based on my knowledge of the characters, how they usually spoke to each other, recollection of the conversation taking place, and the context." How does this use of dialogue affect your understanding of a memoir and its degree of truthfulness?

6. As an engineer, Tom is often occupied with car repairs and constructing improvements for the van. How does this affect their trip? How does Katie feel about all the down time that results?

7. Katie and Tom divide up chores and responsibilities along fairly traditional lines. Why did they do this? What would you have done? How would you have divided the labor with your partner?

8. Were you surprised when Katie and Tom invited their school-aged niece and nephew to join them for the summer? What did the chapters with the children add to your understanding of Tom and Katie's relationship and values?

9. How and why did Tom and Katie's marriage change over the two-year trip? How would their relationship have evolved if they had stayed home? When they return home, Tom and Katie decide on an unconventional lifestyle based on Tom's career. Were you surprised by Katie's eagerness to give up teaching? Do you feel they made the right decision? What choice would you have made?

10. Is this memoir more of a travel story or a relationship story? How did the author blend the two themes? Which aspect interested you the most?

Also by K. Lang-Slattery

Immigrant Soldier, The Story of a Ritchie Boy

Children's books published under the name Katie Lang-Slattery:

Tagalong Caitlin

Caitlin's Buddy

CPSIA information can be obtained
at www.ICGtesting.com
Printed in the USA
LVHW081614130521
687357LV00004B/127